FLAVOURVILLE

FLAVOURVILLE

ECW PRESS
ecwpress.com

FLAVOURVILLE

LESLEY CHESTERMAN

Published by ECW PRESS
2120 Queen Street East, Suite 200, Toronto, Ontario, Canada M4E 1E2

NATIONAL LIBRARY OF CANADA CATALOGUING IN PUBLICATION DATA

Chesterman, Lesley, 1967-
Flavourville: Lesley Chesterman's guide to dining out in Montreal
Includes index. ISBN 1-55022-506-5
Restaurants—Quebec (Province)—Montreal—Guidebooks.
I. Title.
TX907.5C22M6 2002   647.95714'28   C2001-903583-7

Acquisition Editor: Robert Lecker
Copy Editor: Mary Williams
Design and typesetting: Guylaine Régimbald—Solo Design
Production: Heather Bean
Cover illustration: Roger Blachon
Printing: Webcom

This book is set in Minion and Serlio.

The publication of *Flavourville* has been generously supported by the Canada
Council, the Ontario Arts Council, and the Government of Canada through
the Book Publishing Industry Development Program. Canada

DISTRIBUTION

CANADA: Stewart House Publishing Inc., 290 North Queen Street,
Suite 210, Etobicoke, Ontario M9C 5K4

UNITED STATES: Independent Publishers Group, 814 North Franklin Street,
Chicago, Illinois 60610

EUROPE: Turnaround Publisher Services, Unit 3, Olympia Trading Estate,
Coburg Road, Wood Green, London N22 6T2

AUSTRALIA AND NEW ZEALAND: Wakefield Press, 17 Rundle Street
(Box 2066), Kent Town, South Australia 5071

ECW PRESS
ecwpress.com

To all the restaurateurs, chefs, pastry chefs, sous-chefs, commis, maître d's, sommeliers, waiters, busboys, and dishwashers, not to mention the farmers, butchers, cheese makers, and other food suppliers, who have made Montreal one of the world's great restaurant cities.

ACKNOWLEDGMENTS

Thanks to my publisher at ECW Press, Robert Lecker, and editor, Mary Williams, and my editors at the Montreal *Gazette*, David Walker, Ashok Chandwani, and Lucinda Chodan.

A very special thanks to Julian Armstrong for all her insights and guidance.

Thanks also to friends and family members for their dinner company and contribution to my work, especially Sylvia and Anthony Chesterman and Lorraine Chesterman-Holl. For all his help and support, Paul Globus deserves his own sentence so, here you go Paul, your own sentence.

Most of all, I remain eternally grateful to my husband, Bertrand Bazin, and my son, Max, who ate plenty of takeout food while I was out on the town.

CONTENTS

CASUAL DINING

FOREWORD

With over 5,000 establishments ranging from formal French to the laid-back, inexpensive, bring-your-own-wine variety, Montreal's restaurant scene is booming. But our reputation as one of North America's gourmet capitals hardly captures the depth of the culinary scene. This is the city known the world over for smoked meat, bagels, and poutine. And that's only the beginning. Montreal also boasts a wide variety of locally produced luxury foodstuffs, such as raw-milk cheeses, foie gras, venison, and maple syrup. It's the development of these products and their exploitation by local chefs that makes ours such an important and unique North American restaurant city.

Although restaurants are not restricted to any one area of the island city, there are neighbourhood clusters where Montrealers tend to gravitate: Little Italy for its trattorias and open-air markets, Rue St. Denis for its sophisticated bistros and sidewalk cafés, and Boulevard St. Laurent—also known as the Main—for its dozens of trendy hot spots. Two emerging scenes are to be found on the Plateau Mont Royal and in the Gay Village, where a new breed of bistros and boutique restaurants is catering to a young and fashionable crowd up for good food and fine surroundings. Outremont still lays claim to the richest scene outside of the city centre, and Old Montreal is starting to look like the destination of the future.

Faced with the task of reviewing the city's restaurants, I have approached it as a chance to provide a service for the reader. I want to let you know what's going on out there, and which restaurants are worth adding to your list of favourites.

Unlike something always available in its original state (a film or a book), a restaurant is an ever-evolving enterprise. Talk to any restaurateur, and he'll tell you about his new sous-chef, his lunch specials, the latest additions to his wine list, or even the toothpicks he picked up in New York.

One could argue that a restaurant review is dated the minute it's published. Perhaps. My goal, however, is to offer you a brief encounter with each establishment, one that affects all the senses: the look of the decor at La Colombe, a plate presentation at Toqué!, the energy of a room like L'Express, the smell of mussels marinara at Le Latini, the taste of a vanilla-pineapple parfait at Le Lutétia, or the mouth feel of the crusty bread at Le Passe-Partout.

This guide offers a compilation of restaurants rated good to extraordinary at the time they were visited (every review is dated). It's more about quality than quantity. The establishments included here are the ones I believe are worth recommending. There are any number of reasons why a restaurant is not included in this book: out of business, too new to make the publication deadline, still finding its way on the city scene, or going through a renovation or transition.

In the category of casual restaurants, only thirty are included here. This is not intended as a comprehensive listing by any means; rather, it's an overview of some of the places I enjoy when I want to spend less.

Montreal is a city bursting with bright culinary ideas, fascinating chefs, and diverse tastes—a true city of flavours (hence the name of this guide). I invite you to peruse these pages when contemplating a night of celebration or indulgence, a change of pace, or simply a meal away from your own kitchen. A restaurant outing should always be special, a night to remember, and in Montreal you'll seldom find yourself without options or at the point where you've tried everything that's out there. Happy restaurant hopping.

HOW TO USE
THIS BOOK

Note that all restaurants featured here were visited by the author anonymously. All food, wine, and services were paid for in full. Any interviews of restaurant management or staff were conducted after the meals and services had been appraised. Ratings take food, ambience, service, and price into consideration. Menu items and prices are subject to change.

The star ratings:

★★	Good
★★1/2	Good, verging on excellent
★★★	Excellent
★★★1/2	Excellent, verging on extraordinary
★★★★	Extraordinary (one of the best)

The price ratings:

$	Inexpensive, most main courses priced under $10
$ $	Moderate, $10–$20
$ $ $	Expensive, $20–$35
$ $ $ $	Very expensive, $35+

REVIEW COMPONENTS

IN THE KITCHEN · Indicates who's running the show behind the scenes. The restaurant's chef is only listed if he or she has been working as head chef for at least one year. If there is no head chef, none is mentioned.

DECOR, DRESS, AMBIENCE · Montreal has become an increasingly casual dining-out city. If fancy dress is called for, it will be mentioned here. Keep in mind, however, that though jackets are rarely required, jeans, sweatpants, baseball caps, shorts, and running shoes are frowned upon in the majority of the city's finer restaurants.

WINE LIST · A general idea of selection and price is provided here.

DON'T MISS · The dishes listed include favourites tasted at the time of the author's visit. Of course, menu items may vary, but these dishes will give you a sense of the kitchen's strengths (if the duck magret with wild mushrooms was good last year, chances are the duck with red berries will be a winner this year).

WORDS TO THE WISE · Look here for insider tips and general reflections on the restaurant's strengths and weaknesses.

CARDS · "Major cards" means that at least Visa and MasterCard are accepted.

TOP TABLES

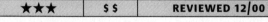

★ ★ ★ | $ $ | REVIEWED 12/00

AREA

SNAPSHOT · Area is a small, 38-seat establishment located in the heart of Montreal's increasingly fashionable Gay Village. Chef Ian Perreault and partner Denis Lévesque have garnered nothing but raves for their restaurant's stylish decor, its innovative cuisine, and the shrewd move of offering excellence and creativity at the midprice level, proving yet again that chef-owned restaurants offer the most confident cuisine and personal dining experiences. In this young chef's hands, cabbage salads taste elegant, pork chops are more toothsome than veal chops, and desserts feel like a necessity rather than an indulgence.

THE BIG PICTURE · Is a chef an artist or merely a skilled manual worker? One could argue that burger flipping requires a certain level of skill. But there are miles between the short-order cook and the experienced chef. Even among the ranks of the pros, there's a wide range of expertise. Compare culinary professionals to musicians. The differences between a commis, a sous-chef, and a chef de cuisine are comparable to those between a section player in the Montreal Symphony Orchestra, the concert master, and conductor Charles Dutoit.

A successful chef develops a signature style, leading us to see food in a new light, be it through interesting flavour combinations, original plate presentations, or a fresh take on the classics. Case in point is chef Ian Perreault of Area.

One of Montreal's most exciting new restaurants, Area offers an eclectic menu, with items listed as either cold, hot, or sweet. Although many dishes could be placed in that most risky of culinary categories, fusion, it turns out the exotic touches in chef Perreault's cuisine are subtle.

Two of the cold starters—crunchy Savoy cabbage with arugula, apples, and smoked duck, and fresh artichoke with marinated calamari and toasted hazelnuts—are made with original, well-matched ingredients. A hot and cold salad consisting of confit of quail with baby potatoes dressed with garlic, olive oil, sel de Guérande, and white balsamic vinegar reduction is, however, a miss. The medley sounds promising, but the dish is dominated by mealy, white-fleshed potatoes.

The deep-fried sweetbreads coated in a gingerbread-crumb crust gets my nomination for starter of the year. Served with a hot quince dipping jelly, every morsel is crisp, melting, spicy, and fruity—the most exciting nuggets around. Curried tempura tiger prawns served in a gold-napkin-lined bamboo steamer basket along with a ramekin of cool pepper-mango salsa is the ideal choice for those who enjoy their food on the spicy side. Also irresistible is a velvety butternut squash soup, tinged with nutmeg and served with sautéed snails and a dribble of sesame oil. Alongside are two fried ravioli, which disappoint only because the goat's cheese filling is a bit skimpy.

Like so many young chefs, Perreault appears to be a garde-manger specialist who excels in the realm of smaller portions. Proof is the main courses, where he occasionally stumbles. The pan-seared rib steak paired with a cupful of sweet balsamic sauce, baby bok choy, and asparagus is tough and has little flavour. A crisp-skinned chicken leg stuffed with pistachio paste is quite nice, but it's served with a dollop of herbed mashed potatoes large enough to feed a family of four. Also trying too hard is a stew of Ricotta-filled ravioli, shredded confit of duck, mushrooms, asparagus, truffle oil, and Parmesan. Not only is there way too much going on here, but also all the elements are soaked in a thick, rich meat sauce.

More reasonably sized and with flavours more vibrant is a smoked and grilled pork chop served with herbed mashed potatoes studded with bacon and diced, sautéed celery root. Also outstanding is the grilled salmon filet, which is fresh, moist, and beautifully enhanced with a candied ginger cream sauce sprinkled with black sesame seeds.

Desserts are another of Area's fortes. Both the berry clafoutis and the oven-baked pineapple seasoned with cinnamon and coffee beans are served with luscious homemade vanilla ice cream. The lemon meringue tart is a revelation. Assembled to order, it offers a delicate tart shell, a potent lemon curd, and a cloud of Italian meringue.

Though waits between courses can be long, service at this sophisticated boutique restaurant is courteous and professional.

IN THE KITCHEN • Chef and co-owner Ian Perreault.

DECOR, DRESS, AMBIENCE • The scene is subdued and sophisticated, with groovy tunes and chattering bilingual patrons providing a pleasant hum in the background. The walls are white-painted brick and lined with slim horizontal mirrors. Other smart features include gauzy white drapes, fresh flower arrangements, and a large, goldfish-filled aquarium. It's all quite Zen, chic, and fabulous.

WINE LIST • The wine list is short, with nicely varied and well-priced bottles, including Chablis, Hautes Côtes-de-Beaune, and Valpolicella priced at under $40.

DON'T MISS • The tempura shrimp, the fried sweetbreads, the grilled pork chop, and the desserts—especially, when available, the lemon meringue tart.

WORDS TO THE WISE • One of the most impressive facets of Area is the creativity-to-value ratio. This generally high-calibre cuisine is a steal at these prices. What's more, the food seems to be steadily improving. This bodes well for the future.

AREA
1429 Rue Amherst (near Ste. Catherine)
Telephone: (514) 890-6691
Open: Lunch, 11:30 A.M.-2:30 P.M., Tuesday to Friday;
dinner, 6 P.M.-11 P.M., Tuesday to Sunday
Wheelchair access: Yes
Reservations: Essential
Cards: All major cards
Price range: Starters, $8-$12; main courses, $16-$20;
desserts, $6

| ★★★★ | $ $ $ $ | REVIEWED 06/99 |

AUBERGE HATLEY

SNAPSHOT · Window boxes cascading with flowers and a breath-taking view of Lac Massawippi await diners at this acclaimed Relais & Château country inn located in North Hatley, a one-and-a-half hour drive from downtown Montreal. The modern French cuisine of chef Alain Labrie features many fresh herbs and greens, which are grown in the on-site greenhouses. Wine is taken seriously at Auberge Hatley. Service, though formal, could not be more hospitable. Though meal prices tend to run high, few restaurants offer a gourmet experience of this calibre.

THE BIG PICTURE · There are good restaurants and there are great restaurants. You can find great food in a good restaurant, but greatness is about more than just what's on the plate. The operation must rate top marks on all counts: a beautiful setting, a warm ambience, superb service, impeccable tableware, an outstanding cellar, and inventive, seasonal cuisine that makes use of the best local ingredients. Auberge Hatley is that kind of place.

How could one ever go back to casual dining after watching tuxedoed waiters move quietly around the well-spaced tables in the auberge's elegant dining room? Crusty rolls from a basket of locally baked bread grace every table. Minutes after arriving, diners are treated to an amuse-bouche made of eggplant, zucchini slices, and grilled goat's cheese. This simple palate teaser, dressed to perfection with a pungent basil oil, starts the meal off on the highest of notes.

Cold starters include a simple goat's cheese salad with tomato confit and wintercress salad, and a duck and foie gras ballotin with a sweet and spicy balsamic vinaigrette. Both are accompanied by lovely greenhouse lettuces, including baby watercress, poirée, and arugula grown in the auberge's nearby commercial greenhouse, Domaine de la Cressonnière.

The second course offers scallops with grapefruit beurre blanc, and a salmon tartare with Oscietra caviar and sour cream. The five seared scallops, topped with a sprinkling of oven-dried orange zest, are arranged in a circle around a mound of sautéed julienne of leek. The tangy grapefruit-butter sauce turns out to be the perfect foil for the tender, sweet scallops.

The salmon tartare is a bit of a letdown. A round of minced salmon is iced with a thick layer of sour cream, masking the subtle flavour of the fish. This also happens to be the second cold starter on the menu; it would be far better followed by a hot appetizer for contrast.

Another excellent starter is a mushroom pithiviers with Madeira sauce. Although the puff pastry is heavier than expected, the torte is packed with a variety of delicious wild mushrooms and served on a large pool of Madeira sauce.

Main courses arrive covered with silver domes, or cloches. The cloches are removed with panache, revealing beautifully presented plates. Two worth sampling are tournedos of duck magret with foie gras and orange sauce, and grilled beef tenderloin with wild mushroom jus.

Topped with a mouthwatering piece of caramelized foie gras, the tender, rosé slices of duck are served with al dente green beans and sautéed mushrooms and potatoes. The beef filet's accompaniments include fresh peas, mushrooms, and soft rounds of beef marrow. The mushroom sauce, carefully spooned around the meat at the table, is light and full flavoured.

As dinner reaches the three-hour mark, the waiter arrives with a selection of over a dozen local and imported raw-milk cheeses, including a ten-year-old Lac St. Jean Cheddar, a Pouligny St. Pierre goat's cheese, a Brie de Meaux, and a Reblochon.

Desserts at Auberge Hatley are as elegant as the surroundings. A rhubarb soup with vanilla iced yogourt is a bit bland; even the yogourt does little to heighten the flavour sensations. A citrus plate comprised of lime sherbet, lemon mousse, and lemon balm crème anglaise is light and refreshing—the perfect end to a wonderful meal.

IN THE KITCHEN · Chef Alain Labrie.

DECOR, DRESS, AMBIENCE · This restaurant's formality belies its hospitable feel. The pale-yellow room is simple and elegantly decorated. Through tall windows there's a breathtaking view of Lac Massawippi as well as elaborate gardens and the surrounding hills. Jackets are required at dinner.

WINE LIST · The wine list consists of page after page of fairly priced, predominantly French wines. Unless you're an expert, leave the choosing to one of the sommeliers, who will not only arrive at your table with full knowledge of your order but also might surprise you by recommending a less expensive bottle than you had planned on.

DON'T MISS · The salads, the seared scallops, the duck foie gras, the beef tenderloin with wild mushroom jus, and the cheese course.

WORDS TO THE WISE · A meal at Auberge Hatley is to die for. It's also to pay for. The total cost for two can top $300. Is it worth it? Absolutely—not only for the food, but also for the experience.

AUBERGE HATLEY
325 Chemin Virgin, North Hatley
Telephone: 1-800-336-2451, or (819) 842-2451
Open: Lunch, noon-2 P.M.; dinner, 6 P.M. to 9 P.M., daily
Wheelchair access: Yes
Reservations: Recommended
Cards: Major cards
Price range: Two set menus, $70 and $105; three-course table d'hôte menu, $55

★ ★ 1/2	$ $	REVIEWED 01/02

AU PIED DE COCHON

SNAPSHOT · Au Pied de Cochon is a restaurant with few pretensions. Artistic-plate-presentation seekers, "heart smart" eaters, and vegetarians be damned. This is a place for pork, duck, venison, even poutine, and the kind of hearty French fare that chefs themselves enjoy after an early-morning excursion to the market, when a bowl of steaming onion soup and a glass of inky Crozes-Hermitage hit the spot better than a croissant and a café au lait. This exciting new bistro/brasserie, like its owner (and the crowd consisting of the Plateau's hippest thirty-and-fortysomethings), has character—a quality all too rare on today's restaurant scene.

THE BIG PICTURE · Restaurant critics receive plenty of letters. They come mostly from readers recommending restaurants they would like to see reviewed. Others, from both restaurant patrons and restaurateurs, offer comments—either glowing or critical—about reviews that run counter to the reader's experience. Once in awhile I receive mail questioning the whereabouts of a favourite chef. Recently, several have started with, "Could you tell me what has become of Martin Picard?"

Besides learning that he was giving the occasional cooking class, I'd heard little about Picard's whereabouts since he left Le Club des Pins in the summer of 2000. Rumours later began circulating that he planned to open a bistro-and-brasserie-style restaurant, on Avenue Duluth, appropriately named Au Pied de Cochon.

Like his local English counterpart, Globe chef David McMillan, Martin Picard is often considered a culinary enfant terrible: a passionate and opinionated young chef who likes things done his way, favouring artisanal meats and produce over standard ingredients and injecting a large dose of personality into every dish. During his three years at Le Club des Pins, he was acclaimed for

his bold take on southern French cuisine, serving whole fish and
chickens baked in a salt crust, lamb shanks slow-cooked in fat
(confit), and duck magrets piled high with wild mushrooms. Hot
foie gras enhanced with lavender honey or chocolate was considered his signature dish.

You'll find such unusual dishes, and plenty of new ones, at his
new restaurant—all reasonably priced at under $20. A recent meal
here started with "oreilles de crisse," half-moon-shaped slices of
deep-fried lard that were dry, supercrisp, and cut into bite-size
pieces far more appealing than the large cabane-à-sucre variety.
Following that bit of indulgence came a superb onion soup filled
with just the right amount of cheese, croutons, and caramelized
onions, everything suspended in a robust of beef broth. A plate of
"cochonailles" included a fine assortment of pork charcuterie
made in-house. My preferred starter was a simple plate of gently
flavoured, thinly sliced smoked ham (credited to a certain Marcel
Picard, a farmer from L'Estrie and no relation to the chef) served
with croutons doused with peppery virgin olive oil.

Main courses included a delicious Alsatian choucroute consisting of tangy fermented cabbage, Strasbourg sausage, baked
ham, and salt pork. The ragoût de pattes de cochon is not the
usual sauce-heavy stew but an assembly of small meatballs and
vegetables topped with a crisp square of breaded, deep-fried—
fatty and gelatinous—pig's feet meat.

As one can expect with any new restaurant, there were a few
disappointments. The duck magret was overcooked and tough,
and the sliced potatoes served underneath were greasy. Fortunately, the dish was topped with a generous mound of delicious
wild mushrooms.

Some dishes could use more seasoning. The foie gras flan
served with a purée of figs and croutons is a case in point; it had
a smooth texture and pleasant flavour but grew dreary after the
first few bites. Although the cassoulet was presented in a beautiful
earthenware casserole filled with tender braised lamb and duck
confit, its white beans and sauce were simply crying out for salt (I
also prefer cassoulet topped with a bread-crumb crust, but that's
a personal preference).

As for dessert, the lemon tart sampled was no more than run-of-the-mill. Far better were the textbook-perfect crème caramel, and the velvety baked apple served atop a butter-soaked slice of pain rustique.

The former owner of Le Club des Pins, Danielle Matte, oversees the dining room and acts as hostess. It's rare to see service provided with such a combination of warmth and professionalism, qualities manifested by the entire wait staff.

IN THE KITCHEN • Chef and owner Martin Picard.

DECOR, DRESS, AMBIENCE • Au Pied de Cochon's original decor is one of its strengths. Napkin rings, menus, and business cards are all emblazoned with an amusing cartoon of the chef, frying pan in hand, riding a smiling pig. Picard was lucky enough to score a locale on one of the city's most popular restaurant strips that once housed a pizzeria, and he puts its wood-burning oven to good use. Large loaves of country bread are sliced on a butcher's block next to a refrigerated takeout counter filled with duck confit, tourtières, and foie gras terrines. Other original touches include numbered wood tables, mirrored walls, and an open kitchen filled with chefs wearing funky floppy hats and T-shirts.

WINE LIST • The wine list is filled with a smartly chosen selection of international wines priced between $28 and $167, with two-thirds of the bottles costing less than $55. Au Pied de Cochon may be Avenue Duluth's only licensed restaurant, but with prices like these, you won't miss bringing your own.

DON'T MISS • The "oreilles de crisse," the "cochonailles" plate, the smoked ham plate, the choucroute, the ragoût de pattes de cochon, the crème caramel, and the baked apple.

WORDS TO THE WISE • Forget working up an appetite by spending an hour hunting for that elusive parking spot on the Plateau. Taking a cab or walking is your best bet. Au Pied de Cochon is a nonsmoking restaurant. As it says on the menu, "The only smoking permitted here is that of the salmon and ham."

AU PIED DE COCHON
536 Avenue Duluth West (near Berri)
Telephone: (514) 281-1114
Open: 5 P.M.-midnight, Tuesday to Sunday
Wheelchair access: Yes
Reservations: Recommended; nonsmoking environment
Cards: Major cards
Price range: Starters, $5-$18; main courses, $11.50-$20;
desserts, $4.75-$8

★★	$ $ $	REVIEWED 08/01

AU TOURNANT DE LA RIVIÈRE

SNAPSHOT · A mere ten minutes from the Champlain Bridge, Carignan's finest restaurant offers classic French food in a contemporary country setting. Wild mushroom dishes and meats are standouts. Also a cut above is the impressive wine list and solicitous service. The tranquil atmosphere picks up on weekends and at Sunday brunch, when reservations are essential.

THE BIG PICTURE · Au Tournant de la Rivière is a very French restaurant. Reading through the menu, one doesn't get the sense that this establishment follows the trend towards market cuisine, as few of the selections (including dessert) are particularly seasonal.

The menu offers either an elaborate multicourse tasting menu, or a four-course table d'hôte that includes soup, starter, main course, and dessert. Although there are a number of luxury ingredients listed (foie gras, wild mushrooms, duck, lobster, sweetbreads), prices are reasonable.

Service is one of the restaurant's drawing cards. Not only are the waitresses courteous, but they also know the menu and wine list inside out, and they take conspicuous pride in their work.

The soups offered include fish soup, cucumber vichyssoise

with shrimp, and minestrone. The fish soup—enhanced with a generous dose of tomato and served with the requisite saffron-filled, garlicky rouille and grated cheese—is pleasant and assertive but too thick to satisfy. Unable to absorb even a single drop of this potage, the croutons sit on the surface instead of slowly sinking through the liquid.

The vichyssoise, by contrast, is light, creamy without being cloying, and refreshing. Topped with a bunch of baby coriander sprouts, its only off note is the half dozen utterly tasteless Matane shrimp. The minestrone is also delicious. The robust chicken broth is filled with a macédoine of fresh vegetables, and the flavour accent comes from a dollop of basil-laden pistou (the French equivalent of—you guessed it—pesto). Every spoonful offers clear, summery flavours. Nice.

Appetizers turn up hits and misses. One of the best is a flaky tart covered with sautéed leeks, goat's cheese, and raisins. Just when I thought I'd had it with insipid goat's cheese starters, along comes one that offers a cheese with enough pungency to take the starring role it deserves. Paired with the melting leeks and sweet raisins, the tangy chèvre makes this dish a real showstopper.

Cannelloni with foie gras and wild mushrooms also benefits from a cheese topping, which in this case turns out to be an orange-coloured, hazelnut-flavoured Mimolette. The cheese shavings garnish two crêpes filled with chopped wild mushrooms and bits of sautéed foie gras served with a creamy mushroom sauce. It's a winning combination of flavours—so earthy and strong—yet none of the many wild mushrooms in the mix come to the fore.

The spiced duck in a croustillant casing is comprised of dark, confit-style shredded duck meat in a phyllo shell, the whole accompanied by no more than a spattering of sauce and a sprinkling of cinnamon. This fails to impress as it's all so dry—simply crying out for a ladleful of sauce—and the strong spice obliterates the duck flavour.

Many main courses seem to suffer from the same fault: vegetables used as an accessory instead of as an integral part of the dish. A generous portion of striped sea bass—cooked to perfection—is marred by a sweet mango sauce and overcooked asparagus spears that add little. The lamb dish (chops and loin) is very good;

the meat is pink, moist, and flavourful. But the potato galette around which the meat is arranged is soggy and tasteless. Although the magret de canard has a fine flavour, the texture is somewhat tough and spongy, and the skin lacks the desired crackly mouth feel.

The cheese course features, among others, a Migneron de Charlevoix and a Sir Laurier d'Arthabaska. Desserts are worth the indulgence. A hot apple tart features thinly sliced apples, a hazelnut filling, a crisp crust, and a scoop of rum ice cream. Also served with rum ice cream are a mellow chocolate soufflé, and a Pavlova consisting of berries, hard meringue, and whipped cream.

IN THE KITCHEN • Chef and owner Jacques Robert.

DECOR, DRESS, AMBIENCE • The decor of this converted blue barn is a conundrum of contemporary styles. It features flying-saucer-shaped light fixtures, wall-to-wall carpeting, yellow stucco walls, red-cushioned wicker chairs, an imposing atrium, and an eclectic selection of paintings hung in every available space. The overriding feel is more modern hotel lobby than country restaurant.

WINE LIST • The uniquely French wine list includes many prestigious and pricey bottles, including the wine world's Big Three — namely, Château Pétrus, Château d'Yquem, and Romanée-Conti. Fortunately, there are many modest selections as well, and the staff is more than happy to consult within your price range.

DON'T MISS • The goat's cheese tart, the lamb, and dishes that include wild mushrooms (mushroom gathering is a passion of the chef's).

WORDS TO THE WISE • Those accustomed to hip and happening surroundings may find Au Tournant de la Rivière a bit stodgy. But stodgy can be good, and many people would be happy to frequent an establishment such as this that offers attentive service and classic French food in a let's-get-away-from-it-all setting.

AU TOURNANT DE LA RIVIÈRE
5070 Salaberry, Carignan
Telephone: (450) 658-7372
Open: Dinner, 6:30 P.M.-9 P.M., Wednesday to Saturday;
Sunday brunch, 11 A.M.-2 P.M.
Wheelchair access: Yes
Reservations: Recommended; essential for brunch
Cards: Major cards
Price range: Four-course table d'hôte menu, $37-$60;
tasting menu, $70

| ★★★1/2 | $ $ $ $ | REVIEWED 01/01 |

BEAVER CLUB

SNAPSHOT · A long-established haunt for the city's business elite, the Beaver Club, located in the Queen Elizabeth Hotel, should also hold a treasured spot on any food-lover's list. The dining room may feel old-fashioned, but the French cuisine, featuring the best Canadian ingredients, can hold its own next to many a modern menu. Service is formal but friendly. Conservative gourmets are sure to find this the ideal spot for an elegant celebration.

THE BIG PICTURE · If the Beaver Club had opened five or ten years ago, it would have been just another hotel restaurant. But this legendary establishment is a Montreal institution. It has become part of our history. For decades, it was the restaurant of choice for the city's movers and shakers. In years past, this was the place where corporate honchos cut deals while indulging in birdbath martinis, oysters Rockefeller, and flambéed steaks — all under the watchful eyes of the stuffed moose heads that lined the walls.

The original Beaver Club was an association formed in 1785 by an elite group of fur traders, Montreal's fur barons. To become a member of this select group, one had to be accepted by unanimous vote. One also had to have wintered in the Northwest Territories and be "vigorous and socially acceptable." The Queen Elizabeth Hotel's Beaver Club restaurant, which opened in 1959, was named after these founding fathers.

Like the original club, the restaurant also counts members among its clientele—today close to 900. Though not required to have wintered on Baffin Island or James Bay, they still represent the city's social elite: captains of industry, politicians, and sports figures. Members' names are engraved on special plates displayed in a glassed-in case at the entrance.

The menu offers a splendid sampling of Canada's top luxury ingredients: Îles de la Madeleine lobster, Malpeque oysters, Charlevoix veal, Abitibi caviar, foie gras, caribou, hare, and more. Though the ingredients are Canadian, many of the underlying accents are French and North American.

What's bound to strike one first about the Beaver Club is the service. The young maître d' is friendly, the waiters are meticulously schooled, and the busboys are efficient. No wonder the bigwigs feel at home.

Soups are irresistible, especially the lentil soup. A shallow bowl dotted with cubes of house-smoked salmon and a dollop of sour cream arrives at the table first. This is followed by a small plate of buttery horseradish croutons. Next comes a silver tureen from which the waiter ladles out the soup. The idea is to drop a crouton into the thick brown mélange and spoon up mouthfuls of the hot, perfectly seasoned liquid accented by, alternately, smoky salmon, rich cream, or crunchy crouton. Divine.

Plate presentations are artfully assembled without being overly fussy. A salad, presented as a bouquet in a wraparound tuile, complete with wispy greens and edible flowers, is the centrepiece of a fan of thinly sliced smoked duck breast and red tuna carpaccio topped with sautéed bolet mushrooms and dressed with a mustard-oil vinaigrette. It's a whimsical combination of flavours and textures—light, tangy, melting, smoky—and easily the most glamorous carpaccio/salad dish around.

When available, don't miss the panfried scallops served with a purée of duck-enhanced beans and beurre blanc swirled with a truffled duck jus. The scallops have a sweet flavour, offset by the earthiness of the bean purée and truffle. It's a dish one could imagine plunging into and rolling around in.

Main courses also score high. How nice to see the waiter masterfully carve the roasted-to-order Cornish hen tableside into four generous pieces and then surround them with roasted root vegetables. It's all so delicious and so very Sunday dinner.

Equally rich and delicious is the Charlevoix veal with Gorgonzola cheese and porcini mushrooms. The thick round of veal loin is panfried to perfection, and its subtle flavour is enhanced (as opposed to masked) by a surprisingly mellow Gorgonzola sauce.

Fish dishes are equally impressive. A flattened salmon scaloppini is seared on one side and glazed with a fish-based savoury sabayon crisscrossed with minced sorrel. The fish could not be fresher, and the sorrel adds a welcome pungent, herbal taste.

Though plated desserts are available, it's hard to pass up the tempting selections on the "chariot de desserts." The chocolate mousse is correct, though the flavour could be more intense. A meringue and whipped cream cake topped with raspberries, strawberries, and fraises des bois is pleasant, even if the meringue is mushy. One of the best desserts is the Ricotta cake, which features a lovely lemony filling. Given the royal treatment, coffee is poured from a silver pot; refills are frequent, and it's served with a selection of sugars, milk, and whipped cream.

IN THE KITCHEN • Executive chef Alain Pignard.

DECOR, DRESS, AMBIENCE • In an effort to rejuvenate the surroundings, much of the sixties Canadiana decor — mounted stuffed animals and fur-pelt-embossed carpeting — has been removed. The back section of the restaurant's cavernous dining room has been sectioned off behind glass doors, creating a more intimate space. The room's colour scheme is a forest-like mix of brown and green, with a bit of life provided by the small flowering plants at every table. Though the overall feel is still Canadian classic, this old-fashioned dining room, with its flaming chafing dishes and rich wood panelling, feels cozy.

WINE LIST • The wine list offers a wide selection of fairly priced, prestigious wines. Wine recommendations are bang-on, and many fine selections are available by the glass.

DON'T MISS • The lentil soup, the Cornish hen, the salmon, and the sweets from the "chariot de desserts."

WORDS TO THE WISE • Though trendsetters and members of the adventurous crowd are likely to shun such a restaurant, gourmets with an eye for tradition are sure to find it an ideal spot for an understated yet elegant celebration. It's unlikely you'll walk away from a meal at the Beaver Club wowed by new flavours or ingredients. But you will eat well in the bosom of a Montreal institution still living up to its fine reputation.

BEAVER CLUB
900 Boulevard René Lévesque West (corner Mansfield, in the Queen Elizabeth Hotel)
Telephone: (514) 861-3511
Open: Lunch, noon-3 P.M., Monday to Friday;
dinner, 6 P.M.-11 P.M, Tuesday to Saturday
Wheelchair access: Yes
Reservations: Recommended; essential at lunch
Cards: Major cards
Price range: Starters, $7.50-$19; main courses, $29-$35;
desserts, $7-$9.95

★ ★ ★ | $ $ $ $ | REVIEWED 12/01

BICE

SNAPSHOT • Show up for an evening at Bice for the food alone, and you'll be missing half the fun. Manager and partner Gianni Caruso has made this restaurant an oasis for the sophisticated crowd, a place for a night of pampering and, of course, to see and be seen. The à la carte menu features a nice mix of nouvelle Italian and authentic fare, with a good choice of starters, pastas, assorted risotti, and plenty of main-course fish and meat dishes. Though the tentlike summer terrace is one of the most stunning dining spaces in the city, the long, candlelit dining room provides a fine wintertime alternative.

THE BIG PICTURE • It feels like ages ago that the space once occupied by the Waddington Gallery was plastered with "Coming Soon" signs promising a Montreal Bice, a new addition to that stylish international restaurant chain (founded in the 1920s in Milan) with branches in the great metropolitan centres—New York, London, Tokyo, and Paris. The signs, which eventually began to crumple and fade, seemed to hang there forever. I had all but given up hope of seeing a restaurant on this elegant strip of Rue Sherbrooke when the good news came that various partners from Primadonna and Mediterraneo were bringing Bice to life.

They pulled it together in record time. Employees were sent for training in Manhattan, and an Italian chef flew in from Milan to get the glamorous party started.

It's taken a few years and a few growing pains for Bice to find solid footing. Two of Bice's former chefs—José Rodriguez and John Ledwell—should be credited for bringing the menu into focus and adding a healthy dose of innovation. Today's chef, Frank Geoffre, appears to be continuing in that vein.

A recent meal with friends started off with a house cocktail (cosmopolitan) and croutons served with chopped fried squid, goat's cheese, and chickpea spread, and a tomato and basil concassé, along with a bowl of fried shiitake mushrooms with pine nuts and garlic. Both the room's sophisticated ambience and the predinner munchies scored high.

The marinated grilled octopus starter was spicy and deliciously tender, and it was accompanied by a spoonful of firm lima beans and a few strips of sweet oven-roasted tomatoes. Also superb was a plate of fried calamari paired with tempura vegetables. The squid rings were toothsome and lightly battered, the vegetables were crisp and not a bit greasy, and the two dipping sauces spiced aïoli and ponzu — provided two marked flavour-enhancers that are worlds apart.

A plate of grilled shrimp served with a savoury bread pudding, rosemary oil, and potato gaufrettes was memorable for the resilient, fresh shrimp. Particularly appreciated was a plate of oysters prepared three ways: traditional, with a bit of spinach; warmed over and sprinkled with truffle oil; and suspended in a glass of cold sake.

For main courses, the carnivore of our group enjoyed the osso buco with risotto Milanese, which featured falling-off-the-bone tender veal shank, and creamy, al dente risotto. My only quibble was that the rice had a strong taste of lemon instead of the saffron so essential to a classic Milanese risotto.

The blackened mahimahi was moist and perfectly cooked, but it's a bland fish, and this filet cried out for additional seasoning, especially salt. Fortunately, it was served with a caramelized leek and chickpea stew, which, when slathered on the fish, enlivened every bite. Also enjoyed was a mound of sautéed red Swiss chard, a delicious vegetable too rarely served in our local Italian restaurants.

Pasta lovers are sure to enjoy Bice's selection of primi piatti, as most of the pasta is made in-house. Though the pappardelle with Mozzarella and tomato cream sauce has long been a favourite, don't overlook another of Bice's signature pastas — veal ravioli (ravioli della Massaia). Unlike so many inferior renditions of this classic, this generous portion offers tender half-moon pasta pillows that are meaty (as opposed to pasty) and smothered in a rich and potent wild mushroom sauce.

I know of no other Italian restaurant that takes as much care with the dessert course as Bice. Pastry chef Rodney Aguilar offers simple and elegant creations presented with flair. The milk chocolate semifreddo with caramel consists of a square of frozen mousse that's unctuous enough to coat the roof of your mouth. Chocolate lovers will be treated to one of the best molten chocolate cakes around, especially since it's paired with an intense pistachio ice cream. A banana parfait glacé filled with lemon cream provides a light finish for those wise enough to avoid the temptation of chocolate at the end of an Italian meal.

Service at Bice is good, if somewhat lacking in enthusiasm. To be fair, the young waiters are usually at hand and make fine menu and wine suggestions.

IN THE KITCHEN · Chef Frank Geoffre.

DECOR, DRESS, AMBIENCE · The decor is very smart, chic in a rather understated way, and perfectly suited to the location. The room, usually packed with downtown's best-dressed diners, follows the Bice formula with bold fresh-flower arrangements, round-back wooden chairs, thick white tablecloths, and a magnificent outdoor terrace. The best seats, next to the front window, offer terrific views of Rue Sherbrooke and the Linton building across the street.

WINE LIST · Bice's predominantly Italian wine list is short but well chosen. You'll find plenty of costly Barolos and Brunellos, but those less willing to splurge are well served, especially for white wines (there's a fine Frescobaldi Chardonnay for $45). Wines by the glass are another good choice here, for they are generously poured and also fairly priced ($7.50).

DON'T MISS · The calamari and tempura vegetables, the oysters prepared three ways, the marinated grilled octopus, the osso buco, the veal ravioli, the pappardelle with Mozzarella and tomato cream sauce, and the desserts.

WORDS TO THE WISE • Many complain that a night out at Bice can be a costly affair. True, but if you order carefully (the pastas are always delicious) you'll end up with a bill on a par with many less extravagant establishments. The lunchtime table d'hôte offers excellent value, and in the summer months lunch on Bice's terrace is unbeatable.

BICE
1504 Rue Sherbrooke West (near Guy)
Telephone: (514) 937-6009
Open: Lunch, noon-3 P.M., Monday to Friday;
dinner, 6 P.M.-11 P.M., daily
Wheelchair access: Yes
Reservations: Recommended
Cards: Major cards
Price range: Starters, $9.50-$17.50; main courses, $22.50-$36; desserts, $8

★★★	$ $ $	REVIEWED 06/00

BISTRO À CHAMPLAIN

SNAPSHOT • If you wanted to build a restaurant around the best wine cellar in the country, you'd have a hard time outdoing Dr. Champlain Charest's Bistro à Champlain. Although the restaurant's name includes the word "bistro," chef Pierre Lavallée's style is hardly casual. Expect inventive market cuisine featuring the best local produce, such as foie gras, fish, red meats, and raw-milk cheeses that simply cry out to be paired with the cellar's fine bottles. Service is first-class, and the romantic country dining room boasts views of Lac Masson and an impressive array of artworks, including paintings by local artist Jean-Paul Riopelle.

THE BIG PICTURE • There are two camps in the rarefied world of gastronomes: the food people (gourmets) and the wine people (oenophiles). The oenophile's world of grapes, corks, breathing, decanting, tannins, nose, bouquet, and vintage has little to do with the gourmet's world of choice ingredients, plate presentations, sweetness, saltiness, temperature, and crunch. Although both worlds deal with complexity of flavour (call it the over-active-tastebud syndrome), each firmly believes that the other is a mere complement to itself.

Entering the dining room of Bistro à Champlain, one senses immediately which camp one has penetrated. Wine remains this restaurant's raison d'être, a point punched home when a wine list as imposing as *The Book of Kells* is placed reverentially in the centre of the table. One could spend hours studying this list without sampling a drop. The selection is outstanding: page after page of the best that money can buy. Flipping through, one is blinded by zeros. Prices range from the marginally affordable to the second-mortgage-on-the-house variety. A methuselah of 1990 Romanée-Conti is listed at a stratospheric $60,000. The good news is that there's plenty of choice for those with $50-a-bottle budgets.

Although pairing food with such heady wines can be difficult, chef Pierre Lavallée is up to the challenge. Despite the establishment's name, his menu shuns bistro standards like steak frites and crème caramel, instead featuring beautifully presented, refined Quebec market cuisine. Lavallée exploits his ingredients with gusto. Ultrafresh bluefin tuna is covered with a coriander, chive, and dill crust and seared "à l'unilatéral" (on one side), resulting in the tenderest bite of fish this side of sashimi. Its inventive accompaniments include marinated, julienned daikon, deep-fried leek, ratatouille, and local milkweed pods, the taste of which is best described as a cross between asparagus and broccoli.

Luscious, asparagus-topped seared scallops surround a salmon-wrapped timbale of sea urchin roe, the arrangement set on a pool of rich Chardonnay butter. A generous portion of pan-seared foie gras, decorated with a tarot root chip and a slice of oven-dried blood orange, is paired with a peach, currant, pine nut, and ground cherry compote marinated in Cabernet Sauvignon vinegar. The marriage of earthy and fruity flavours is excellent, but the foie gras, especially the thin parts, is just this side of overcooked, resulting in a bitter taste. Also disappointing is a crab bisque with morels. Not only does this watery soup lack the body of a bisque and the flavour of either crab or highly perfumed morel mushrooms, but the bowl is also covered in a puff pastry crust that lacks flakiness.

By contrast, the main courses deliver. The cider and mustard-grain roasted sweetbreads are perfectly prepared—soft and sweet—and they are served with a mille-feuille composed of tomato concassé and smoky sautéed apples stacked between layers of tarot chips. Mallard duck (known in French as "colvert") is presented two ways: with the breast thinly sliced and fanned around a delicious parsnip-green-apple purée, and with the leg, as a confit, placed beside a few brown-butter-coated girolle mushrooms. Although the confit is a bit dry, the breast meat has a delicious, full flavour.

Two other offerings, venison and beef, are expertly cooked to the ideal medium-rare. The venison tournedos is served with glazed carrots, a purée of Ratte potatoes enhanced with bits of black truffle, and a potent sauce flavoured with bittersweet chocolate and juniper berries. Here's a terrific dish that cries out for one of the bank-breaking bottles of red wine from the cellar. So does the filet of beef. This pan-seared filet, no larger than the size of a child's fist, is the increasingly popular and ever-so-flavourful Angus beef. Equally bold are the accompaniments: smoky grilled artichokes with Parmigiano-Reggiano, and a miniature version of the caramel-coloured galette of thin potato slices known as "pommes Anna."

Expect another moment of wine envy when sampling the outstanding selection of cheeses from Fromagerie du Marché in St. Jerôme, including a Mi-Carême, a three-year-old Perron Cheddar, an aged Victor et Berthold, and a cinder-coated Valençai goat's cheese. On the same high note are the desserts, all made in-house and served with coulis, crème anglaise, and fresh fruit. A warm apple and pear tarte Tatin provides the ideal tangy contrast to the delectable homemade vanilla ice cream. The Valrhona chocolate mi-cuit features thick cake on the outside, molten chocolate on the inside. Coffee nougat glacée with pistachios and a caramel spice sauce provides the only spicy note — reminiscent of gingerbread, and most enjoyable.

Befitting such a fine dining experience, service at Bistro à Champlain is first-class. And, if you're lucky, you might be invited to tour the magnificent wine cellar at the end of the meal, where you may just meet Dr. Charest himself, glass in hand.

IN THE KITCHEN • Chef Pierre Lavallée.

DECOR, DRESS, AMBIENCE • Beauty, be it visual or olfactory, appears to be the foundation of Dr. Charest's bistro. The restaurant is located on scenic Lac Masson, about an hour's drive from Montreal. The interior is rustic yet elegant, with log-cabin walls, crystal chandeliers, and large original paintings by Miró, Sam Francis, Joan Mitchell, Quebec artists Louis Gosselin and Louise Prescott, as well as the most famous Lac Masson resident, Jean-Paul Riopelle (the Riopelle connection is all the more intriguing when we consider that he is one of an esteemed group of artists who, since World War II, have been asked to create labels for the great Bordeaux wine Château Mouton-Rothschild).

WINE LIST • With its 35,000-bottle wine cellar, Canada's only *Wine Spectator* magazine Grand Award, and more than 100 six-liter bottles (known as methuselahs) of the world's most prestigious wine, Domaine de la Romanée-Conti, this famed Laurentian establishment is a wine-lover's paradise.

DON'T MISS • The wine-friendly meats and cheese course, the Château d'Yquem offered by the glass, and an after-dinner tour of the wine cellar.

WORDS TO THE WISE • Yes, the wine list is a great drawing card for oenophiles, but those who live in the food-lover's camp will not be disappointed. Consider inviting along a nondrinking friend to do the driving, as the hour-long road trip could be a bit chancy after such a night of indulgence.

BISTRO À CHAMPLAIN
75 Chemin Masson, Ste. Marguerite du Lac Masson
Telephone: (450) 228-4988
Open: Summer, 6 P.M.-9:30 P.M., daily; winter, 6 P.M.-9:30 P.M.,
Thursday to Sunday
Wheelchair access: Yes
Reservations: Recommended
Cards: Major cards
Price range: Starters, $8-$26; main courses, $21-$36;
desserts, $9-$12; six-course tasting menu, $72.50

★★	$ $	REVIEWED 04/00

BISTRO ON THE AVENUE

SNAPSHOT • Arguably Westmount's most popular restaurant, this Greene Avenue eatery offers inexpensive, creative comfort food in a relaxed neighbourhood setting. There's a definite "scene" here. The crowd consists primarily of middle-aged couples with stylish haircuts, expensive sweaters, understated jewellry, and designer handbags. Though the steak frites and daily specials rise above standard fare, there's no doubt that this restaurant's main draw is the friendly atmosphere and the stellar service. Reservations are essential.

THE BIG PICTURE • At a time when so many turn to restaurants for a last-minute meal, who besides the flush and the overindulgent can handle a fancy dinner more than once a week? The solution for many appears to be the casual and inexpensive bistro. These are the establishments that specialize in simple food and a relaxing ambience, the perfect recipe for those not up to making anything but reservations for dinner. And those reservations are as difficult to garner as reservations for the top restaurants—a good indication of just how starved Montrealers are for honest, unpretentious fare. The harbinger of the "bistro à l'américaine" style is Westmount's Bistro on the Avenue, a well-loved restaurant celebrating its twelfth anniversary this year.

Expect to be given the once-over when walking to your table, as most of the patrons are regulars, and they greet each other and the wait staff by name. But as cliquish as the place may sound, the ambience is relaxed and welcoming.

There are two menus offered at lunch and dinner. The main menu includes hamburgers, salads, sandwiches, and hot dishes, such as chicken pot pie, steak, and salmon; and there is a list of daily specials representing some exciting alternatives to the standard fare.

At a recent dinner, I noticed a handsome, rumpled-suited businessman at the next table, looking down at his plate of Arctic char. The fish was stacked on a swirl of mashed potatoes and carrots, with small mounds of chopped beets around the sides. "What an interesting presentation," he said to his companion. He was right. It *was* original—especially for a bistro—and, at $16.95, much less expensive than a similar dish downtown.

Equally impressive from a presentation perspective is the papaya and shrimp appetizer. A colourful, papaya-based salsa provides a gentle boost to three tender, medium-sized grilled shrimp. The whole is topped with an airy pile of julienned, deep-fried squash, which provides a pleasant crunch with every bite. Though not as playful as the papaya and shrimp dish, the cold seafood salad, composed of cold seared tuna, mussels, a lone scallop and a mound of baby lettuce, is another satisfying, high-quality starter.

Among the main-menu appetizers are crab cakes with mustard-dill sauce, which, though crisp and grease-free, have little taste of crab, and another old-fashioned offering, phyllo-wrapped herbed goat's cheese, which tastes as tired as it sounds. I'm not wild about the spinach salad either. Tossed with grated Cheddar, bacon bits, and raw sliced mushrooms, this well-known combination might have worked if not for the sweet honey dressing, bereft of even an ounce of tang to bolster such neutral ingredients.

Fish dishes are the high point of the main-course selections. The Arctic char, mentioned earlier, is delicate, moist, and pleasantly salty, and the accompanying mashed potatoes are light and well seasoned. My favourite fish dish is the mahimahi. Ultrafresh and lightly grilled, it's not only juicy and meltingly tender, but also smartly paired with fluffy Basmati rice, sautéed Swiss chard, and al dente asparagus.

Meats are less predictable. Rabbit, served with a pile of stuffing and heavy blue cheese mashed potatoes, is unevenly cooked. The legs are meaty and moist, but the saddle is dry and tasteless. Osso buco is pink on the outside, brown on the inside—something I've never seen before. The marrow, a favourite of osso buco lovers, is minimal, and the nutty flavour of the accompanying flageolet beans is completely wiped out by an overabundance of fennel. An exception to the mediocre meat offerings is the steak. The generous, medium-rare strip loin is thick and full flavoured. Naturally, it's served with thin homemade fries, more tender than crisp, and an addictive garlicky mayonnaise.

Desserts are of the American variety—rich and sinful. The apple Frangelico cheesecake is pleasant but has no discernible flavour of that heavenly hazelnut liquor. Coffee crème brûlée is also faintly flavoured, and drastically overbruléed. Flourless chocolate cake and chocolate pecan tart are for those who like heavy, fudgy-textured desserts. The most elegant choice is the smooth mango sorbet. Served in a small tulip cup, this may be the perfect treat to soothe a tired palate. Coffee is excellent.

Service at Bistro on the Avenue is casual, efficient, and friendly. Though the restaurant can often be packed to the rafters, seldom does one feel rushed or neglected. Making the experience even more memorable are the little touches, such as allowing you to sample a wine before ordering a full bottle.

IN THE KITCHEN · Chefs Guy Lavoie and Clinton Hughes.

DECOR, DRESS, AMBIENCE · Noise levels at the bistro are high, creating an exciting buzz. This is definitely the Anglo set, and most of the conversations seem to revolve around the stock market. The convivial mood is fortified by such reliable tokens of bistro-ness as a long bar packed with talkative locals, large framed mirrors (to help you spy on your neighbour across the room), posters of Impressionist paintings, green-vinyl banquettes, black-boards, and ceiling fans, all surrounded by bright, sponge-painted yellow walls.

WINE LIST · The wine list is affordable but not especially interesting. The costliest reds, a Chianti Classico Brolio at $42 and a Californian Fetzer at $38, are ordinary at best. It's surprising that such an upscale crowd hasn't requested a bit more variety.

DON'T MISS · The steak frites. Otherwise, skip the printed menu and go for one of the 14 daily specials.

WORDS TO THE WISE · There are highs and lows here, but with prices like these it's hard to be disappointed. Bistro on the Avenue proves that the middle ground between luxury fare and fast food is the place to be. If I lived nearby, I wouldn't hesitate to come here for a casual meal—provided I could get a last-minute reservation.

BISTRO ON THE AVENUE
1362 Avenue Greene (near Sherbrooke)
Telephone: (514) 939-6451
Open: 11:30 A.M.-10:30 P.M., Monday to Saturday;
10:30 A.M.-10 P.M., Sunday
Wheelchair access: No
Reservations: Essential
Cards: All major cards
Price range: Starters, $4.50-$9.95; main courses, $9.95-$16.95; desserts, $3.75-$5.25

★★	$ $ $	REVIEWED 07/00

BUONNA NOTTE

SNAPSHOT • Gorgeous waitresses, loud music, casual Italian food, and an industrial decor set the scene for the Main's trendiest eatery. After ten successful years on Boulevard St. Laurent, Buonna Notte could be considered a Montreal institution (but don't tell the trendies who look like they've just discovered the place). What's the secret of its success? Making it all feel new and exciting, night after night. And making sure that its brand of cool is accessible to all. Friendly is in, pretentious is out. That's the golden rule that seems to keep them coming back for more.

THE BIG PICTURE • On your typical happening night at Buonna Notte, many of the young turks in attendance look like they've just died and gone to heaven. It might have something to do with the gorgeous waitress/models, who wear hot pink and lavender sheaths cut low in the neckline and high on the leg. Or maybe it's the pulsating background music that makes conversation conveniently impossible. Patrons gaze reverently at the auto- graphed plates on display in the entranceway, signed by such high priests of hip as Jim Carrey, Nicolas Cage, and Bono — a reassur- ing sign that they're at the epicentre of Montreal cool.

Buonna Notte caters to those for whom dining out is a rite of passage while providing an exciting night on the Main for the more experienced — a walk on the wild side. But this scene isn't for everyone. If you reserve a table for 8 P.M. on a busy night, you'll be faced with crowds, low lights, and loud background music. When ordering, you'll probably have to strain to catch the waitress's description of the specials. By 9 P.M., you won't see much of what's put in front of you or be able to communicate with your dining companions without yelling. In short, it's not everyone's idea of a relaxing time.

Happily, the only sense that's not impaired in this environ- ment is one's sense of taste. The menu is filled with popular mod- ern Italian dishes — pastas, pizzas, meats, fish — but the most interesting choices are the daily specials. Recent offerings have in-cluded a carpaccio of swordfish topped with olive oil, orange juice, and zest. Soft and citrusy, it's an ideal summer starter, and, at $7.50, it's an affordable experiment for carpaccio novices. The classic carpaccio also gets novel treatment here. Paper-thin slices of raw beef are replaced by chunkier morsels that are lightly seared and tossed with the usual sidekicks, arugula and Parmesan shavings.

Equally original is a plate of wild mushrooms with polenta. The firm polenta is shaped into a round container, sliced in half, and filled with sautéed portebellini and Parisian mushrooms. Al-though the polenta is excellent, rich and well-seasoned, the por-tion is too large. The mushrooms, piping hot and mixed with concassé of tomatoes, lack seasoning, and the swirl of reduced balsamic vinegar fails to provide the desired kick.

Artichoke croquettes served with goat's cheese are crisp and grease-free but taste not a bit of artichoke. Nonetheless, the subtle flavour of these crispy green disks makes a nice foil for the strong cheese. The tuna salad could use some attention, as the tuna is canned, the garnish of black and green olives is excessively salty, and the mix of julienned carrots, designer lettuce, and sliced celery is lacklustre.

Main courses are much better. The veal chop is expensive by global standards but worth every penny. Pounded to perfection, the meat is tender, flavourful, and rosé in the centre—just the way it ought to be. The huge chop is topped with a delicious heap of portebellini, oyster, and Parisian mushrooms along with baby new potatoes, and the mix is enlivened by a bold herb-lemon sea-soning. Yum.

Sophisticated palates, shunning the pizza, will no doubt hone in on the mezzaluna pasta. The five plump pockets are filled with gamy guinea fowl and served with a cream-based mushroom sauce—excellent.

Desserts are surprisingly subdued for such a funky place. The "Bongo Bongo" does not live up to its exotic name. It's just a large profiterole with chocolate sauce, okay vanilla ice cream, and tough choux pastry. Those who don't like their desserts chewy, ooey, and gooey should abstain. My favourite is a simple Ricotta cheesecake with pine nuts. Its sweet taste and dry texture are ideally offset by a tangy red fruit coulis.

Hats off to Buonna Notte's waitresses. Friendly and efficient, they provide service with a smile despite working the night shift in dainty mules. The hectic scene is such that the timing of the courses can be a bit prolonged. And the fact that patrons tend to monopolize the attention of such cool chicks is understandable.

IN THE KITCHEN • Chef Renato Pellizzari.

DECOR, DRESS, AMBIENCE • The decor here is industrial bistro: a mix of open pipes, mirrors, ceiling fans, and turquoise-and-maroon walls illuminated by spotlights and votive candles. Needless to say, there's an ashtray on every table (salt and pepper shakers are available upon request). Open floor-to-ceiling windows face a raucous strip of the Main (where hard-revving motorcycles abound), making it difficult to judge whether noise levels are higher inside or outside.

WINE LIST • Buonna Notte's wine list features an impressive array of Italian wines (many privately imported): Champagne, Barolos, and Brunellos for the visiting celebs, and inexpensive Chiantis for the newcomers to the scene.

DON'T MISS • The daily specials and pastas are probably your best bet.

WORDS TO THE WISE • It would be easy to categorize this restaurant as just another trendy hot spot. But Buonna Notte has been going strong for years now, while wannabes surrounding it on St. Laurent have come and gone. It's not the best restaurant for a quiet evening with grandma, but it's *the* place for those who want to feel they're in the right place at the right time.

BUONNA NOTTE
3518 Boulevard St. Laurent (near Sherbrooke)
Telephone: (514) 848-0644
Open: Lunch, noon-3 P.M., Monday to Saturday;
dinner, 5:30 P.M.-1 A.M., Saturday, 5:30 P.M.– midnight,
Sunday to Friday.
Wheelchair access: Yes
Reservations: Essential
Cards: Major cards
Price range: Starters, $6-$14.50; main courses, $10.25-$31;
desserts $5-$7.50

★★★	$ $	REVIEWED 12/99

CAFÉ MASSAWIPPI

SNAPSHOT • There's plenty going on behind the wide porch and
lace curtains of North Hatley's Café Massawippi. Chefs/owners
Dominic Tremblay and Maryse Carrier's original, high-end cuisine is offered at prices well below what you'll pay in the big city.
And though the setting and ambience are country casual, the
cooking and service offer the utmost in professionalism.

THE BIG PICTURE • Take a look at many of Montreal's top
restaurants and you'll notice that most are chef-owned. From the
choice of napkins and cutlery to the flavour of the tuile propped
on your dessert, chef-owners offer their patrons a highly person-
alized dining experience. Call it purity of vision.

It's a tough gig. At a time when four-leaf clovers and uni-
corns are easier to come by than bank loans for restaurants, chef-
entrepreneurs have to be careful. Yet for a chef to make a mark, a
certain amount of creative risk taking is imperative. If the chef is
talented enough to manage the financial responsibilities while
reaching the level of maturity in his or her cooking required to
produce a menu that is both unique and desirable, then a star is
born. Café Massawippi is a case in point.

The monthly menu (written on a chalkboard beside the front door) offers a table d'hôte format that includes appetizers, main courses, desserts, and coffee. Dinner for two with wine will probably cost less than $100, which is roughly half the price of dinner at one of Montreal's top restaurants. What's more, the ingredients favoured by this kitchen — lamb, sweetbreads, oysters, fresh salmon, duck — are first-class.

Dinner starts off with delicious homemade focaccia and an amuse-bouche such as a cream of zucchini soup with smoked herring, or chicken-liver pâté served with a curried raisin chutney.

The artfully presented appetizers always draw raves. Standouts include a spring roll filled with goat's cheese and spinach set atop a fresh salad of delicately dressed apples, raisins, and sliced Belgian salsify, and a large cod raviole with lime vinaigrette served with braised fennel, eggplant, and tomato coulis. The best starter is the "terrine mystère." The mystery meat turns out to be lamb. A terrine made with lamb? Yes, and once you taste the perfectly seasoned meat accented with caraway seeds and a spoonful of cranberry salsa you'll wonder why everyone isn't making this dish.

The phyllo beggar's purse of lamb sweetbreads and kidneys is less successful in that the sweetbreads are dry and overcooked. A seafood risotto, served in a lovely lidded porcelain pot, is packed with shrimp, mussels, and clams, but the underlying bed of risotto is mushy.

Main courses follow in the same creative style as the starters. This is typified by the pavé of perfectly cooked salmon topped with deep-fried rice noodles and served with spinach and sautéed red peppers and Ratte potatoes. Another good choice is the thinly sliced magret of duck served with celery root purée, sautéed spinach, and a phyllo turnover filled with herbed mushrooms.

Of the homemade desserts, the gentle ginger crème brûlée and the warm chocolate cream topped with light hazelnut-chocolate ice cream are both enjoyable. The waffle points with sautéed pumpkin, the tiramisu, and a mirliton with mandarins all sound great and look fantastic but fall short in the flavour department. A nice alternative to dessert is the cheese course, which includes some of Quebec's best cheeses.

Service in this convivial country setting is casual, efficient, and friendly.

IN THE KITCHEN • Chefs and co-owners Dominic Tremblay and Maryse Carrier.

DECOR, DRESS, AMBIENCE • The setting is more homey bistro than café. This restaurant resides in a country house with the requisite front porch and lacey drapes. But if this is Holly Hobby style, she's certainly all grown up. From the large and colourful prints (some quite risqué) hung on the putty-coloured walls to the young, attractive wait staff and the stylish modern food, there's an undeniable feeling of experimentation in the air.

WINE LIST • The short, eclectic wine list is reasonably priced, with well-chosen bottles (and a few half bottles) from California, France, and Italy. Wines by the glass are also available for as little as five dollars.

DON'T MISS • The goat's cheese spring roll, the lamb terrine, the salmon, and the ginger crème brûlée.

WORDS TO THE WISE • Granted, the food might benefit from a simplified approach with more of an emphasis on pronounced, pure flavours; that said, however, this is a gutsy little restaurant, offering original, high-end cuisine at some of the best prices around. Be warned: Café Massawippi is only open for dinner; unless you have accommodations nearby or are planning a visit to the area, the drive to and from Montreal can be arduous, especially in winter.

CAFÉ MASSAWIPPI
3050 Chemin Capelton, North Hatley
Telephone: (819) 842-4528
Open: 6 P.M.-10 P.M., Wednesday to Saturday
Wheelchair access: Yes
Reservations: Essential
Cards: All major cards
Price range: Three-course table d'hôte menu, $27-$36

★★ | $ $ | **REVIEWED 08/01**

CHAO PHRAYA

SNAPSHOT · Few customers seem concerned with details of Thai table etiquette at Outremont's stylish Chao Phraya. And, judging from the tame menu selections, the restaurant itself does not seem overly concerned with authenticity. What the crowds appear to be drawn to here is the light, health-conscious nature of Thai cuisine, and its exotic flavours—ginger, coconut, lemongrass, peanut, chilies—which excite the palate and rejuvenate the senses. This makes Chao Phraya one of the best restaurants for a casual meal, especially during the hot summer weather.

THE BIG PICTURE · As you enter Chao Phraya, the first thing that hits you is the seductive aromas. Those lovely smells emanate from the 150 items listed on the menu (though most of the main courses are interchangeable, depending on the choice of meat).

Prices and portion sizes are reasonable, so ordering a variety of dishes to share family style is an excellent way to sample the many facets of this cuisine. Don't worry about leftovers; it's considered good manners in Thai circles to leave food on the plate— proof of your host's generosity (doggy bags are provided for those who enjoy cold pad Thai with their morning Rice Krispies).

Salads provide a fine start to the meal. The duck salad, made with spicy roast duck, red onions, mint leaves, chives, and coriander, is excellent. More typically Thai is a salad of green mango, onions, hot chilies, and dry shrimp. Unfortunately, it has a fishy aftertaste, which points to an excess of bottled fish sauce, for there's nary a shrimp in the mix. Also, the dish is overly sweet, and the mango has little or no mango flavour.

If it's flavour you're after, don't skip the soup course. The hot and sour wonton soup looks plain enough, but it packs a punch of sour, salty, and spicy, with the added aromatic kick of lemongrass. Also outstanding is the hot and sour chicken soup with coconut milk. The cooling nature of the milk neutralizes the spice, and every spoonful comes up with a lily-white morsel of chicken breast—a concert of tastes in perfect harmony.

Of the hot appetizers, the breaded shrimp are fleshy, tender, and tasty, though hardly enhanced by the sweet plum dipping sauce. The overstuffed imperial rolls are also lacking tastewise. Packed with cabbage, noodles, and shredded carrot, they have no discernible seasoning.

One of the best-loved Thai appetizers is chicken satay. Though moist, this version features grilled meat that lacks any of the desirable charred markings or flavour. The accompanying peanut sauce tastes more of coconut than of peanut, and the overriding taste sensation is sweet as opposed to spicy (Thai cuisine has a reputation for being fiery, but this tame dish is nothing more than pleasant).

Main-course dishes include more highs and lows. The sautéed pork with ginger and onions would be better with a sauce thick enough to coat the meat and vegetables; as served, it gathers in a puddle at the bottom of the plate. The sautéed chicken with peanut sauce and crispy spinach sounds better than it tastes. As with the satay, the sauce lacks character, and a bit of texture would have provided a nice contrast to the flaccid chicken. The spinach, which appears to have been sprinkled with sugar, is too sweet even for even the most well-developed sweet tooth. Also suffering in the flavour department is that Thai restaurant signature dish, pad Thai. Again, it's bland; the duck pieces within are especially lacklustre.

Those up for spicy may enjoy the sautéed roast duck with hot chili and basil, known in Thai as "ped pad kha pao." It arrives glistening on a beautiful pedestal plate. Unfortunately, all the heat (spice) appears to be emanating from the crust of chili powder on the duck, not from any layering of spices or dried chili peppers.

Without a doubt, this restaurant's forte is curries. The panang beef curry is superb. Spooned over the excellent steamed rice, the meat is tender and the sauce, a blend of coconut milk, curry paste, sweet basil, and peanuts, is as delicious as an Indian curry but even more aromatic. Chicken in a red curry sauce is another winner. This mélange is fruitier than the panang curry and well matched with chicken; it includes more fragrant basil leaves, red pepper, and pineapple.

After this plethora of novel taste sensations, the only dessert that seems appropriate is fried bananas with ice cream. Nothing too exciting here, but who goes to a Thai resto for the desserts? In my book, jasmine tea or a fruity liqueur would be more than sufficient.

IN THE KITCHEN · Chef Piao Rattanasamy.

DECOR, DRESS, AMBIENCE · This restaurant is usually crowded with casually dressed diners. The long rectangular room is elegant, though not exotic enough to transport you to faraway lands for the duration of your meal.

WINE LIST · The wine list is short but affordable; a bottle of Californian Cabernet Sauvignon provides a neutral backdrop for the meal's diverse flavours.

DON'T MISS · The duck salad, the soups, and the curries.

WORDS TO THE WISE · Though in this busy room one can sometimes feel neglected, service at Chao Phraya is, on the whole, quite good. If you're a seeker of exotica, there are discoveries to be made. Just don't be blinded by the crowds and lengthy menu into thinking that this is the last word in Thai cuisine.

CHAO PHRAYA
50 Avenue Laurier West (corner Clark)
Telephone: (514) 272-5339
Open: 5 P.M.-10 P.M., daily
Wheelchair access: No
Reservations: Essential
Cards: Major cards
Price range: Starters, $3.95-$9.95; main courses, $7.95-$16.95; desserts, $1.50-$5.95

★★1/2	$ $ $	REVIEWED 12/99

CHEZ DELMO

SNAPSHOT · Look no further than the huge, flat Dover sole pictured on the menu for the specialty of the house: fish. This historic Old Montreal restaurant, a favourite of local businessmen and lawyers, has classic French seafood, a civilized atmosphere, and solicitous service. The trout and Dover sole are sublime. At lunch, join the regulars at the bar for oysters, lobster sandwiches on brown bread, beer, and coleslaw.

THE BIG PICTURE · Many of the city's finer restaurants are examples of an international type. L'Express is pure Paris bistro. Lucca reminds us of the best Italian trattorias. Milos has already reproduced its neo-Greco digs in New York City. But if there's one restaurant absolutely rooted to its Montreal heritage, it would have to be Chez Delmo.

Located on Rue Notre Dame West, a stone's throw from Notre Dame Cathedral, in the heart of what was once Montreal's busy financial and business district, Chez Delmo is a restaurant from a bygone era. Entering the place is like stepping into a sepia-toned photograph taken at the turn of the last century. This three-floor establishment opened in 1902 as a private English gentlemen's club. The ground floor was for drinking. On the second floor, they gambled. And the top floor was—well, let's just say that the top floor was the only floor where women were allowed. Today, puritans among us will be happy to know that the second and third floors are empty, and that the only thing one can do at Chez Delmo is enjoy a fine meal.

There are reasons this long-standing restaurant still attracts loyal patrons; the menu features solid French food, the service is attentive, and the atmosphere and sound level are civilized—save for at the lunch hour, when the two-martini crowd lets loose. Rumour has it that Chez Delmo's frequent customers are given preferential treatment, but in my experience, one couldn't ask for better service or a warmer welcome. The red-jacketed waiters are seasoned professionals whose serving skills leave little to be desired.

You won't find Chilean sea bass or grilled swordfish at Chez Delmo. Things are kept simple here—classic French all the way, with cooking terms like "meunière," "St. Jacques," and "Nantua" sprinkled throughout the menu.

What better way is there to start a meal in a French seafood restaurant than with oysters? The six lovely Malpeque oysters served at Chez Delmo arrive on crushed ice and are fresh, plump, and briny. The large, thin slice of smoked salmon is also excellent, but considering that many restaurants are now smoking their own salmon, it's difficult to wax enthusiastic over this offering.

The fish soups—clam chowder and lobster bisque—prove that seasoning is the forte of this kitchen. All have a wonderful depth of flavour and are expertly salted. The lobster bisque is creamy, hot, and filled with chunks of lobster meat. The clam chowder is chock-full of clams, but it should be thicker to earn the name chowder.

Main courses, similarly, are classic French favourites. Two of the house specialties, gratinéed shrimp Nantua and Dover sole, could not be more different. The shrimp dish consists of the small variety of the crustacean smothered in a cup's worth of thick béchamel-based sauce. The generous portion is barely gratinéed and the rich and delicious sauce, which is enriched with crayfish, Cognac, and cream, completely overwhelms the shrimp.

In complete contrast is the Dover sole meunière. This lightly floured fish is sautéed in butter and served with brown-butter sauce on the side. Quickly and expertly boned at the table, the fine, firm-textured specimen is cooked to perfection, offering delicate flavour and a melt-in-the-mouth texture. Believe it or not, the trout, prepared in the same manner, is even better. The rosy flesh is tender and succulent, and the taste is divine.

The grilled sea scallops could use a bit of love and attention. The six chunky mollusks are properly grilled, but they sit naked, crying out for sauce. The one offered, a ramekin of that onion-and-caper-laden mayonnaise, tartar sauce, is about as heavy as it gets.

Another choice from the grill, halibut, must be popular with weight-watching patrons, for it's also served sans sauce. But this light and tender fish doesn't need any. The accompanying vegetables — fine French green beans and carrots — are perfectly cooked in the al dente, nouvelle cuisine style. The homemade French fries are thin, crisp, and tasty — the real McCoy.

A word of caution: don't be tempted by the small selection of meat dishes on this menu. The steaks can be fatty, sinewy, and tough, even if the accompanying pepper sauce is just as it should be — Cognac-enhanced and creamy, with a sweet, potent pepper flavour.

The desserts here are run-of-the-mill samples from the most basic French repertoire and are a bit of a letdown. The crème caramel is awfully sweet, the apple tart has a soggy crust, and the profiteroles are made with choux pastry that lacks the desirable crunchiness. You might prefer to skip dessert altogether and savour the delicious coffee instead.

IN THE KITCHEN • Chef Enzo Bertoli.

DECOR, DRESS, AMBIENCE • The restaurant is divided into two rooms, each with a different mood and decor. The front room, with its two New York-style mahogany bars, is masculine-Anglo-urban, while the dining room behind is old-fashioned-feminine-French-country. At lunchtime, many businessmen and lawyers from the nearby office towers and the Palais de Justice eat at the bar, preferring the clubby atmosphere up front. At dinner, the dimly lit dining room, with its high-backed wooden chairs, flower-print wallpaper, pale-yellow wainscoting, and antique serving platters propped around its perimeter, has a decidedly romantic, Old World ambience.

WINE LIST • The single-page wine list offers favourites from Bordeaux, the Loire Valley, Alsace, and Burgundy. I'd recommend the Sancerre, which not only provides good value but also marries well with most fish dishes.

DON'T MISS · The oysters, the lobster bisque, the halibut, and the sole or trout meunière.

WORDS TO THE WISE · While some may welcome Chez Delmo's old-fashioned style, those who favour more experimental and adventurous cuisine are likely to find it a bit too conservative. Whatever the case, fish lovers should give Chez Delmo a try. Go for lunch, find a seat between two lawyers at the bar, enjoy the lobster bisque, and soak up the soul of Old Montreal.

CHEZ DELMO
211-215 Rue Notre Dame West (near St. François Xavier)
Telephone: (514) 849-4061
Open: Lunch, 11:30 A.M.-2:30 P.M., Monday to Friday; dinner, 5:30 P.M.-10 P.M., Tuesday to Sunday
Wheelchair access: Yes
Reservations: Recommended
Cards: Major cards
Price range: Starters, $4.75-$14.75; main courses, $15.75-$29.95; desserts, $4.75-$5.25

| ★★ | $ $ $ | REVIEWED 12/00 |

CHEZ L'ÉPICIER

SNAPSHOT · This establishment bills itself as a restaurant/bar/gourmet grocery store—hence the name, Chez L'Épicier. The menu features inventive fusion cuisine that will either thrill your palate or leave it wanting. The sophisticated crowd is made up of more locals than tourists. The award-winning decor is young and modern and beautifully suited to the restaurant's classic old-stone-house setting.

THE BIG PICTURE • If you add curry spices to a béarnaise sauce is it still a béarnaise? Can a tarte Tatin be made with anything but apples? Are pickles an essential ingredient of relish? Purists will have one answer to these questions, while those who favour innovation will have another. In an effort to be different or creative, many chefs have strayed from the tried and true. But, seated in front of a plate of these newfangled offerings, one may question whether too many liberties have been taken with traditional fare.

One of Montreal's newer and more fashionable restaurants, Chez L'Épicier, takes the brave step of attempting to modernize the classics. On the menu, French culinary terms such as "pot-au-feu," "Tatin," and "bourguignon" butt up against "maki," "wonton," "ponzu," and other such exotic descriptors. The house philosophy may best be summed up in one particular menu item: foie gras glazed with tandoori caramel and banana madeleine. It would be easy to carp about such confused, fusion-style cuisine. There's always the chance, however, that one day someone will master these intriguing combinations.

Obviously, the city's diners are ready for experimentation, for last-minute reservations can be hard to come by here. On most nights, the place is packed with a primarily French, sophisticated, fortysomething crowd.

At Chez L'Épicier there's often more flash than substance. The previously mentioned seared foie gras arrives barely warm and with a sauce bereft of any of the spices associated with tandoori cooking. The accompaniments include orange halves and a banana chip, which better serve as decorations than flavour enhancements. The madeleine suffers as a savoury sponge, for its lack of sweetness results in a rubbery texture and its banana flavour is nonexistent. Better to keep those madeleines where they belong—on the petit four plate.

A second starter, a fish cake, is also served with a cookie: a shortbread fried in sesame and saffron oil. The fish cake has a light texture and flavour enhanced with the sweetness of carrot, but it's fried and therefore already dry. Adding another dry element is like adding whipped cream to a meringue pie. What this dish could use is a sauce or mayonnaise. Even the accompanying mound of marinated vegetables seems like an afterthought.

The fondant of St. Benoit du Lac blue cheese with dried rabbit is another fried galette that suffers for similar reasons. Here the dryness is alleviated somewhat by diced eggplant, which is described on the menu as a relish. The best of the starters turns out to be a hearty corn chowder drizzled with a faintly flavoured lobster oil and topped with a corn and tomato salsa. The chef credits this dish to the innovative American chef Charlie Trotter, which may explain his devotion to a medley of styles.

When the main courses arrive, you might find yourself searching for the ingredients described on the menu. Take, for instance, the Quebec lamb Tatin with endives, black olive emulsion, cream of cauliflower, and milk of nutmeg. Although it sounds intriguing, what comes on the plate is a mound of shredded cooked lamb meat topped with a few braised endive leaves, a cloud of puréed cauliflower, and a robust lamb sauce. The black olive emulsion and milk of nutmeg are nowhere in sight.

Equally mysterious is the filet mignon in a pepper-garlic crust with root vegetable bourguignon and nut vinegar béarnaise. The filet mignon is tender and cooked to the requisite medium-rare, but the sauce around the stew of root vegetables contains an off note: a spice in the curry family. "Béarnaise" is a complete misnomer, since it has none of the lively tarragon flavour and buttery richness of the classic sauce.

In welcome contrast come two stewed dishes. Sweetbreads braised in a mixture of apple juice and fresh thyme are served with a delicious vegetable stew of blue potatoes, snow peas, carrots, and beans. Every bite is heavenly. Also memorable is a salmon stew. The many morsels of pink fish are fresh tasting and delicate. The vegetables — salsify, snow peas, carrots, baby red potatoes, and green beans — are suspended in a light cream sauce perfumed with mustard and fresh mint. This simple dish proves that when the kitchen restrains its penchant for excess, the food and its ingredients really shine.

Desserts are given high marks for conception and low marks for execution. An apple and pecan crumble, which offers a sweet mix of apples and pecans, is heavy going, as the mix is weighed down by an overabundance of oatmeal. Served with a lively coconut-milk sorbet, the coconut marble cake has the desirable soft-filling consistency, but the chocolate flavour is obliterated by a shot of rum worthy of a Caribbean barman.

Service at Chez L'Épicier is uneven and can lag towards the end of the meal. But this is a young restaurant, and one can't help but be charmed by the many original touches: menus printed on small grocery bags, bread served in tin buckets, and miniature boxwood plants on every table. Then there's the food, which can vary greatly depending on how you feel about fusion and what combination of wild and wonderful flavours you're treated to on a particular night.

IN THE KITCHEN · Chef and co-owner Laurent Godbout.

DECOR, DRESS, AMBIENCE · The restaurant's award-winning decor is showcased in two high-ceilinged rooms with large picture windows, thick stone-and-brick walls, chicken-wire-wrapped light fixtures, and pillars painted swimming-pool blue. Shelves abound and are filled with cooking magazines and pricy imported food-stuffs.

WINE LIST · The wine list includes a small but impressive selection of interesting, food-friendly bottles, such as as a Cahors Château du Cèdre. All wines are reasonably priced.

DON'T MISS · The corn chowder, the sweetbread stew, the salmon stew, and the chocolate-sesame frozen nougat.

WORDS TO THE WISE · Chez L'Épicier is a much-needed addition to the staid, tourist-driven Old Montreal dining scene. It's an original restaurant that shows promise, even if the kitchen sometimes appears to be trying too hard.

CHEZ L'ÉPICIER

311 Rue St. Paul East (near St. Claude)
Telephone: (514) 878-2232
Open: Lunch, 11:30 A.M.-2 P.M., Monday to Friday;
dinner, 6 P.M.-10 P.M., daily
Wheelchair access: No
Reservations: Essential
Cards: Major cards
Price range: Starters, $4-$16; main courses, $16-$28;
desserts, $6-$14

★★1/2	$ $ $	REVIEWED 11/01

CHEZ QUEUX

SNAPSHOT • Housed in a building that dates from 1862, Chez Queux may appear to be another of Old Montreal's dusty French restaurants, a place for tourists who want their pepper steaks flambéed tableside and their waiters to wear tuxedos. You'll find both at Chez Queux, but only the most cynical gourmets will fail to notice this restaurant's charm and savoir faire. Service is superb, the wine list is impressive, and the delicious, old-fashioned French food makes all that fussy fusion food look downright silly. At Chez Queux, you can relax in your high-backed chair, peruse the retro-luxe menu, soak up the château-like decor, and prepare yourself for a night of pampering. In summertime, consider a meal on the terrace, with its superb views of the Old Port and Place Jacques Cartier.

THE BIG PICTURE • People who dine out frequently can develop a pushy attitude towards a restaurant's wait staff. They hand the maître d' their coat before someone offers to take it. Once seated, they blurt out a request for a cocktail, scan the menu in seconds, request an update on the specials, fill their own wine glass, and ask that that the bill be brought along with dessert. All in all, they do their utmost to take control of the evening rather than let the waiter dictate the pace of events.

But can we blame them? Though the level of service in Montreal restaurants is generally quite high, there's no denying that many waiters are losing control of their customers. Not so at Chez Queux. The last time I dined there I encountered a waiter who controlled every aspect of the evening, transforming what could have been just another old-fashioned French dinner into one of my most memorable experiences of the year.

The waiter in question was as unassuming as they come. He looked like an easy target for my foul mood. He inquired in a soft voice if we'd like an aperitif. "Perrier," I said. He returned with the Perrier and asked if we'd be interested in a taste of Beaujolais Nouveau. Okay, I nodded, but only one glass to share. He was back, seconds later, with three glasses and poured a generous half glass in each. "What the . . . ," I whispered under my breath before I heard him say, "Here you are, one glass for three." Nice touch.

Our orders were taken in due time. I asked about the châteaubriand for two. He described the preparation of this thick beef filet in detail and offered to find a cut that would serve the three of us (how accommodating). I quizzed him about the catch of the day. Tuna, he answered. Prepared how? Grilled. Then came the ultimate test: wine consultation. Having scanned Chez Queux's ample, award-winning list, I knew that the under-$50 selections paled next to the impressive, three-digit Burgundies and Bordeaux. I asked for something good—something interesting—for no more than $50. He suggested a very special Bordeaux for $45. A good Bordeaux for $45? I hesitated and offered to up my rate to $60.

He returned with the starters: shellfish bisque, sweetbreads, and a goat's cheese salad. "Where's the wine?" I whispered to my companions through clenched teeth. Just then, I heard the gentle pop of a cork and my glass being filled for tasting. Lo and behold, it was the $45 Bordeaux—and it was delicious. "I saved you a few dollars," the waiter whispered to my dining companions with a knowing smile.

After the wine episode, the man could do no wrong in my books. I sat back, relaxed, and enjoyed the food.

The bisque was wonderful: light in texture, bursting with rich shellfish flavour, and without a trace of bitterness. The sweetbreads were also divine. Served with lightly sautéed mâche, a handful of orange and grapefruit supremes, and a dribbling of citrus juice, the two flattened lobes were crisp and assertively salted. The goat's cheese salad was everything a goat's cheese salad should be. The oak leaf lettuce was crunchy, fresh, and laced with a gentle vinaigrette, and the large round of goat's cheese was a variety that's neither insipid nor overly strong.

The main courses were also very good. The grilled tuna, topped with a dash of pesto, was moist and cooked to the requested medium-rare. Its accompaniments included a generous mound of wild rice, carrots, and asparagus — nothing revolutionary, yet delightful nonetheless.

The châteaubriand, dished up tableside, was the standout of the evening. Our waiter cut the filet mignon into six thick slices, set them on a pool of béarnaise sauce, and spooned around a square of dauphinoise potatoes, green beans, carrots, and asparagus. Each plate was then reheated before being set in front of us. The perfectly rosé meat was tender and full of flavour, and the vegetables were excellent: piping hot, well seasoned, and al dente. The béarnaise sauce, however, was a disappointment. Not only did it lack a pronounced tarragon flavour, but the heat of the plate caused it to separate. Dommage!

When I inquired about the cheese course, the waiter once again seized the opportunity to strut his stuff. He showed up with a fine selection and, before we knew it, he started slicing away, insisting we try this and that with our last few sips of wine. With aplomb, he sold us a course we were all too full to consider. But again he was right; the cheeses — a combination of French and local varieties — really hit the spot.

For dessert we couldn't resist a simple lemon tart (delicious) and that old French favourite, crêpes Suzette (good, if a bit bitter).

IN THE KITCHEN · Chef Jean-Paul Aubry.

DECOR, DRESS, AMBIENCE • Chez Queux is a good-old-days French restaurant with stone-and-wood-panelled-walls, heavy drapes, thronelike chairs, heavy chandeliers, fireplaces, and red carpeting. There's more of a perfume in the air than a crackle, and the background music is Mozart, not Madonna.

WINE LIST • With over 300 selections to choose from, this establishment (a *Wine Spectator* Award of Excellence winner since 1996) has almost every bottle an oenophile could desire. Those on a budget are equally well served and should not hesitate to ask the waiter for suggestions within their price range.

DON'T MISS • The goat's cheese salad, the sweetbread starter, the shellfish bisque, the châteaubriand, the cheese course, and the lemon tart.

WORDS TO THE WISE • Parking in this sector of Old Montreal can be trying. Your best bet is to walk or take a cab (or a calèche). Chez Queux is not the newest or hottest place in town, yet, with such comforting food and confident service, it shows us how pleasant it can be to just let go, sit back, and be pampered.

CHEZ QUEUX
158 Rue St. Paul East (near Place Jacques Cartier)
Telephone: (514) 866-5194
Open: Lunch, 11:30 A.M.-3 P.M. (Sunday brunch);
dinner, 5 P.M.-11 P.M., daily
Wheelchair access: No
Reservations: Recommended
Cards: All major cards
Price range: Starters, $4.50-$14.95; main courses, $24.95-$35; desserts, $4.75-$7

| ★★ | $ $ | REVIEWED 06/00 |

CHINE TOQUE

SNAPSHOT · This modern Chinese and Szechwan restaurant located on the downtown edge of Westmount offers a fine array of North American Chinese favourites. One taste of the delicious vegetable spring rolls and feather-light wontons shows that this restaurant gives Chinese food the attention it deserves. Chine Toque is a good choice for anyone interested in delving into the wider world of Chinese food. But if it's the outer reaches of the experience you're after, the lovely decor and friendly service may not be enough to satisfy your search for spice.

THE BIG PICTURE · We've all tasted Chinese food in one form or another. Those two words, "Chinese food," fall on a continuum stretching from wonton soup, chicken chow mein, and egg rolls on one end, to shark's fin, fermented bean curd, and thousand-year-old eggs on the other. In our fair city, the ubiquitous "mets Chinois" notwithstanding, the fastest-growing trend appears to be upscale Cantonese and Szechwan restaurants with a decor more reminiscent of an elegant uptown eatery than the pagoda palaces of yesteryear.

At Chine Toque there are few clues to indicate that this is a Chinese restaurant. The absence of chinoiserie in the decor extends to the menu, for it contains not a single Chinese character. The first hint of Asiatic flavour comes from the dishes themselves. All the well-known North American Chinese favourites are here: sesame beef, dumplings, spring rolls, spareribs, and the chicken named after that mysterious Chinese military man, General Tao.

Like the postmodernist setting, the food is scaled down to the taste of the locals — a crowd that has little in common with the diehard chop suey and dim sum lovers who seek out the exotic in the esoteric haunts of Chinatown. This fact is brought home when a request for spicy dishes results in food that's low on the heat scale. Nonetheless, Chine Toque's "contemporary Chinese cuisine" does quite well.

Take the vegetable soup, which is filled with thinly sliced strips of bok choy, carrot, snow pea, and cucumber. The broth offers a delicate medley of vegetable flavours, the most pronounced being cucumber. The wonton soup is one of the best around. Made with a clear, piping hot chicken broth topped with shreds of lettuce and a sprinkling of scallions, this version also includes delicate wontons filled with chicken as opposed to pork. The hot and sour soup, too, is top-notch. Made hot and sour by the addition of vinegar and freshly ground pepper, it's ideally seasoned, and the accumulation of heat reaches a pleasant peak with the final mouthful.

Of the hot hors d'oeuvres sampled, the crisp vegetable spring rolls are practically grease-free and are delicious when dunked in the fruity, Day-Glo-yellow plum sauce. The chicken spring rolls are also excellent, especially since they contain visible chunks of chicken meat—a rarity on the spring roll circuit. The steamed dumplings—pork served with a vinegar and ginger sauce, and shrimp with a hot mustard dip—offer pairings with lively flavour combinations. The problem here is the dumpling wrappers, which are thick and chewy. Chicken dumplings with peanut butter sauce fare somewhat better. These dumplings (the same as the ones in the wonton soup) are very good, but the weak peanut sauce makes a drab accompaniment to the delicate flavour of the chicken.

Although the deep-fried Pekinese boned spareribs coated in a sweet and spicy soy sauce are also nice, many of the ribs are fatty underneath the crispy coating. Equally cloying are the deep-fried squid rings. The thick breading hides a thin circle of squid that tastes more like a donut than a seafood starter when dipped into the accompanying red cherry sauce.

Though admittedly heavy and calorific, breaded and fried dishes coated in sweet/hot sauces are well-known Szechwan favourites. At Chine Toque, the crispy sesame beef glazed in a sauce that enhances the meat flavour without overwhelming it is superb. The General Tao's chicken is made with white breast meat and sautéed with peppers and green onions. Though this version is pleasantly light on the breading, it lacks aggressive spicing to counter the sweetness.

Szechwan-style shrimp are correctly spiced thanks to a much-needed dose of hot Szechwan pepper. Stir-fried chicken with honey mustard sauce is heavy on the potent, bright-yellow mustard and light (very light) on the honey. Double-cooked Szechwan pork pairs barbecued pork in a stir-fry with peppers, bamboo shoots, and green onions. Once again, the sauce is sweet and spicy, but the double-cooking method results in pork that's stringy and dry.

Vegetable dishes are uniformly excellent, especially the traditional yu-hsiang eggplant, which combines al dente eggplant bâtonnets with a sweet garlic sauce. Also first-rate are the steamed rice noodles topped with stir-fried sliced carrots, bok choy, celery, baby corn, and small "cloud ear" fungus (which do indeed look like puffy black clouds in the colourful mixture).

Desserts are simple. The vanilla ice cream is rich and delicious. Canned lichees are, well, canned lichees—supersweet and gelatinous. Fortune cookies and Chinese tea provide a nice finish to a copious meal.

Service is gracious and professional. Not only is the sake properly decanted, but also all dishes are expertly served to each diner at the table, and any questions about menu items are answered in detail.

IN THE KITCHEN · Chef Chong Lei.

DECOR, DRESS, AMBIENCE · The walls are sunny yellow, and there's a large bar at the entrance. The furniture is of the nouveau-resto-chic variety, with polished blond wood, sleek lines, and tables covered in thick white linen. The recessed halogen lights cast an appealing glow over the three separate rooms, which are divided by sticklike partitions and the occasional potted palm. Tables are set with both cutlery and chopsticks, and Natalie Cole sings the easy-listening background tunes.

WINE LIST · The wine list is pretty basic: one type of sake, six choices of red and whites wines, and two house wines that are also available by the glass.

DON'T MISS · The wonton and hot and sour soups, the spring rolls, the sesame beef, and the vegetable dishes.

WORDS TO THE WISE · My major complaint about Chine Toque would be the nature of the menu. Unlike many Chinese restaurants, Chine Toque offers no set-price, multiportion tasting menus; every dish here is à la carte—a costly proposition if you want a wide sampling. Tempted by so many offerings, you might end up with a steep bill and too much food (the staff is only too happy to provide doggy bags, and half orders are available).

CHINE TOQUE
4050 Rue Ste. Catherine West (near Atwater)
Telephone: (514) 989-5999
Open: Lunch, 11:30 A.M.-3 P.M., Monday to Friday; dinner,
5:30 P.M.-10 P.M., Sunday to Thursday, and 5:30 P.M.-11 P.M.,
Friday and Saturday
Wheelchair access: Yes
Reservations: Recommended
Cards: All major cards (and Interac)
Price range: Starters, $3.25-$6.85; main courses, $10.80-$14.80; desserts, $3.25-$3.50; four-course dinner menu, $41.99 for two

★★★	$ $ $	REVIEWED 08/01

CHORUS

SNAPSHOT · Formerly Jongleux Café, Chorus carries on with a fully renovated decor and a new chef and co-owner, Thierry Baron. Expect outstanding nouvelle cuisine featuring the best local ingredients coupled with charming, professional service at this gem of a restaurant.

THE BIG PICTURE · Chorus is an apt name for this establishment. Why? Because it strikes a chord that so many restaurants fail to achieve. I'm referring to the fundamental principal of success —namely, that flawless teamwork is the essence of the business. That the former Jongleux Café was renamed for the supporting cast as opposed to a new star chef speaks volumes.

After the untimely death of her former partner and chef, the renowned Nicolas Jongleux, owner Patricia Hovington had to re-think her restaurant's formula—and quickly—to keep the fickle gourmets on side. Hovington had no choice but to wipe the slate clean and start over.

Though the restaurant claims its cuisine is still inspired by Jongleux, chef/partner Thierry Baron's style is quite different. Plates are artfully assembled, nouvelle cuisine style, and they feature many of the best local ingredients, courtesy of organic farmers Pierre-André Daignault, François Brouillard, and Stephen Homer.

Baron's take on salade Niçoise is good fun. Not only does he pare down the portion, but he also fancies it up, replacing canned tuna with seared and sliced fresh red tuna loin, and hard-boiled chicken eggs with quail eggs. Add to that the usual Niçoise suspects—potatoes, red peppers, Niçoise lettuce, olives, green beans, tomatoes—and you've got one terrific and original starter.

Equally appealing is the beet and Chaource cheese mille-feuille with mustard sprouts. The bright-yellow beets are sliced thin and used to sandwich layers of creamy Chaource. The consistency is lovely and melting, but what seduces here is the contrast between the sweetness of the beets and the pungency and saltiness of the cheese.

Those up for more in the way of mouth feel should try the duck tartare with figs. The duck is cut into tiny cubes that dance on the palate before slithering down the throat with the jammy figs. Adding to the flavour is a smoky-tasting papadam that offers a much-needed crunch.

Main courses don't disappoint either. A medium-sized venison chop is tender, full flavoured, and roasted to the requisite medium-rare. It's an elegant piece of meat, good enough to outshine many a filet mignon. The accompaniments—potato and prosciutto pancakes and caramelized carrots—are also first-class.

Crisp panfried sweetbreads with girolle mushrooms and sherry wine sauce arrive on a rectangular dish arranged in two straight rows. Though a bit salty, they are nonetheless light and delicious, and not the least bit spongy. The accompanying barley risotto cake is also faultless. It's less filling than the rice version, and Baron laces it with a heavenly dose of Parmesan, topping the lot with asparagus tips.

The rabbit stuffed with shiitake mushrooms, sesame, and cabbage is, in a word, superb. Rabbit is so often dry and overcooked. Here the saddle is rolled with mushrooms, seared, and sliced into rounds. Served alongside is a mound of rabbit confit with julienned carrots and daikon, whose sesame flavour melds beautifully with the wild ginger sauce. Think Asian spring roll, only more luxurious.

Desserts are good, though not quite up to the level of the savoury plates. Warm chocolate tourte, a Jongleux specialty, is just this side of overcooked. The raspberry crème brûlée is runny and undercooked, but it's served with a raspberry and butter-cookie sandwich that will leave you pining for more.

Though the cuisine at Chorus is now entirely Thierry Baron's, there remain details to remind us of the old Jongleux Café: the antique teacups, the bowls and plates of many different shapes and sizes, and the beautiful glass case in the dining room overflowing with cookbooks. Then there are the young waitresses, a Jongleux Café trademark, intended to give the place a fresh feel. Their kindness and professionalism is still refreshing.

IN THE KITCHEN · Chef and co-owner Thierry Baron.

DECOR, DRESS, AMBIENCE · Gold-framed mirrors of various sizes adorn the dark-blue walls, and halogen lamps are suspended from a thin-wire grid that runs the length of the room. It's all quite modern and grown up, verging on the Gothic, like something out of an Edward Gorey illustration. The ambience is relaxed and calm, especially on weeknights and at lunch, making this the right restaurant for an intimate meal with that special someone.

WINE LIST · When last visited, Chorus had a wine list that was short, confusing, and pricey. I'm told they are working to improve the situation with input from renowned local sommelier Don-Jean Léandri.

DON'T MISS · The salade Niçoise, the stuffed rabbit (when available), and the house specialty, beer-braised pig's cheeks. Most everything is outstanding, and the market-style menu changes seasonally.

WORDS TO THE WISE · In such a small restaurant, it's hard to miss the cash register and coffee machine churning away in the background. But these are quibbles next to the generally high quality of the cuisine.

CHORUS
3434 Rue St. Denis (near Sherbrooke)
Telephone: (514) 841-8080
Open: 6 P.M.-11 P.M., daily; after Labour Day, lunch,
noon-2:30 P.M. and dinner, 6 P.M.-11 P.M., Monday to Saturday
Wheelchair access: No
Reservations: Recommended
Cards: Major cards
Price range: Starters, $7-$14; main courses, $23-$32; desserts,
$6.50-$8; tasting menus, $55 and $65

| ★★★ | $ $ $ | REVIEWED 08/01 |

CUBE

SNAPSHOT • Cube is one of the most interesting and ambitious restaurants to appear in a long while. Quebec chef Claude Pelletier (formerly of Mediterraneo) is an innovator whose following among foodies is well deserved. Ingredients are an obvious inspiration, and Pelletier is keen on showing their many sides. The seasonal menu changes frequently, and the lunch menu is revamped daily. Raw-bar items and tapas are served in the second-floor bar. Despite the fashionable crowd, the atmosphere is unpretentious.
THE BIG PICTURE • The rumours about Cube hit the streets about six months before it opened in July 2001. Unlike the advance hype for hot spots like Queue de Cheval and Newtown, Cube generated a flood of local foodie gossip, focusing on the comings and goings of Montreal chef (and Cube partner) Claude Pelletier and his plans for a new modern restaurant in Old Montreal's oh-so-chic Hôtel St. Paul. So, with all the talk, the place would be either a revelation or a letdown. But fans of Pelletier's modern American cuisine—who were giddy with anticipation—needn't have worried. Cube is a winner.

Reading over the menu, one senses that this is no repeat of Pelletier's past performances. At Mediterraneo, Pelletier was revered for turning out hundreds of plates for a hip crowd that was perhaps more drawn to the restaurant's atmosphere and location than to the ultimate gourmet experience. At Cube, his market-based cuisine is pared down, bold, and perfectly in keeping with the minimalist decor. In this bleak setting, it provides all the colour and shows a newfound maturity—an intellectual bent—based on his curiosity, technique, and experimental nature.

Salmon three ways (marinated, tartare, carpaccio), veal three ways (sweetbreads, braised breast, tournedos Rossini), and pan-seared foie gras with Granny Smith apple (sauce, sorbet, matchstick slices) feature an ingredient theme with preparation variations. The salmon starter is dominated by a marvelously fresh and vibrant tartare; one might gladly trade in the marinated salmon or carpaccio for a full plate of the stuff. On the veal plate, the crisp sweetbreads stand head and shoulders above the tournedos Rossini and the braised meat. Not that the tournedos topped with a foie gras and truffle crouton and the melting braised meat sweetened with raisins aren't delicious. They certainly are. It's just that the sweetbreads are even better, and two bites aren't enough when you've tasted sweetbreads this divine.

The foie gras is far more successful, for the main ingredient, the liver, takes the starring role, and the Granny Smith fixings provide support. And what delicious liver it is—full flavoured, without a trace of bitterness, crisp on the outside and rosé within.

Pelletier's organic tomato starter features a green zebra tomato layered with buffalo Mozzarella, a cup of tomato broth with sliced tomatoes, sautéed yellow cherry tomatoes with sliced beets, and a tablespoon of tomato concassé with basil. In the middle sits an incongruous quenelle of horseradish sorbet. It's all quite nice—full marks for creativity—but everything competes for first place. Moreover, the green tomato is practically tasteless, the broth has an unpleasant earthiness, and the beets outshine the tomatoes in the third dish. Only the spoonful of concassé is memorable.

Although the chef's novel approach with these threesomes is commendable, when you have a dish that works, it's nice to get your tongue around more than a few bites. The wild mushroom tart starter with truffle oil, Cheddar, and arugula features a cracker-like tart shell filled with a generous portion of sautéed portobello, shiitake, and girolle mushrooms. The tart is set atop a few poached leeks, arugula, and baby beet leaves, the whole surrounded by an intense truffle sauce, resulting in a starter that's perfect in every way.

The main-course duck magret—served with faro, rapini, cauliflower purée, and a passion fruit sauce—is good, if a bit underseasoned. The roasted striped bass doesn't disappoint. The skin is fried to a crisp, the flesh is moist and melting, and the subtle flavour is ideally enhanced with a lemon and herb broth. The accompanying white cannellini beans are prepared al dente, providing a welcome contrast to the soft fish.

The best desserts are a caramelized banana with a chocolate "moelleux" cake, a peanut tuile and vanilla ice cream, and another of those experimental threesomes featuring Illy coffee and Italian Domori chocolate, which includes a mocha crème brûlée layered with a frothy cappucino-style topping, a tart filled with mocha ganache, coffee-chocolate gelato, and a biscotti. The original touch here is that the sugar is used sparingly, allowing all the fruity and earthy chocolate and coffee flavours a chance to come to the fore.

Those not up for dessert may prefer to settle for the excellent espresso and a few of the complimentary chocolate truffles.

IN THE KITCHEN • Chef and co-owner Claude Pelletier.

DECOR, DRESS, AMBIENCE • The style is casual-chic and dress should follow suit. The low-lit room features high ceilings, concrete-grey walls, picture windows, square mirrors, thick white drapes, and enough sparkling votive candles to add a touch of glamour and take a minimum of ten years off every babe on the scene.

WINE LIST • Cube's wine list is short and filled with many obscure selections that cry out for explanations from a schooled sommelier.

DON'T MISS • The foie gras, the fish dishes, the chocolate desserts, and the homemade ice cream.

WORDS TO THE WISE • Dishes tend to be "cheffy" — the kind of stuff that sounds exciting when conceived in the kitchen by a bunch of keeners in aprons and funny hats but a bit frustrating for customers used to the standard meat, veg, and starch combination. The cheeses offered (only one from Quebec) are all too easy to pass up. Service is friendly and smooth, but waits can be long between courses.

CUBE
355 Rue McGill (corner Place d'Youville, in the Hôtel St. Paul)
Telephone: (514) 876-2823
Open: Lunch, 11:30 A.M.-2:30 P.M., Monday to Friday; dinner,
6 P.M.-11 P.M. daily; brunch, 11:30 A.M.-2 P.M., Saturday and
Sunday
Wheelchair access: No
Reservations: Essential
Cards: Major cards
Price range: Starters, $7-$120 (caviar); main courses, $24-$30;
desserts, $7-$10

★★1/2	$ $ $	REVIEWED 11/00

DA EMMA

SNAPSHOT · There are beautiful restaurants, dreary restaurants, old-fashioned restaurants, and modern, minimalist restaurants. Da Emma doesn't fit into any of these categories. Rather, it offers the unique combination of authentic Nothern Italian comfort food in a "cool" basement setting. One gets the feeling you're part of dinner party set in a fabulous apartment where, behind the kitchen door, mama's doing all the cooking. Service provides just the right balance between Italian charm and professional polish. The wine list is impressive, with a wide selection at many price points.

THE BIG PICTURE · Home-cooked meals — especially Italian ones — are the meals many of us find most appealing. Restaurant food is another story. It's seared, broiled, charred, carved, blanched, grilled, stir-fried, blowtorched, and caramelized. It's flashy fare — often exciting — yet it's often prepared without the love and attention given the handmade pastas, hearty ragus, slow-braised meats, and simple vegetable casseroles of home. For most of us, however, eating out is about more than just good food. There's the setting, the service, the wine list, and the ambience — factors that rarely come into play around the family table. An interesting experiment would be to transfer home cooking into a magnificent restaurant setting. The closest you'll come to that in Montreal is at the Old Montreal Italian restaurant Da Emma.

Befitting the homey atmosphere, the waiters have a way of making all feel welcome. At the outset of the meal, one will arrive at your table with delicious bruschetta: grilled bread, salted diced tomato, and virgin olive oil. He'll then bring over a small blackboard that lists the menu in Italian. While translating the dishes —six appetizers, three pastas, and a wide selection of meats and fish—he might just personalize the selections with a running commentary such as, "The fettuccini with porcini is my dad's favourite," or, "The meatloaf is too heavy," or, "The lamb and pork dishes come in Flintstone-sized portions." You'd think he was talking about his own mother's cooking.

An appetizer of prosciutto with buffalo Mozzarella is as plain as they come, just a few paper-thin slices of tender, if somewhat fatty, cured meat blanketing fresh Mozzarella quarters. Although the combination is unusual, these first-rate ingredients share a similar melting quality that makes the dish appealing. A little more daring is the standard tomato and Mozzarella pairing. The large rounds of ripe tomato topped with thick slices of cheese have a gentle taste that's boosted by a chiffonade of basil and a dribbling of fruity olive oil—so simple, yet so satisfying.

Da Emma's more elaborate starters are even better. The clear fish soup filled with shreds of fish and stelline pasta has a delicate, haunting flavour. The octopus, stripped of its tentacles and cut into thick slices, is poached in a delicious white wine and vegetable broth. And a half portion of porcini pasta features al dente strands of fettuccini covered in a subtle cream sauce filled with sautéed peppery porcini.

The tomato-sauced pastas are less successful. A serving of veal agnolotti turns out to be a deep bowl of homemade pasta pockets drowned in a rather acidic, sluggish meat sauce. Gnocchi topped with a similar tomato sauce without the meat (pomodoro) also falls flat. The gnocchi are excellent—light and spongy—but their neutral flavour calls for a more complex sauce that doesn't grow tiresome after the first few mouthfuls.

Save for one off note, the "straccetti rughetta" (a hot and cold mix of arugula and bland beef strips sautéed with onions and white wine), meat and fish choices turn up consistent winners. All are shining examples of Italian home cooking, with fine ingredients treated in a pure and unaffected manner.

The salmon steaks are grilled to perfection: moist on the inside and ever-so-lightly crusted on the outside. Osso buco is prepared northern style, with the veal shanks braised in white wine until meltingly tender, and it's served with a plateful of peas and sliced carrots. A side of roast suckling pig arrives in a large, glistening, honey-coloured slab. It's all there: the loin, three chops, and the liver—an anatomy lesson on a plate. The meat, which requires a bit of patience to carve into bite-size pieces, is both flavourful and succulent. The bits around the bone are especially tasty. Take note, however: despite the Italian custom of small meat portions, this dish is generous enough to share.

Desserts include a good tiramisu with the lingering anise flavour of Sambucca. The panna cotta is a variation of the classic cream, as it's cooked, crème-caramel style, on a layer of liquid caramel. The pineapple sorbet is a bit insipid, and its consistency is off-puttingly crusty. Coffee in all its forms—espresso, decaf, cappuccino, filtered—is excellent.

IN THE KITCHEN • Chefs and co-owners Emma and Lorenzo Risa.

DECOR, DRESS, AMBIENCE • The basement setting is eclectic: stone walls, cement pillars, a black wooden floor, wooden wine coolers, and white-linen-covered tables. Dean Martin tunes play softly in the background. The fetching Italian waiters, clad head-to-toe in black, hair slicked back à la Rudolf Valentino, aren't too hard on the eyes either.

WINE LIST • Da Emma's wine list comprises an impressive array of fine Italian wines and enough inexpensive bottles to keep everyone happy.

DON'T MISS • The Mozzarella salads, the grilled salmon, the suckling pig, the tiramisu, and the panna cotta.

WORDS TO THE WISE • All in all, a meal here has plenty to offer in terms of how close it comes to the simplicity of top-quality Italian home cooking. For those of us not fortunate enough to have Italian mothers, Da Emma provides a warm and satisfying experience—the ideal spot to come home to.

DA EMMA
777 Rue de la Commune West (near Prince)
Telephone: (514) 392-1568
Open: Lunch, 11 A.M.-2 P.M., Monday to Friday; dinner, 6 P.M.-
11 P.M., Monday to Saturday
Wheelchair access: Yes
Reservations: Essential
Cards: Major cards
Price range: Starters, $4-$19; main courses, $14-$34;
desserts, $4-$10

★★1/2	$ $	REVIEWED 02/00

DELFINO

SNAPSHOT • When was the last time a chef came to your table to pop open a scallop shell? For that matter, how many chefs are buying scallops in the shell? Very few, except for the one at Delfino, a 26-seat neighbourhood restaurant that offers simply prepared, fin-flapping fresh fish and seafood at reasonable prices (but don't get too excited about the scallops; the menu is seasonal and changes daily). Add to that a reasonably priced wine list and an outdoor terrace, and the result is one of the most appealing seafood restaurants in town.

THE BIG PICTURE · Delfino is a seafood restaurant in its purest form. Fish lovers are in for a treat, for few other restaurants offer such fresh fare. Chef George Georgi buys only the best, changing his daily menu accordingly. So if the scallops aren't perfect that day, he might buy mahimahi, and if he does, you're in luck—it's sublime.

Starters provide a clue to the chef's Mediterranean background. Kalamata olives, hummus, taramasalata, and pita bread arrive gratis at the outset of the meal. Following that, there's saganaki, a Greek specialty consisting of a thick slice of fried Kasseri cheese sprinkled with lemon juice. The Italian/Mediterranean favourite of grilled zucchini, mushrooms, and peppers could use a few more minutes on the grill. The leek soup tastes more of fennel than leek and is underseasoned. In complete contrast is the velvety clam chowder. This French-style chaudière de moules (as opposed to the thicker New England chowder) has an intense, sweet, clam-flavoured base and is filled with a mixture of onions, potato cubes, and clams. Delicious.

Appetizers play no more than a supporting role at Delfino and are easily forgotten when the fish arrives. Served grilled, Cajun style, or sautéed (Provençal or meunière style), all fish and seafood dishes are accompanied by a timbale of delicate Basmati rice aromatized with star anise, a row of thin French green beans, and a mound of sautéed spinach. Excellent homemade French fries are also available.

Cajun mahimahi is blackened and coated in subtle smokey-flavoured spices. Though similar to red meat in appearance and thickness, the firm white flesh is moist and flavourful, without a trace of unpleasant fishiness—the hallmark of freshness. A large filet of loup de mer is equally moist and has that sweet sea flavour. Every mouthful is as light as a cloud.

I know of no other restaurant serving this quality of fresh Atlantic scallops. Seven plump specimens, reaching up to an inch and a half in diameter, are served grilled with no more than a spoonful of extra-virgin olive oil. They are hot, tender, and sweet enough to stick to your teeth.

When available, the Provençal-style black sea bass should not be missed. This popular American saltwater fish is lightly pan-fried and moistened with just enough garlic-butter-wine sauce to enliven the unctuous flesh without overwhelming it.

For dessert, the tarte Tatin is good, if hardly glamorous appearancewise. The chocolate mousse is pleasant, but it would benefit from a better quality chocolate. The cheesecake may be the best choice here.

Service is puzzling. Though competent, the waiters often seem hurried and indifferent. That said, Delfino is a restaurant one could visit often. Recently, yellowtail, Mediterranean bass, and the chef's favourite, grilled pompano, were on the menu. The Cajun red snapper also sounded promising, and if one is feeling macho, there's always the grilled mackerel.

IN THE KITCHEN • Chef and owner George Georgi.

DECOR, DRESS, AMBIENCE • This casual restaurant is tucked away on a residential street in the chic banlieu of Outremont. The Art Deco decor is as simple as the food, with dark-caramel wood panels, large mirrors, and dim lighting accented by flickering votive candles on every table. There's a pleasant feeling of intimacy in a space this petite, but noise levels can sometimes be a problem.

WINE LIST • Though short, the wine list offers terrific value; most of the wines are sold at no more than twice their retail price. The Sancerre or Chablis Premier Cru are a perfect match for seafood.

DON'T MISS • The grilled octopus, the scallops, the loup de mer, the Cajun mahimahi, and the catch of the day.

WORDS TO THE WISE • Landlubbers and vegetarians be warned: there are no nonseafood items on this menu. If you're one of the many skeptical Montrealers who believe scales are for musicians, I can't think of a better place to take the plunge.

DELFINO
1231 Avenue Lajoie (near Bloomfield)
Telephone: (514) 277-5888
Open: Lunch, noon-2 P.M., Thursday and Friday;
dinner, 5 P.M.-10 P.M., Tuesday to Saturday
Wheelchair access: Yes
Reservations: Recommended
Cards: Major cards
Price Range: Starters, $3-$11; main courses, $17-$27;
desserts, $3.50-$4

★★	$ $ $	REVIEWED 10/99

DESJARDINS

SNAPSHOT • A Montreal institution since 1892, this well-loved seafood restaurant is renowned for its lobster; the grilled fish and sushi are also very good. The ambience is one of old-fashioned elegance, and the waiters are veterans who know many customers by name. No wonder Desjardins remains a popular destination for the businessman's lunch.

THE BIG PICTURE • Fish has become impossibly chic. It's the new meat, the ne-plus-ultra item on many restaurant menus. At the better establishments, one can enjoy exotic specimens, grilled to perfection, served with a stack of designer vegetables, and dressed with a squirt of lemon and the best extra-virgin olive oil.

Diehard fish lovers, the kind who'll eat mackerel, sardines, and monkfish liver, insist on two conditions for the ultimate piscine experience: the fish must be incredibly fresh as well as perfectly cooked. For this reason, many people prefer to go out to eat fish. Not only are fish dishes challenging for the home cook, but also restaurant chefs are the ones nabbing the freshest specimens.

So what of the old seafood restaurants like Desjardins? Here is an elegant establishment that still favours the lobster tanks, crab legs, and foil-wrapped baked potatoes of the seventies. But

Desjardins has also made the wise decision of adding modern dishes to its repertoire, such as grilled tuna, swordfish, and the trendiest fish favourite of recent years: sushi.

The menu is substantial, with a wide variety of fish and seafood. There's also a small selection of sushi and sashimi listed on the back of the menu, and a few meat and chicken dishes to keep the carnivores at bay.

Though classical next to the offerings of some cutting-edge Montreal sushi emporiums, the sushi and sashimi starter offers excellent value. Every bite is fresh, clean on the palate, and well seasoned, with just enough wasabi to enhance without over-whelming.

The other starters aren't nearly as exciting. The clam chowder is watery and lacks both character and flavour. An avocado crab salad is passable. The moules marinière are small, undersalted, and missing the parsley or any other herb so integral to a good marinière.

Main courses fare better. The grilled tuna steak is moist, firm, and not the least bit flaky.

The catch of the day—cod—is also perfectly cooked and has a wonderful creamy, melt-in-your-mouth texture—the hallmark of superfresh cod. Its flavour is so delicate that a squirt of fresh lemon nearly overwhelms the subtle taste. The seared scallops meunière aren't as successful. The scallops are rubbery and lack sweetness, but they are saved by a pool of excellent meunière sauce.

Desjardins offers a wide selection of lobster dishes, from boiled, broiled, cardinal, and Newburg, to sashimi lobster and lobster tempura. The classic Thermidor consists of lobster meat in a white-wine-based mushroom cream sauce topped with Parmesan cheese and gratinéed in its shell. The meat is tender, not in the least bit rubbery, and the accompanying sauce is rich and creamy, though slightly undersalted. It's a dish from the past, granted, but still rather nice.

Desserts could use some attention. The crumbly baked cheese-cake is served with runny homemade jam. The crème caramel looks more like a pile of smooth vanilla cream. And a poire Belle Hélène, which tastes of store-bought everything (ice cream, poached pears, chocolate sauce), is served in a sundae boat more in keeping with the local soda fountain than an elegant restaurant like Desjardins.

Service is uniformly friendly and efficient. The veteran waiters serve up not only food, but also quips, jokes, and anecdotes worthy of a Catskill comic.

IN THE KITCHEN • Chef Tadayuki Endo.

DECOR, DRESS, AMBIENCE • Unlike the townhouses that surround it on lower Rue Makay, Desjardins looks like a Canadian national park tourist office. The large, square dining room, with its cascading drapes, floor-to-ceiling windows, fieldstone walls, and kitchy chandeliers has a cozy retro feel. One can easily imagine a group of old-style politicians at a corner table ready to cut a deal over some serious surf and turf.

WINE LIST • The wine list is short and rather pricey. Unless money isn't an issue, go for the Bourgogne Aligoté, not the most scintillating of wines but a good all-around choice for fish. There is also a nice white Burgundy available for six dollars a glass.

DON'T MISS • The lobster, the grilled fish, and the sushi.

WORDS TO THE WISE • Desjardins may not be the place for trend-conscious diners, but it is a lobster-lover's paradise. The no-nonsense food is quite good, and it's sure to impress a-fishionados of any stripe.

DESJARDINS
1175 Rue Mackay (near Ste. Catherine)
Telephone: (514) 866-9741
Open: Lunch, 11 A.M.-2:30 P.M., Monday to Friday;
dinner, 5 P.M.-11 P.M., daily
Wheelchair access: Yes
Reservations: Recommended
Cards: All major cards
Price range: Starters, $4.50-$17.50; main courses, $18.95-$39.50;
desserts, $5

★★	$ $ $	REVIEWED 07/00

FAROS

SNAPSHOT • Faros is good-time, let-your-hair-down kind of restaurant. It's popular with families, couples, and friends— many of them regulars. This Greek bistro features the token stucco walls, fishing nets, and blue-and-white checkered table-cloths. Favoured dishes include tzatziki, grilled vegetables, lamb, and whole grilled fish. Service is friendly and efficient and, as an added bonus, there's free valet parking.

THE BIG PICTURE • Have you ever heard of menu envy? It happens to every restaurant-goer sooner or later. Menu envy is when you've made the wrong menu selection and end up stewing in your own juices, coveting all the dishes around you.

One of the worst places for menu envy is the Mile End Greek seafood restaurant Faros. While slicing through your spanakopita, you may notice a platter of grilled mushrooms and peppers arriving at the next table. Your spanakopita is okay, but the food on that platter is far more tantalizing. And it might happen again with the main courses, when you see a charred swordfish steak that looks a lot sexier than your simple filet of striped bass.

Zucchini, eggplant, and tzatziki are listed separately on the menu. Who knew the three could be served together in a mound of deep-fried splendor? The regulars, that's who! On nights when most restaurants can count their customers on two hands, Faros is usually packed. You'll be lucky to get a table without a reservation. Noise levels are high, and everyone—families, couples, friends— appears to be having a heck of a time. You'll see the regulars greet the staff and each other by name across the 67-seat room. Handsome blue-shirted waiters race by, deftly balancing large platters.

Many customers order without even opening the menu. It's a good idea, as this menu lists dishes in the most simple terms ("zucchini," "exotic salad," "black sea bass"). The waiter's ready suggestions and a quick look around provide all the information you need.

You probably won't notice many of the regulars eating spanakopita, because this version of the classic spinach and Feta cheese pie is overcooked and underseasoned. The grilled Mexican jumbo shrimp are far more popular, as the meaty crustaceans are ultrafresh, lightly charred, and enhanced with just a sprinkling of chopped parsley and lemon juice.

While most everyone orders the grilled mushrooms and peppers, the fried zucchini and eggplant, stacked around a dollop of tzatziki, are a lot more fun. The vegetables are expertly fried—dry and crisp—and the tzatziki has a gentle garlic flavour.

The heaped plates of fried calamari sure look tempting. Of course, looks can be deceiving. The calamari, though tender and tasty, are greasy and unevenly battered. With so many excellent renditions of this dish around town, Faros's offering is no more than mediocre.

The star of any meal here is sure to be the whole grilled fish. The striped bass, large enough for two, is served plated, boned, and adorned with nothing more than a spoonful of capers and a wedge of lemon. The fish is perfectly cooked: large, delicate chunks of meat come away from the skin with ease, and every bite is moist and melting. The only ingredient missing to enliven the overall flavour is a splash of olive oil.

The swordfish steak is a bit of a tease. The steak is thick but small—no bigger than a large apple. The meat is indeed expertly charred, but it's cooked past the medium-rare that's ideal for swordfish. The flavour is unappealingly fishy, and the steak is salted enough to render it almost inedible. The accompaniments include run-of-the-mill rice pilaf and vegetables: broccoli, carrots, cauliflower, corn, beets.

A pleasant and unexpected surprise for a seafood restaurant is a plate of grilled lamb chops. These three thick chops are succulent, full flavoured, and perfectly rosé. The dish is marred, however, by the same lacklustre rice and vegetables as the fish.

At dessert time, you'll be tempted by the classic baklava and the many colourful fruit plates. Although they look appetizing, be warned: the fruit—kiwi, golden cherries, apricots—can be past its prime, and the baklava is usually soggy and cloyingly sweet.

Service is excellent—from the friendly parking attendant out front (Faros offers free valet parking) to the charming indoor wait staff. One rarely encounters such a genuine and eager team.

IN THE KITCHEN • Chef Benny Kazerouni.

DECOR, DRESS, AMBIENCE • With its arched windows, stained glass panels, fruit-and-vegetable displays, blue-and-white table-cloths, and stucco-and-brick walls, Faros is Montreal's Greek bistro extraordinaire. It has a relaxed and casual atmosphere, and dinner here can remind you of a big family get-together.

WINE LIST • The list is short but sweet, with about 50 selections of Greek, Californian, French, and Chilean wines. There's also a separate "owner's list" for those willing to splurge.

DON'T MISS • The grilled vegetables, the tzatziki plate, the grilled whole fish, and the lamb chops.

WORDS TO THE WISE • At the end of your meal, with its many highs and lows, take another look around at the animated crowd enjoying the copious platters of grilled everything, and take a guess why this restaurant is so popular. I'd say it's the increasing popularity of Mediterranean food combined with professional but casual service. For those whose spirits could use a lift, this little Greek bistro is just the ticket.

FAROS
362 Avenue Fairmount West (near Hutchison)
Telephone: (514) 270-8437
Open: Lunch, noon-2 P.M., Monday to Friday; dinner, 6 P.M.-10:30 P.M., Monday to Wednesday, and 6 P.M.-11 P.M. Thursday to Sunday
Wheelchair access: No
Reservations: Essential
Cards: All major cards
Price range: Starters, $4.95-$13.95; main courses, $16-$36 (fresh fish and shrimp priced by the pound); desserts, $2-$5.50

★★★	$ $ $	REVIEWED 10/99

FERREIRA CAFÉ TRATTORIA

SNAPSHOT · Read through the menu at Café Ferreira and you'll wonder where else Portuguese cuisine is given such star treatment. What customers can look forward to at this downtown hot spot is some of Montreal's most stylish food in a beautiful Mediterranean-style setting. Chef Marino Tavares has adapted many simple and traditional Portuguese dishes to today's tastes, interpreting the classics with a contemporary edge. Add to this a cosmopolitan crowd, an enthusiastic and knowledgeable wait staff, and a comprehensive selection of Portuguese wines and rare ports, and you have one of the city's most exciting and popular restaurants.

THE BIG PICTURE · The first thing to hit you at the entranceway of Ferreira Café and Trattoria (known to regulars as Café Ferreira) is the wonderfully welcoming aroma of grilled seafood. The mood here is sophisticated, with bluesy background music and soft lighting. Suave, blue-shirted waiters glide around tables filled with upscale cosmopolitan types quaffing red wine and feasting on seafood. In an open kitchen on the mezzanine, chefs are busy assembling plates.

Café Ferreira is doing for Portuguese cuisine what Milos did for Greek—giving it style. There are plenty of meat dishes, soups, and salads, but the main attractions here are the fish and seafood specials. On most nights, customers are offered not one, but eight "catches of the day." Start the night out with a glass of white port, the ideal match for the salty olives and lupini beans served gratis at the outset of the meal. Appetizers include a Mediterranean favourite, grilled squid, which is served with a light tomato sauce. The flavour is fresh and smoky, and the texture is soft, chewy, and not the least bit rubbery.

A chouriço sausage, grilled and flambéed with brandy at the table, is served on a bed of lime-flavoured lentils with a spicy tomato sauce. This Portuguese sausage, traditionally made with smoked pork seasoned with paprika, crushed pepper, garlic, and other spices, is surprisingly fatty and bland. The limey lentils topped with the leftover brandy also taste strange. Perhaps a spicier sausage might have enlivened the dish.

Considered by many to be Portugal's national dish is caldo verde, a soup consisting of a potato-based broth with olive oil, shredded kale, and a thick round of sausage. The soup is thick and the cabbage is finely sliced, but the greens are off-puttingly bitter, and, again, the sausage is bland.

The best of the appetizers, and one of the most typically Portuguese, is the grilled sardines. Dwarfing the minuscule canned variety, these four large specimens, served on a bed of arugula and sprinkled with sea salt, are moist, flaky, and pungent—simply superb.

Main courses are impressive. The seafood rice (Ferreira's most popular dish) arrives at the table in a small cast-iron pot, which is uncovered to reveal clams, mussels, baby squid, small shrimp, and prawns atop plenty of white rice—the Portuguese equivalent of Spanish paella. The waiter skilfully spoons the colourful mixture onto a plate. The mollusks are perfectly cooked and seasoned and served with an aromatic fish broth. It's all heavenly, save for the prawns, which can be overcooked and floury.

Another potted rice dish, duck rice, is more typical of northern Portugal, as meat is used instead of seafood. The boneless pieces of duck meat, served with sautéed mushroom halves, have a delicious strong and sweet flavour. The accompanying rice, served risotto style, is Italian Arborio, and the mushrooms are shiitake. An interesting twist on tradition here: the concept is Portuguese but the ingredients are multiethnic.

The yellowfin tuna is the specialty of the house and doesn't disappoint. The grilled slab of pink tuna is coated with white and black crushed peppercorns and served very rare. The fish is stacked between sautéed baby pak choy and a crisp galette of shredded potatoes, and it's topped with a lively salad of diced cucumber, pineapple, and tomatoes with coriander leaves and chives. The presentation, finished off with sweet-potato chips, is spectacular. The fresh, sweet accents of the salad contrast beautifully with the rich-flavoured fish and earthy galette.

Desserts include a perfectly cooked miniature crème caramel, a natas tartlet with a baked custard centre (found in every local Portuguese bakery), a delicate fruit tart, and a decadent chocolate pudding cake. Three homemade sorbets—mango, raspberry, and honey-orange, are flavourful, creamy, and not in the least bit icy.

The enthusiastic young waiters, many of whom are of Portuguese descent, not only know their way around the menu and wine list but also seem everpresent without hovering.

IN THE KITCHEN • Chef Marino Tavaras.

DECOR, DRESS, AMBIENCE • Apart from the appetizing smell and the crowds, what's sure to impress first-time diners is the decor. The room is framed by long sunflower-yellow walls and a terra-cotta-tiled floor. The accents—a collage of broken plates near the entrance, a stunning tile fresco of a mountaintop village behind the bar, and comfortable wide-backed chairs—are all a vivid shade of Mediterranean royal blue.

WINE LIST • The wine list is faithful to the concept, and it's no surprise that the pages are dominated by privately imported Portuguese wines listed by region. If you need help, don't hesitate to ask your waiter for advice. Port connoisseurs are definitely in for a treat, with bottles priced from $60 to $4,000, and a wide selection offered by the glass.

DON'T MISS • The grilled squid, the grilled tuna, the sardines, the duck or seafood rice, and the desserts.

WORDS TO THE WISE • With a formula this promising, Café Ferreira is one of the most engaging restaurants in Montreal. The food is not always rock solid, but it has been improving steadily

every year. Autograph seekers take note: this is a favourite haunt
of visiting celebrities and movie stars.

FERREIRA CAFÉ TRATTORIA
1446 Rue Peel (near de Maisonneuve)
Telephone: (514) 848-0988
Open: 11:30 A.M.-11 P.M., Monday to Friday; 5 P.M.-11 P.M.,
Saturday
Wheelchair access: No
Reservations: Essential
Cards: All major cards
Price range: Starters, $5-$13; main courses, $15-$37;
desserts, average $7; lunch table d'hôte menu, $14-$22; dinner
table d'hôte menu, $25-$35

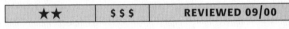

| ★★ | $ $ $ | REVIEWED 09/00 |

FOUQUET'S

SNAPSHOT • A satellite operation of the famed Parisian celebrity-
and-tourist-packed Champs Élysées café, Fouquet's boasts an elegant Belle Époque decor and a prime downtown location. The
overly simple menu offers predictable French dishes that are ideal
for out-of-towners but all too commonplace for sophisticated
local gourmets. Service is formal and friendly. The lunchtime
table d'hôte offers good value.

THE BIG PICTURE • Many restaurants appear to be playing it
safe these days, avoiding risks by offering a menu of "greatest hits"
over original compositions. So common are these generic menus
that if aliens landed in Montreal, they'd think we lived on a restaurant diet of sweetbreads, smoked salmon, scallops, carpaccio, and
crème brûlée.

A prime example of this is found at Fouquet's. This downtown
restaurant seems to be trying to sell its glamorous name as opposed to an original menu. In Paris, its namesake is a Champs

Élysées café/restaurant known as a glittering celebrity hangout (though, in reality, the majority of the patrons are tourists). Fouquet's of Montreal has been in business for three years, but last year it was taken over by the proprietors of the Parisian establishment, Groupe Lucien Barrière.

To further emphasize the French connection, the Montreal restaurant incorporates pastel murals picturing the Parisian café. The only element missing is the crowd, for Fouquet's dining room often sits empty. The greeting at the door is friendly, and service is solicitous and thoroughly professional. The location, next to that high temple of elegance, Holt Renfrew, is ideal for the ladies who lunch.

For such an aesthetically pleasing establishment, the food is surprisingly ordinary. Take, for example, the soups. Vegetable soup is the litmus test for any kitchen, and this version fails due to its lack of seasoning—especially salt. The fish soup looks terrific: deep-orange coloured and correctly served with tender pieces of white fish, fresh croutons, and a spicy, garlicky rouille. But after a few spoonfuls it fails to deliver. The flavour is weak and one-dimensional, lacking any interesting accent, such as saffron or pastis. Equally dreary is the mixed salad, which consists of a supermarket-variety green lettuce and radicchio mix dressed with a run-of-the-mill vinaigrette.

Sometimes ordinary is okay. Lunchtime table d'hôte main courses include some simple dishes with few faults. The grilled entrecôte topped with a sprinkling of thyme is a fine cut of meat, perfectly grilled to the requested "blue" (rare). A swordfish steak "à la plancha" (pan-seared) is fresh, moist, and meaty. The fish and steak are served with a jardinière of vegetables—broccoli, cauliflower, carrots, zucchini—that are all well cooked and seasoned. Only the tired house French fries disappoint.

To be fair, some dishes, like the roasted magret de canard, are a cut above. The meaty, pink duck breast is served fanned atop a beautiful array of turned vegetables. It's well enhanced by an old-fashioned grainy mustard sauce—an unusual combination, but a surprisingly good one.

Another notable dish is the hot and cold foie gras starter, which includes a crisp panfried piece of duck liver and a smooth, masterfully deveined slice of terrine. Every bite is rich and delicious. The accompaniments are a bit puzzling, though. The plate is garnished with a mound of caramelized endive (which tastes sautéed, rather than caramelized), a few asparagus spears, and a fan of tomato slices—simple vegetables that hardly complement the richness of foie gras.

With a menu this predictable, one is tempted to sample any dish that sounds adventurous. The waiter describes one offering as "veal-and-Ricotta-filled pasta pockets with a North African sauce." Unfortunately, what arrives is a plate containing four overstuffed, Ricotta-filled pasta pockets coated in a cloying curry cream sauce. Where's the veal? And since when is curry a specialty of North Africa?

Of the desserts, only one—a crisp, thin apple tart with vanilla ice cream—stands out. The others don't quite make it. The homemade sorbets—mango and raspberry—are set in a stale tulip biscuit. The crème brûlée is overbruléed and curdled. The soft chocolate cake lacks an oozing centre and, as strange as it may sound, any chocolate flavour.

IN THE KITCHEN · Chef Céline Cosseron.

DECOR, DRESS, AMBIENCE · The Belle Époque decor is highlighted by table lamps and scarlet banquettes. The tables are set with Fouquet's signature Limoges china, and the walls are hung with a series of black-and-white photographs of bleary-eyed French celebrities sipping Champagne in the maison mère. It's all quite French, chic, and authentic, and if it weren't for the scaled-down size and lack of Gitane cigarette smoke in the air, you could easily imagine yourself in the City of Lights.

WINE LIST · The wine list at Fouquet's contains many bottles under $40 in addition to private imports at more exorbitant prices. Wines by the glass are not listed, but there are always a few open bottles on hand.

DON'T MISS · The foie gras, the duck with mustard sauce, the grilled steak, and the thin apple tart.

WORDS TO THE WISE · Interestingly enough, the word "brasserie" is emblazoned in bold letters on the cover of Fouquet's menu. So where are the brasserie essentials? The late-night hours, the extensive choice of beers, ciders, sauerkraut, and oysters? It seems as though this elegant restaurant is in the midst of an identity crisis. Let's hope it soon finds its place on the downtown restaurant scene.

FOUQUET'S

2180 Rue de la Montagne (near Sherbrooke)
Telephone: (514) 284-2132
Open: Lunch, noon-3 P.M., Monday to Friday; dinner, 6 P.M.-
11:00 P.M., Monday to Saturday
Wheelchair access: No
Reservations: Recommended
Cards: All major cards
Price range: Starters, $9.75-$26.75; main courses, $22.75-$36;
desserts, $5.75-$8.75

★★1/2	$ $ $	REVIEWED 03/01

GIBBYS

SNAPSHOT · Gibbys is one of Montreal's most popular steak houses, if not its most popular restaurant. The establishment's rustic Old Montreal setting, its roaring fireplaces and wood-beamed ceilings, make it a preferred destination for tourists and celebrating locals, who keep coming in droves for pickles, steaks, Monte Carlo potatoes, and delicious fresh fish. Service is friendly and efficient. Reservations are essential, and there's free valet parking.

THE BIG PICTURE · What's the most difficult reservation to get in Montreal? For a weekend table at Toqué!, you'll have to plan a few weeks ahead. Outremont's La Chronique can be equally trying. But considering the number of seats available, the toughest table to book in Montreal might just be at the Old Montreal steak house Gibbys.

Though gourmets wouldn't necessarily place this or any of the city's steak houses on a list of Montreal's top ten restaurants, in this case the crowds do the talking. The popularity of Gibbys reaches far and wide. It's the number-one dining destination for many American and Canadian tourists, and it is loved—dearly loved—by hundreds of locals. The winning formula of what is arguably Montreal's most popular restaurant (now 30 years strong) is that customers are offered a fully satisfying dining experience. Gibbys aims to please—not the foodies, perhaps, but certainly the majority, "Monsieur et Madame Tout-le-Monde."

However old-fashioned they may be, onion soup, snails, shrimp cocktail, pepper steak, and cheesecake still appear popular with most people. Cholesterol watchers and calorie counters can choose from a separate fish menu that features some seven fresh specimens, from swordfish and striped bass to salmon and tuna, all of which are available poached with dill, grilled, or blackened with Cajun spices.

Starters are an unnecessary indulgence at Gibbys, as a generous house salad is offered with every main course. But those with a hearty appetite can try the Provençal mussels, which are broiled in the shell with garlic butter, bacon, and shallots. The mussels are plump and soft, and the garlicky sauce is delicious enough to lick off the plate.

The onion soup features a light beef broth, an abundance of caramelized onions, and the obligatory cheesy crouton raft. The shrimp bisque has a pronounced flavour and the few crustaceans strewn within are tender. Unfortunately, it has an overly thick consistency and a high cream content that only adds to its cloying richness.

At Gibbys, main courses are the raison d'être. Those up for the ultimate carnivore experience should try the New York cut sirloin coated with garlic and spices and grilled medium-rare. The steak has a wonderful texture, well crusted on the outside and tender on the inside—every bite melts in the mouth. Accompaniments include a handful of broccoli, a crumb-coated broiled tomato, and a stuffed baked potato (the renowned Monte Carlo). As an added flavour enhancement, request a side order of béarnaise, which has the correct pronounced tarragon flavour.

The sauce Diane isn't in the same league as the béarnaise. This Cognac, mushroom, and cream sauce served with a filet mignon is too rich, skimpy on the Cognac, and filled with sliced Parisian mushrooms that add little. The accompanying French fries are equally lacklustre.

Surprisingly enough, one of the best main courses is the fish. The Arctic char with Cajun spices is a generous filet seasoned just this side of spicy. It's cooked to perfection — delicate, moist, and flavourful.

The American-style desserts are nothing to write home about. A large slice of Key lime pie has a fluffy, faintly flavoured filling that pales next to the tangy, custard-like filling of the real McCoy. The New York-style cheesecake is the type of cake you'd expect in a deli, not in an upscale restaurant. The hot apple "croute" consists of a puff pastry vol-au-vent shell filled with soggy sautéed apples and an overdose of cream, whipped and iced. A large mint leaf is wedged into the mix — a futile gesture if ever there was one.

Despite the lack of passion on the dessert list, Gibbys betters the competition in many other departments. Service is efficient and refreshingly unpretentious. Valet parking is free, and everyone from the coat-check girl to the busy hostess at the entrance is friendly and welcoming.

DECOR, DRESS, AMBIENCE • Seated in one of the restaurant's stone-walled, low-ceilinged, wood-beamed dining rooms, you'll see families with sparkling birthday cakes being photographed by waiters, and couples holding hands, soaking up the romantic candlelit atmosphere. One who cringes at the thought of either of these scenarios might find it all a bit saccharine, but there's also a sense of fun at Gibbys, a sort of good-times gregariousness, as appealing as the sight of the generous plates of food, the long-skirted waitresses, and the complimentary bowls of dill pickles, sour cream, and bacon bits at every table.

WINE LIST • The wine list is fairly priced, with a variety of bottles from all corners of the globe at price points starting under $30.

DON'T MISS • The Provençal mussels, the fish, and the steaks. Calorie counters should skip the rich sauces in favour of a Monte Carlo potato.

WORDS TO THE WISE • Owners Gibby and Alan Rosenberg have come up with a restaurant recipe that really seems to work: good food and warm service in a relaxed setting. It may take a few calls to get in, but when you do, you'll be satisfied.

GIBBYS
298 Place d'Youville (near McGill)
Telephone: (514) 282-1837
Open: 4:30 P.M.-11 P.M., Sunday to Thursday; 4:30 P.M.-11:30 P.M., Friday to Saturday
Wheelchair access: Yes
Reservations: Essential
Cards: Major cards
Price range: Starters, $6.50-$12.75; main courses, $19.95-$42.75; desserts, $4.50-$7.95

★★★	$ $ $	REVIEWED 08/00

GLOBE

SNAPSHOT • Look beyond the glamorous clientele, the see-and-be-seen atmosphere, and the pulsating background music in this Boulevard St. Laurent pleasure dome, and you're sure to find what counts: the food. Chef David McMillan offers some of Montreal's most innovative North American-style cuisine prepared with first-rate organic, and primarily local, ingredients. Service is laid-back and friendly, and the wine list offers many original selections. This is one of the city's most exciting restaurants.

THE BIG PICTURE · Looking around the vast, high-ceilinged space of Globe, you'll probably spot a tall, broad-shouldered young man in a golf shirt and a blue dishwasher's apron. He might be by the door greeting customers or talking to a passerby on the street. Or he might be chatting with diners, extolling the virtues of a new Canadian wine or discussing the pros and cons of pan-seared Quebec foie gras. The blue-aproned man in question is David McMillan, Globe's chef, and the person who, over the past five years, has made this restaurant one of the most intriguing and successful on the Main.

McMillan is not your everyday chef. The choice of golf shirt — as opposed to starched white vest, chef's hat, and checkered pants — speaks volumes. His attitude is casual. This applies to his taste in food as well. Those who label his ingredient-driven dishes as market cuisine might be missing the bigger picture. Here's a chef who's not afraid to serve meat with that Anglo Sunday-dinner favourite, gravy.

Globe's initial slogan was "Think Global, Eat Local," but McMillan has slowly dropped all foreign accents from his cooking in favour of a no-nonsense North American style. Qualifiers like "crispy," "oven roasted," and "garlic rubbed" enhance mouth-watering menu descriptions. Just look at what he's doing with potatoes: not only are they roasted and French fried, but they're also dirty mashed, whipped, crushed, and hash browned. And what other high-end Montreal restaurant is offering homemade alphabet soup as a starter?

McMillan's ideas may be simple, but their composition is first-class. As stated on the menu, ingredients are organic, and all meats and fowl are free-range and come from local farmers. Plate presentations aren't fussy — no tuiles or marbled sauces. Portions are generous, certainly more in line with comfort food than haute cuisine. McMillan's only fault is that occasionally his dishes appear to be no more than an assembly of lovely ingredients, like a party filled with good-looking people who have little in common. But this chef is a risktaker, and when his experiments fly, they fly high.

For starters, try the endive salad tossed with fresh walnuts, green-apple bâtonnets, and sliced grapes. Within the curved endive leaves are nestled small chunks of Stilton cheese, which provide a pungent kick. A pair of shrimp, leek, and potato cakes served with cold shrimp, pickled new onions, and a mound of shaved celery offer three well-balanced flavours in two golden, grease-free parcels. Served alongside are a few squiggles of delicious aïoli.

The baked tomato with fresh and dried Ricotta and braised Île Verte lamb provides a terrific mix of flavours and textures. The soft Ricotta is cold and creamy, the dried Ricotta is salty and crumbly; the plump tomato conveys the fresh taste of summer, and the tender chunks of lamb add an assertive, meaty note. The best taste comes last, when the tomato and lamb juices, the bits of Ricotta, and the few droplets of oil are swirled and slurped up along with the mirepoix of vegetables at the bottom.

Main courses are McMillan's forte, especially braised meats. The slow-cooked rabbit — a large leg and a herbed-stuffed loin — is amazing. Rabbit is so often either dry or tasteless, but this meat, topped with crisp fried pancetta and served with excellent Parmesan risotto, sautéed chanterelles, rapini, spinach, and green beans, is melt-in-the-mouth tender.

Baby back ribs served with a red wine sauce, Ricotta gnocchi, and baby beets are a triumph. The slow-braised pork is succulent, full flavoured, and enhanced with the rich wine-based sauce. If McMillan were barbecuing these ribs, one wonders what sort of barbecue sauce he'd use. A clue may come from the quince and honey paste brushed onto the crispy Peking duck. This dish is, hands down, the most exciting on the menu. After a few tangy, sweet bites of the duck, you'll question whether you'll ever be able to enjoy it prepared any other way.

Two other dishes, brick-roasted Cornish hen and seared filet of halibut, seem timid next to the three preceding showstoppers. The deboned hen arrives splayed over a bed of hash-brown potatoes and sautéed Swiss chard. It's nice, but here the common pairing of chicken and potatoes makes you yearn for one of McMillan's interesting flavour combos. So does the fish. Though it's perfectly cooked and juicy, with a delicious crusty coating, the subtle flavour will leave fish lovers wanting more.

McMillan's desserts are simple and well chosen. Warm chocolate torte with espresso ice cream has never budged from this menu and remains the perfect rendition of this popular dessert. Chocolate pôt de crème, served with a oversized biscotti, is also exemplary.

Though subdued, service is friendly and professional. The young wait staff may have the right look, but they could use a bit more confidence.

IN THE KITCHEN · Chef David McMillan.

DECOR, DRESS, AMBIENCE · On busy nights, Globe's environment is dark, noisy, and crowded. It's also trendy enough to make you second-guess your choice of footwear. Not everyone is here for a gourmet experience, and if you are, you may be distracted. What a shame, since the star of the show is really what's on the plate and not whichever visiting celebrity is holding court from one of the cushy red-and-blue banquettes along the wall. Even though the staff and chef McMillan go out of their way to welcome all, the pervading atmosphere is definitely "see and be seen."

WINE LIST · The wine list grows more complex every year. Wine aficionados may find McMillan's suggestions illuminating, as wine is one of his passions. There's also a long list of spirits and house cocktails—not surprising, since this restaurants boasts one of Montreal's most vibrant after-hours bar scenes.

DON'T MISS · The endive salad, the Peking duck, and the warm chocolate torte. The daily specials are also a good bet.

WORDS TO THE WISE · If you're up for a bit of fun with your dinner, by all means visit Globe late in the week or on a weekend. If you're looking for a gourmet experience, you might prefer eating early in the night and early in the week. A word of advice: this is more a place to take a friend eager to soak up the action on the Main—not necessarily your mother, unless she dresses like Cher.

GLOBE
3455 Boulevard St. Laurent (near Sherbrooke)
Telephone: (514) 284-3823
Open: 6 P.M.-11 P.M., daily
Wheelchair access: No
Reservations: Essential
Cards: All major cards
Price range: Starters, $7-$15; main courses, $18-$30; desserts, $8

★★1/2	$ $ $	REVIEWED 03/01

GUY & DODO MORALI

SNAPSHOT • Although Guy & Dodo Morali has a large and loyal following among the power-lunch crowd, many Montrealers may never have heard of it. The reason? The restaurant's location — inside the Cours Mont Royal. Yet this hidden gem epitomizes French savoir faire, offering traditional French cuisine and some of the friendliest service in the city. Standouts on the menu include the fish dishes and the exceptional confit de canard.

THE BIG PICTURE • In Montreal's shops and boutiques, you'll find many people who've mastered the French art of salesmanship. These are the commerçants who, while wrapping up your purchase, politely inquire, "And with that, Madam?" Yet the most endearing of these personalities are often found in restaurants. The maître d' at Le Grand Café, for example, offers waiting patrons a complimentary glass of wine. Then there's the owner of Le Bistingo, who will always try to find you a table, even when his restaurant is full. Add to this list the owners and wait staff of Guy & Dodo Morali. This downtown restaurant is *the* place to come to experience friendly French service at its best.

The room is overseen by Dodo Morali herself. The tall, stylish blond patronne is easy to spot as she greets regulars at the door by name or hands out boxes of homemade chocolates to tourists. She often appears tableside to take your order, her eyes sparkling as she tantalizes with recommendations from the table d'hôte, nodding and smiling in approval when someone chooses the house specialty, confit de canard.

The menu is classic French, more haute cuisine than bistro. Of the starters, the clam chowder is creamy and filled to overflowing with potatoes and tender clams. The excellent boudin blanc (veal sausage) arrives sliced and arranged in a circle around a pile of melting caramelized onions. Also memorable is the duck terrine, which is wonderfully chunky and flavourful. Less successful is the cream of carrot soup (a bit bland), the oeufs mayonnaise (better labelled "mayonnaise oeufs"), and the seared scallops with sea salt (stringy and too salty for my taste).

Main courses are excellent. The salmon Wellington, a puff-pastry-wrapped layering of spinach, moist salmon, and julienned vegetables, is a lovely light dish, far more appealing than its old-fashioned beef counterpart. Halibut amandine, a panfried filet topped with toasted, slivered almonds and served on a bed of tender julienned vegetables, is fresh, buttery, and melting. The côte de veau Normande is a thick veal chop sliced and sauced with a Calvados veal jus, sautéed mushrooms, and apple slices. A side dish of creamy scalloped potatoes adds a welcome touch of excess.

And the confit de canard? Terrific—all crackling skin and glistening dark meat. (Although confit purists would stop here, with maybe a bouquet of watercress to refresh the palate between bites, the waiter adds a brown, meat-based sauce espagnol that obliterates the flavour of the duck and softens the crispness of the skin.) Equally appealing are the panfried sliced potatoes, caram-elized onions, and sautéed Parisian and oyster mushrooms.

Desserts include a fine crème caramel, an okay tarte Tatin (the crust can be a bit soggy and the apples on the dry side), an excel-lent molten chocolate cake served in a ramekin, and that well-loved French bistro classic, floating islands.

At coffee time, Dodo Morali reappears, all smiles, with a plate of tuiles, while chef Guy Morali makes his way around the room, greeting diners by name, with the comfortable air of a man surrounded by friends.

IN THE KITCHEN • Chef and owner Guy Morali.

DECOR, DRESS, AMBIENCE • With its cream walls, wood panelling, wide bar laden with open wine bottles and fancy liqueurs, small shaded lamps, and wooden ducks on every table, the setting is straight out of a French thriller. One can just picture Belmondo, playing a spy, seated in one of the well-worn leather banquettes or high-backed chairs.

WINE LIST • Selections are diverse and well priced, with the added bonus that every wine listed is available by the glass.

DON'T MISS • The clam chowder, the confit de canard (skip the sauce), the fish, and the simple desserts, like the crème caramel.

WORDS TO THE WISE • Guy & Dodo Morali is a restaurant that pampers its customers and makes them feel like valued guests. Apparently, this establishment draws not only locals but also many out-of-towners, who come for a dose of genuine French charm as well as for the food.

GUY & DODO MORALI
1444 Rue Metcalfe, or 1455 Rue Peel (in the Cours Mont Royal)
Telephone: (514) 842-3636
Open: Lunch, 11:30 A.M.-3 P.M., Monday to Friday; dinner,
5:30 P.M.-10:30 P.M., Monday to Friday, and 6 P.M.-10:30 P.M.,
Saturday
Wheelchair access: Yes
Reservations: Recommended
Cards: Major cards
Price range: Starters, $6.50-$24.50; main courses, $10.50-$38.80;
desserts, $6.50-$12.80

★★1/2	$ $ $ $	REVIEWED 09/99

IL CAMPARI CENTRO

SNAPSHOT · One of downtown Montreal's top Italian restaurants, Il Campari serves upscale classic Italian cuisine in a luxurious setting. The wine list is extensive and the service is exceptionally polished and friendly. Hockey fans take note: the Molson Centre is but a stone's throw away.

THE BIG PICTURE · What serious cook hasn't tried to re-create a restaurant dish at home? In my case, there have been many. But I will always remember the first — penne Campari, from Il Campari, located on the corner of Côte des Neiges and Van Horne. Here was the perfect pasta dish: tiny tubes of penne drenched in a creamy tomato sauce chock-full of sautéed mushrooms and sliced pancetta. I had almost succeeded in cracking the code when Il Campari moved downtown, changing its name to Il Campari Centro.

The new location is an open room that seats about 90 diners and features an elevated outdoor terrace overlooking Rue de la Montagne. There's a long list of daily specials along with à la carte listings of traditional Italian soups, salads, meat, fish, and, surprisingly, only eight pasta dishes.

Of the starters, the calamari fritti is excellent. The golden fried squid are crisp, tender, and salty, and without a trace of grease left in their wake. Other favourites include a full-flavoured lentil soup, and a fresh spinach salad with a delicious creamy vinaigrette. A plate of prosciutto and melon is also exceptional. The thin slices of top-quality prosciutto are served with sections of luscious late-summer melon. A few strawberry quarters add an original sweet note to the dish (another Il Campari concept worth trying at home).

The beef and tuna carpaccio plates miss the mark because both feature more arugula than meat (they might better be described as salads). The vinaigrette, messily piped around the border of each, seems superfluous—hardly worth the effort.

By contrast, two main-course dishes, ravioli with Gorgonzola and penne with green peas, are quite nice. The ravioli is homemade and stuffed with a delicious, surprisingly subtle Gorgonzola filling. The penne, served with fresh peas and sautéed pancetta, is good but dry, simply crying out for more sauce. The portion is also small for a main course.

The risotto with porcini mushrooms is mushroom heaven—a walk in the woods. The large portion of creamy rice is packed with slices of fresh, expensive porcini mushrooms. The overall effect is sufficiently powerful to send your olfactory senses into overdrive.

Il Campari Centro offers several versions of that old Canadian Italian favourite, veal scaloppini. Here's a dish that's difficult to get excited about. Some of the sauces, however, such as the mustard cream sauce, are very good. So are the accompanying grilled peppers, wilted spinach, cauliflower, and broccoli.

As is the case in many of Montreal's Italian restaurants, desserts are a minor player on the menu. The obligatory tiramisu is fluffy like a mousse and frozen in the middle. There's an interesting frozen chocolate mousse that's creamy, along the lines of a semifreddo, and it packs a wonderful hazelnut kick.

Service at Il Campari Centro is excellent. The waiters, fine Italian gentlemen all, could show many in the Montreal service community a thing or two. Cutlery is discreetly replaced, wine is poured with care, and the occasional jokes are perfectly timed.

IN THE KITCHEN • Chef Antonio Santa.

DECOR, DRESS, AMBIENCE • The luxurious setting features wood-panelled walls, stained glass windows, and racks of expensive wine. The diners are tourists and locals, especially those with tickets to an event at the Molson Centre, located a few blocks away.

WINE LIST • Wines are expensive, with full bottles costing close to triple their retail price. A few less-expensive bottles and several half bottles (only one red) are available. Wines by the glass are disappointing. It's worth enquiring about the unlisted and relatively inexpensive imports that are available from time to time.

DON'T MISS • The prosciutto and melon, the pasta (especially the penne Campari), the mushroom risotto, the veal with mustard cream sauce, and the iced chocolate mousse.

WORDS TO THE WISE • While Il Campari Centro is not the most cutting-edge restaurant in town, it's not the most old-fashioned either. Generally speaking, the food is delicious and the stellar service leaves nothing to be desired. Another plus is the location. Unlike nearby Rue Crescent, with its boisterous bar scene, lower Rue de la Montagne has a charm all its own. For summertime dining, the small front terrace is hard to beat.

IL CAMPARI CENTRO
1177 Rue de la Montagne (near René Lévesque)
Telephone: (514) 868-1177
Open: 11:30 A.M.-11 P.M., Monday to Friday;
5 P.M.-midnight, Saturday
Wheelchair access: No
Reservations: Recommended
Cards: All major cards
Price range: Starters, $6.50-$17.50; main courses, $15.50-$39;
desserts, $4.50-$8.50; three-course table d'hôte menu, $19.50-$35

| ★★ | $ $ | REVIEWED 02/01 |

IL CORTILE

SNAPSHOT • This is the Italian restaurant we're all looking for: a place with friendly waiters, a welcoming ambience, a comprehensive Italian wine list, and a menu featuring authentic, affordable Italian fare. The daily market menu is made up of classic favourites, including buffalo Mozzarella and tomatoes, Caesar salad, stracciatella, as well as various pasta and veal dishes. The decor is as elegant as the crowd, which includes many business types and museum-going ladies who lunch.

THE BIG PICTURE • Il Cortile is one of Montreal's little secrets —a real find, tucked away down a corridor in the basement of a Rue Sherbrooke gallery of stores fronted by a chocolate shop. At lunch, almost every table is filled, and waiters whiz past carrying colourful and appetizing plates. When the sun sets, everything changes: the lights are low and the room is usually empty—you'd never know it was the same restaurant. Obviously, lunch is Il Cortile's raison d'être.

The daily market menu is set out table d'hôte style, with starters included in the price of the main course. Nothing is complicated here; it's all quite simple—as Italian cuisine should be. The caprese salad, made of ripe tomatoes, creamy Mozzarella, and mesclun, is dressed with an assertive balsamic vinaigrette. A plate of prosciutto and Parmesan offers a generous portion of paper-thin prosciutto slices and chunks of buttery, fresh Parmesan— two of Italy's finest foodstuffs, which meld together, mouthful after mouthful.

Some of the other starters could use some fine-tuning. The egg and chicken-broth soup, stracciatella, is filled with over-cooked spinach and mushy zucchini. Given the neon colour of the broth, one might suspect commercial chicken stock played a role in its composition. The Ricotta filling of a crêpe served with a saffron hollandaise is in desperate need of seasoning—even just salt and pepper. A small serving of melanzane (grilled eggplant and zucchini topped with tomato sauce and cheese) is covered in insipid Provolone.

Two main-course pastas, linguini pomodoro e basilico and fazzoletti (Ricotta and spinach pasta pockets), prove that home-made pastas are the way to go at Il Cortile. The linguini is a generous bowl of thin noodles topped with fresh basil and plenty of chunky tomato sauce. This is pasta at its simplest and most appealing. The fazzoletti offers a classic Ricotta and spinach filling loosely wrapped in sheets of fresh pasta and topped with more of the wonderful red sauce, obviously made with fresh tomatoes.

A house specialty, gnocchetti with Gorgonzola sauce, features bite-size gnocchi made in-house with semolina flour and Ricotta as opposed to the standard heavier potato dough. Although the dumplings are indeed less filling than most, this time the sauce fails to impress. Not only has it separated into an oily, creamy puddle, but also the Gorgonzola flavour is faint.

One dish that many Italian restaurants rarely prepare correctly is risotto. In fact, given the odd exception (such as at Le Latini) you'll taste some of the best risotto dishes in non-Italian restaurants. Il Cortile is no exception. Though the risotto primavera looks promising—glistening and loaded with mushrooms, zucchini, and spinach—the consistency of the rice is mushy, and it lacks the required creamy starchiness. One might even question whether the correct Arborio rice was used.

The veal scaloppini is lightly sautéed and drizzled with lemon, white wine, and pan juices. The accompaniments include sautéed zucchini strips and red peppers. It's good, but about as exciting as North American pork chops and applesauce.

With a cup of espresso, don't miss the tiramisu, which, unlike many dull versions of this popular dessert, is fresh, moist, heavy on the cake, and creamy enough to make it all come together. There's also a fine three-chocolate mousse cake (very eighties) and an icy lemon sorbet.

IN THE KITCHEN · Chef and owner France DeCrescentis.

DECOR, DRESS, AMBIENCE · The restaurant is small—just 46 seats. The bright room features an elaborately tiled floor and bar, and floor-to-ceiling windows that face a small courtyard, which comes to life (and doubles the seating capacity) in the summer. Dark-green wooden venetian blinds, oil paintings, and Italian wine bottles of various sizes add an air of sophistication. If it weren't for the well-dressed patrons chatting loudly in both French and English (often on cell phones), you could imagine you were in a bourgeois restaurant in downtown Milan.

WINE LIST · Il Cortile offers a comprehensive selection of fine Italian wines at many price points. There are also six reasonably priced choices by the glass: three red and three white.

DON'T MISS · The starters, the homemade pastas, and the heavenly tiramisu.

WORDS TO THE WISE · Dinner and lunch at Il Cortile are night-and-day experiences. The former limps along, never quite taking flight, while the latter is good in just about every respect. It's obvious that this establishment is catering to the lunch crowd. So do lunch and enjoy. One insider's tip: if you open it, the bottle of San Pellegrino that has been placed on your table (and every other table in the place) will make its way onto your bill.

IL CORTILE
1442 Rue Sherbrooke West (in the Passage du Musée)
Telephone: (514) 843-8230
Open: 11 A.M.-11 P.M., daily
Wheelchair access: Yes
Reservations: Recommended; essential at lunch
Cards: Major cards
Price range: Lunch table d'hôte menu, $12-$17; main courses (starters included), $17-$28; desserts, $5

★★1/2	$ $ $ $	REVIEWED 12/00

IL MULINO

SNAPSHOT · Il Mulino is a homey neighbourhood restaurant located on the quiet corner of St. Zotique and Alma in the heart of Little Italy. Renowned for over a decade for its "cucina rustica," using only the best market ingredients, this well-loved restaurant's new owners aim to preserve the high quality—with prices to match.

THE BIG PICTURE · A critically acclaimed restaurant changing hands is enough to cause a stir on the fine-dining scene, especially a Montreal institution like Il Mulino, an establishment that has been family owned and operated for over a decade. Owners Francesca and Maria Mazza turned this unpretentious neighbourhood restaurant into one of the city's top Italian eateries, where authentic Calabrian cuisine made from the freshest market ingredients attracted a faithful following. Recently, restaurateur and Mazza family friend Aniello Covone, along with partner and chef Tony De Rose, took over the reins.

Since the new owner's goal is to preserve Il Mulino's strong points—namely, unpretentious Italian cuisine combined with warm and watchful service—not much has changed. Mr. Covone's greeting is welcoming, and his lengthy menu explanations and wine suggestions are more than helpful.

The daily menu offers Italian market cuisine with nary a pompous name or a fussy presentation in sight. After elaborate French meals, there's no denying the appeal of Italian "cucina rustica." But let's not confuse rustic or simple with inexpensive, for the ingredients at Il Mulino are high quality, which means that prices are bound to be steep as well.

Since starter and main-course portions are large, it's best to avoid filling up on the excellent house foccacia and opt for the complimentary olives or peppers instead (be warned: the peppers are hot enough to be classified as lethal weapons). To begin, it's hard to resist the homemade gnocchi, described by Mr. Covone as "the lightest in town." He may be right. The large potato dumplings are a delight: melt-in-the-mouth tender and not in the least bit gummy (a common gnocchi pitfall). But gnocchi tend to be bland, and they require a bold sauce. The tomato-basil sauce offered here is just too insipid to make the dish memorable. For the same reason, the "paccheri polpette" (large, smooth, rigatoni-like pasta tubes) also falls short. The tomato sauce is again lacklustre, and the dish's two large veal meatballs, though tasty, are barely warm.

These same meatballs, scaled down in size, make a second appearance in a bowl of vegetable soup. Served in a homemade broth filled with chunky vegetables, the herb-enhanced mini meatballs add heartiness to this robust winter soup.

Other winning appetizers include grilled scallops, antipasto, and "crostini con fegatini di feaona" (toasted bread with sautéed guinea-hen livers). The large diver scallops, served with tangy pink grapefruit segments, have a caramelized crust and translucent centre — perfection on a plate. The antipasto selection is served on two plates: one with buffalo Mozzarella and freshly sliced prosciutto, and the other with grilled mushrooms, peppers, and eggplant, boosted with dribbles of thick, sweet, aged balsamic vinegar.

When available, the sautéed guinea-hen livers are not to be missed. Tender, sweet, and without a trace of bitterness, the little livers, which are sautéed with mushrooms and onions and placed atop a large crouton, offer a rare taste of an authentic favourite.

Unfortunately, the many high notes hit by the starters don't follow through to the main courses. The fish soup, "zuppa di pesca," consists of a large bowl of saffron-flavoured broth filled with clams, mussels, scampi, as well as pieces of salmon, bass, and monkfish. Though the monkfish and scampi are both tender and tasty, the mussels are dry, the clams sandy, and the salmon overcooked. The delicious garlic, tomato, and saffron broth turns out to be the best part of the mix.

Reading the menu description "roast veal with cipollini," one would expect sliced veal roast with a handful of sweet, flat cipollini onions. What arrives instead are two large and thick roasted veal chops and a few roasted shallots. The meat has a rich flavour, but it's also dense and dry. Far better is the osso buco with risotto, which is served only on Wednesdays. In this veal dish, the meat is juicy and falling off the bone.

A sweetbread-and-mushroom-filled tortelli (a large tortellini) is served with a veal jus enhanced with tomato and cream. Though the pasta wrapping is excellent, the flavour of the sweetbread filling is a little too subtle, and it has a mushy consistency. What a shame, since this luxury ingredient's appeal is its light and spongy texture.

Desserts, so rarely given full play in Italian restaurants, are taken seriously at Il Mulino. The tiramisu has a pronounced coffee flavour, a silky texture, and a cake base that hasn't been soaked to death. The apple tart is also dreamy, thanks to its delicate, buttery crust. But the best is the semifreddo. It's cool, creamy, and chock-full of caramelized hazelnuts — heaven, when savoured alongside a smooth, inky espresso.

One of Il Mulino's most appealing aspects is the service. Timing between courses is ideal, wine is carefully decanted and poured, and everyone, especially Mr. Covone, does his best to make sure you're comfortable and well fed.

IN THE KITCHEN · Chef Tony De Rose.

DECOR, DRESS, AMBIENCE · Small and square, the stucco-ceilinged room is lined with wooden armoires, a small bar, and, on the back wall, a rack containing books and numerous bottles of wine. There are no more than 14 tables here, all covered in immaculate starched white linen. The restaurant is usually packed with regulars, including many Italian families, who are greeted by Mr. Covone with smiles and handshakes in the true "sympatico" Italian fashion.

WINE LIST · The primarily Italian selections include about two dozen bottles of red and white wine priced between $30 and $70. There are also close to 50 private imports (including many rare wines and magnums) from $100 to $400.

DON'T MISS · The homemade gnocchi, the sautéed guinea-hen livers, the scallops, the antipasto, the osso bucco, and the desserts.

WORDS TO THE WISE · Considering the short transition period from the old to the new guard, it's possible that the chef has yet to come into his own. And when he does, Il Mulino might very well assume the lofty perch it enjoyed during its illustrious past.

IL MULINO
236 Rue St. Zotique East (corner Alma)
Telephone: (514) 273-5776
Open: Lunch, noon-3 P.M. ; dinner, 6 P.M.-10 P.M. Tuesday
to Saturday
Wheelchair access: Yes
Reservations: Essential
Cards: Major cards
Price range: Starters, $10-$22; main courses, $28-$38;
desserts, $5-$6

★★	$ $ $	REVIEWED 10/00

KATSURA

SNAPSHOT · Katsura is the place where a young, attractive, upscale crowd flocks to feast on excellent sushi and sashimi. Japanese standbys like tempura and teriyaki are less successful. The setting, with its private tatami rooms and comely waitresses padding along in silk kimonos, is always glamorous. The lunchtime table d'hôte menu offers good value.

THE BIG PICTURE · The crowd at Katsura would be the envy of many a restaurateur. Here the patrons are attractive, upscale, adventurous, and young. This is one of the rare places in Montreal where you'll notice twentysomethings dining in couples as opposed to family groups. It appears that members of the new generation of high-end restaurant-goers are cutting their teeth on Japanese food—and, more specifically, on sushi. Who would have imagined that the natural progression from pizza and French fries would lead to dried seaweed, vinegared rice, and raw fish.

Katsura has more in its corner than maki and hand rolls. This is also one of the most glamorous restaurants in town. But as stunning a setting as Katsura provides, the food is another story. It hasn't changed much in ten years ago. If anything, it's gotten a bit dreary. There's an unfortunate assembly-line feel to much of the cuisine. True, Westerners accustomed to rich, filling sauces often find Japanese food insipid, but unless you soak your food in the provided sauces (many of them bottled), you're sure to notice that some dishes don't live up to their exotic names and descriptions.

Hot appetizers are especially lacklustre. The brochettes of chicken yakatori taste only sweet, and the skewered shrimp benefit little from a weak ginger sauce. Two dumplings, panfried minced pork (yaki gyouza) and steamed shrimp (wafu shumai) arrive as hot parcels, looking plump and seductive. Too bad the pork filling is as dull and pasty as canned ravioli, and the shrimp dumplings impart little taste of shrimp.

Chicken tatsuta-age promises fried chicken marinated in gingered soy sauce, but the pieces that arrive taste no different from chicken nuggets. The fried squid (karamari) are tender, fresh, and benefit from a spicy sauce. Unfortunately the dish is stone cold, as is a plate of assorted tempura, which might just be the greasiest version of this popular Japanese classic you've ever tasted.

Anything to recommend? The deep-fried Japanese-style spring rolls are quite good. They're hot, supercrisp, and filled with bits of chicken and vegetable. The beef sashimi provides a pleasant start to a meal, though the lightly grilled meat could certainly be a bit more tender. A small portion of crab sunomono offers a mix of sweet (crab) and sour (vinegar) offset by cool, refreshing cucumber and potent seaweed. The soups, including samashi, a clear fish broth enhanced with tiny shrimp, and akadashi, an opaque soybean soup, are also quite good.

Main courses are uneven as well. Tempura, served as a main course, arrives hot, but is again greasy and lacking the sought-after light, lacy coating. The only high point of the dish is the jumbo shrimp, which are both fresh tasting and tender, despite the heavy batter. Although the chicken teriyaki is less salty than I remember it being on earlier visits the meat lacks the promised charcoal-broiled flavour. It's served with two tough stalks of broccoli and some grilled green peppers. The accompanying fried onions are cold and taste as though they were fried at 6 P.M.—Japanese time.

Toban yaki arrives at the table in a wide, single-size earthenware donabe casserole and is set upon a lit stand. The top is removed to unveil a shallow pool of simmering stock filled with steamed mushrooms, scallions, onions, carrots, leeks, zucchini, a boneless and skinless chicken breast, chunks of beef, and a miniature lamb chop. The accompaniments for this Japanese pot au feu are a bowl of white rice and three sauces: ginger, mustard, and chili. This offering has few redeeming qualities. There's not an ounce of seasoning to wake up the flavours. The stock is especially watery. And two of the three sauces are poor matches for the overcooked meat and vegetables (only the ginger sauce works). It's a dish that makes spa food look decadent.

So, with all these negatives, why is Katsura packing them in night after night? In a word, sushi. It may not be the most adventurous in town, but it is very good, impeccably fresh, and masterfully prepared. And the people who come here know it, for you'll see sushi (not toban yaki) on almost every table.

Connoisseurs might prefer to skip the sushi dinner (which offers a small, tame selection of standard nigiri sushi and cucumber and tuna maki) and opt for the à la carte selections. Set atop perfectly seasoned and cooked rice are melting slices of salmon, tuna, hamachi, sole, and shrimp. The grilled eel—unagi—is terrific —both sweet and spicy.

Katsura's maki rolls are only served in portions of four, six, or eight large pieces. Favourites include the spicy tuna roll, the Katsura roll, the Montreal roll, and an especially spicy kamikaze roll. The only roll that falls flat is the bagel roll. This is a reverse roll made with smoked salmon, cucumber, sesame, and a nugget of cream cheese that weighs the whole thing down (where did they get this recipe—Beauty's?).

A slice of melon is the best way to end your meal at Katsura. Of the iced desserts, vanilla ice cream was the clear winner over a sweet orange sorbet and an off-puttingly bitter green tea ice cream.

DECOR, DRESS, AMBIENCE • The decor, with its checkered dark-wood panels, cherry-coloured chairs, slanted ceiling, and delicate Japanese prints, is the most elegant of its genre. Spacious tatami rooms line the right side of the restaurant, providing an intimate setting for groups unwilling to compete with the elevated noise levels on crowded nights. Even the serving dishes, from the lacquered soup bowls and sushi trays to the hand-painted glazed platters and casseroles, are exquisite.

DON'T MISS • The soups, the beef sashimi, the spring rolls, and, of course, the sushi.

WINE LIST • Most customers drink Japanese beer or sake (two varieties, served hot and cold). There are also ten white and eight red wines priced between $27 and $60.

WORDS TO THE WISE • Is Katsura's courteous and efficient service, first-class decor, and better-than-average sushi enough to compensate for the lapses of its kitchen? Yes and no. If you're a connoisseur of Japanese food, you might want to venture further afield. But if it's a civilized evening you're looking for, or if you're curious about some of the more exotic aspects of the fine-dining scene, you may find yourself making regular trips here.

KATSURA
2170 Rue de la Montagne (near Sherbrooke)
Telephone: (514) 849-1172
Open: Lunch, 11:30 A.M.-2:30 P.M., Monday to Friday;
dinner, 5:30 P.M.-10 P.M., Monday to Thursday, 5:30 P.M.-11 P.M.,
Saturday, and 5:30 P.M.-9:30 P.M., Sunday
Wheelchair access: No
Reservations: Essential
Cards: Major cards
Price range: Starters, $1.75-$9.50; main courses, $11-$27;
desserts, $3-$5; complete dinners, $27-$31

★★1/2	$ $ $	REVIEWED 06/01

LA BASTIDE

SNAPSHOT · It might take a few tries to garner a reservation at Avenue Bernard's newest restaurant, La Bastide. Since its opening in May 2001, the place has been praised to the hilt by local French restaurant critics. What everyone is gushing about is the win-win formula: an imaginative southwestern French menu, a welcoming staff, a relaxing decor, and reasonable prices. It isn't yet perfection, but once a few kinks are ironed out, this unpretentious Mile End restaurant may soon live up to its hype.

THE BIG PICTURE · "Bienvenue!" exclaims Pierre Vesperini, La Bastide's tall, dark, bushy-haired, blue-eyed, well-built owner. "Come, we have a table for you on the terrace," says the affable Frenchman, bounding along like an excited Labrador retriever. Vesperini's enthusiasm is infectious. You'll find yourself bounding along behind him with an eager smile on your face.

La Bastide's menu is short, with added seasonal specials and wines offered by the waiter at the outset of the meal. Chef Alexandre Loiseau's cuisine is flavourful as opposed to fancy—more earthy than ethereal.

Starters are light and bright. A cold tomato soup sprinkled with chives has a clear fruity flavour and a smooth texture, every slurp enlivening the taste buds. Paper-thin shaved fennel dressed with truffle oil offers a simple yet complex flavour sensation. Add a few moist-and-meaty chunks of grilled tuna and you've got one superb appetizer. Grilled vegetable terrine is another stunner. With its layers of zucchini, mushrooms, eggplant, and the most flavourful red peppers imaginable, this colourful square, enhanced with a dribble of balsamic vinegar, puts all those tired grilled vegetable platters to shame.

The "assiette de cochonnailles," served in a deep Moroccan bowl, is a medley of cold meats, including rosette de Lyon and

Morteau sausages, Bayonne ham, thinly sliced smoked lard, and chorizo. Each bite is garlicky, spicy, and salty—delicious sandwiched between thick slices of pain de campagne.

The half-smoked, half-seared salmon is sublime. The pink flesh comes apart in silky, perfectly undercooked morsels. The flavour is rich, pleasantly smoky, and almost sweet. The texture is melting. To accompany the delicate fish, Loiseau adds a cool cucumber sauce enhanced with that most elegant (and underexploited) of herbs: sorrel.

Main courses turn up hearty fare, the kind of food big boys enjoy—like pork chops, beef stew, sausage, and bavettes. Ideally cooked magret de canard (we're talking crisp skin, pink flesh, and little fat) is served with an original accompaniment—red rice. Daube de boeuf (beef stew) is perfection: the braised meat is tender, the sauce is thick and flavourful, and the turned vegetables are al dente.

Unfortunately, all is not rosy. Save for the occasional charred morsel, the tapas-style grilled calamari is practically tasteless. A thick pork chop served with corn cakes is also dreary, underseasoned, and slightly overcooked—much less interesting than a home-grilled supermarket chop. The halibut cheeks are stringy and bland. It's amazing that this dud originated from the same kitchen that produced the accompanying lentils, which are creamy and delicious.

In the tradition of classic French dining, the cheese course is the indispensable third act. La Bastide offers a small choice of Quebec cheeses paired with a delightful raisin chutney and assorted breads—ideal for polishing off a bottle of wine or glass of port before delving into the sweet finale.

But don't get your hopes up. Desserts fall short of expectations. A frothy cream enhanced with orange flower water is sour, no better than plain yogourt. A chocolate pot de crème filled with mushy bits of plum is in desperate need of some kind of garnish. And a frozen vanilla parfait with griottines (Kirsch-soaked cherries) is okay, but its coffee sauce is a bad idea. The best way to end the meal here is with the excellent espresso.

Despite the uneven food and slow service, this restaurant has charm to spare. At the end of the meal, Mr. Vesperini has been known to regale customers with descriptions of the restaurant's transformation from a Portuguese social club, reeling off details like the number of nails he used in the Gyprock walls he installed and outlining his ambitious plans for the future.

IN THE KITCHEN • Chef Alexandre Loiseau.

DECOR, DRESS, AMBIENCE • The restaurant's sparsely elegant decor features a welcoming bar, white walls, high ceilings, chic beige chairs, swooping drapes, and large framed mirrors. The terrace is equally arresting: more billowing drapes, cotton table-cloths, gleaming silver and stemware—a regular oasis on a lack-lustre stretch of Mile End. The ambience is laid-back; dress is casual-elegant, and Pierre Vesperini and his staff couldn't be more welcoming.

WINE LIST • The wine list is short, fairly priced, and interesting. One hopes the selection will steadily increase, and that they'll stop serving the red wine straight from the refrigerator.

DON'T MISS • The half-smoked, half-seared salmon, the "assi-ette de cochonnailles," and the daube de boeuf, which is satisfying in both hot and cold weather.

WORDS TO THE WISE • La Bastide is a new restaurant, and there are still a few cracks in the plaster. Waits between courses on busy nights are lengthy, and snaring a last-minute reservation can be difficult—especially on weekends. There's no restaurant this side of the Atlantic that can maintain the expectations created for La Bastide. Nonetheless, the balance sheet is encouraging, and the management seems to know that while food trends wax and wane, enthusiasm and hospitality will win out in the end.

LA BASTIDE
151 Avenue Bernard West (near Waverly)
Telephone: (514) 271-4934
Open: 5 P.M.-midnight, Tuesday to Sunday
Wheelchair access: No
Reservations: Recommended
Cards: Major cards
Price range: Starters, $8-$10; main courses, $22-$25;
desserts, $6-$9; three-course table d'hôte menu, $20

★★★	$ $ $	REVIEWED 10/01

LA CANTINA

SNAPSHOT • Situated just north of Boulevard Métropolitain, La Cantina is a well-kept secret from those of us who spend most of our time in Montreal's downtown core. The tables are filled and the place is buzzing almost every night. The unpretentious menu includes Italian Canadian favourites such as antipasto, stracciatella, Caesar salad, fettuccini Gigi, as well as veal scaloppini and grilled meats. Not only is the food first-class and the wine list well chosen, but also the service displays the utmost courteousness and professionalism.

THE BIG PICTURE • Shopping at Jean Talon Market in the heart of Montreal's Little Italy, I always end my rounds at my favourite Italian butcher and grocery store, Capitol. If I'm lucky, I run into owner Tony Ledonne, who is always ready to show me the newest products, talk to me about olive oils and pastas, or offer me a sliver of fresh Parmesan or a spoonful of aged balsamic vinegar.

Not long ago, our usual product-based discussion turned to the local Italian restaurant scene. We generally agreed on the establishments we favour, but when he mentioned La Cantina, I drew a blank. His eyebrows rose over his glasses in disbelief, and he suggested that I try it out. Since Tony is the man who introduced me to the caviar of risotto rice, Carnaroli, as well as "mosto d'uva" sauce and the glories of imported Ricotta, if he says go, I'm there.

My first visit was on a Friday night. After a warm greeting at the door from co-owner Dominico Fazioli, I moved through the front room, past the kitchen, to a second dining room, where I spotted two portly men tucking into heaping plates of spaghetti, a magnificent prosciutto di Parma ready for slicing, and an enormous coffee machine pumping out espressos full throttle. As they say in Italian, the scene was "molto sympatico!"

La Cantina's table d'hôte features simple dishes like baked portobello mushrooms, arugula and Parmesan salad, tortellini with salmon, and fegato al balsamico (calf's liver with balsamic vinegar). Most of the dishes are good; some are magnificent.

The antipasto plate is exemplary. It includes fried calamari, which are crisp on the outside and tender within, ripe tomatoes with Mozzarella, fragrant and salty prosciutto di Parma, grilled and skinned red peppers, and marinated strips of eggplant that have no trace of stringiness or bitterness.

The marinated and grilled octopus is also superb. Its texture is tender and meaty, and its flavour is fresh and smoky. A salad consisting of arugula, bresaola (air-dried beef filet), and slices of Parmigiano-Reggiano is dressed with a vibrant, lemony vinaigrette. Also delicious are the mussels, which arrive steaming hot and laden with sautéed garlic and a chunky marinara sauce.

Main courses include pastas, veal dishes, and a pancetta and trevise risotto. The linguini with clam sauce is chock-full of clams and features a balanced red sauce and al dente pasta. Nice. The ravioli alla Caprese consists of tender pasta pillows filled with cheese, more of the wonderful house tomato sauce, and a few slices of melted Mozzarella. To complement this main course, consider ordering the homemade meatballs, which are perfectly seasoned and light in texture; they provide a bit of backbone to the ravioli.

The veal stew features toothsome meat coated in a tomato-based sauce that's zesty and well seasoned. It's served with crisp fried potatoes and undressed steamed spinach. La Cantina's veal chop arrives glistening, and each pink-tinged morsel turns out to be juicy, full flavoured, and melt-in-the-mouth tender.

The risotto is good, not great. Although cooked to perfection

—every creamy bite is filled with dozens of grains of melting rice—the stock used is weak, the bits of pancetta and trevise are few and far between, and the buttery flavour can be overbearing.

Desserts at La Cantina are simple and satisfying—as Italian desserts should be. Not to be missed is the crème caramel, which is silky smooth and offers a pleasant contrast between assertive caramel sauce and gentle vanilla flan. The tiramisu is also praiseworthy, even if less creamy than the best. The chocolate-hazelnut semifreddo is rich and creamy, though not cloyingly so. Fullbodied and strong, without a hint of bitterness, the espresso is the ideal accompaniment to these wondrous creams.

IN THE KITCHEN · Chefs Marco Bitetti, Donato Ruberto, Maltese Diego, and Igniazio Logiudice.

DECOR, DRESS, AMBIENCE · The decor of the long, rectangular dining room is quaint and traditional. Hung from the beamed ceilings are steak-house chandeliers. The chairs are covered in flowered tapestry fabric, and oil paintings—large and small (along with photos of visiting celebrities, including a nice one of Charles Aznavour)—line the walls. Although the room is often crowded, noise levels are tolerable, and the ambience maintains a romantic feel, with small oil lamps adding a warm glow to every table.

WINE LIST · The wine list is short, but over half of the wines available are private imports and therefore not listed. The selections are primarily reds, 70% Italian and 30% Californian, and prices range from $24 to $1,000. Ask your waiter for suggestions.

DON'T MISS · The antipasto, the grilled octopus, the pastas (with homemade meatballs), the veal chop, and the semifreddo.

WORDS TO THE WISE · True, you won't find the fanciest tableware or elaborate plate presentations here. But La Cantina does offer top-of-the-line ingredients and just about everything else one expects of a fine Italian restaurant, including an ambience that will make you feel very much a part of Montreal's big and boisterous Italian family.

LA CANTINA
9090 Boulevard St. Laurent (near Legendre)
Telephone: (514) 382-3618
Open: Lunch, 11:30 A.M.-3 P.M., Monday to Friday;
dinner, 5 P.M.-11 P.M., Monday to Friday, and 5 P.M.-10 P.M.,
Saturday and Sunday
Wheelchair access: Yes
Reservations: Essential
Cards: Major cards
Price range: Starters, $4.50-$13.95; main courses, $8.75-$36;
desserts, $3.50-$8.50

★★★1/2	$ $ $	REVIEWED 06/00

LA CHRONIQUE

SNAPSHOT • Over the past five years, this 40-seat establishment, located on a quiet stretch of fashionable Avenue Laurier, between du Parc and St. Urbain, has emerged from obscurity to become one of Montreal's top restaurants. How? It might have something to do with the combination of chef Marc de Canck's imaginative market cuisine, the unpretentious setting, the friendly, professional service, and an extensive, affordable wine list with numerous selections available by the glass. Take note: the menu on Fridays and Saturdays is a four-course, $55 prix fixe.

THE BIG PICTURE • There's a fruit and vegetable store on the south side of Jean Talon Market called Chez Louis, where many of the city's top chefs shop for such choice ingredients as cipollini onions, Ratte potatoes, white asparagus, out-of-season berries, and more. On the counter, between the bottles of truffle oil and aged balsamic vinegar, there's one cookbook for sale: *La Chronique: Livre de cuisine aux saveurs d'ici et d'ailleurs* by Montreal chef Marc de Canck. "He's one of our favourite customers," says the owner, Charles Gingras. "He only buys the best."

The setting of de Canck's restaurant, La Chronique, is so dis-armingly low-key that first-time visitors might not know they're in for the best. Prices offer no clues, either, for they are lower than those of many of the city's high-end places.

In its early days, La Chronique was often described as "a poor man's Toqué!" This no longer holds true, as de Canck has devel-oped a style all his own. Built on his Belgian background and heavily influenced by his 17 years on the North American scene, his cooking puts a modern, experimental twist on market cuisine, resulting in some of the most inspired and exciting dishes around.

Chef de Canck's cuisine shines brightest with fish and seafood starters. One of the most memorable is the refreshing combina-tion of lobster (claw and medallion) with a lime, hazelnut, and vanilla vinaigrette, accompanied by a row of al dente, mouse-tail-thin asparagus tips. Another pairs a tartare of potent green-tea-smoked scallops with hot, medium-rare seared scallops—an exemplary modern dish that successfully displays the contrasting flavours, textures, and temperatures that can be drawn from a single luxury ingredient.

An equally opulent staple treated in the hot and cold manner is the sashimi salmon. The raw fish is rubbed with coarsely ground pepper, coriander, and mustard seed as well as an exhila-rating dose of sea salt. It's then seared, spice-side down, to form a blackened, cooked layer on one side and a tender, raw one on the other (à l'unilatéral). Wow! It's no surprise that this is one of the most popular dishes on the menu.

Served with a lacy potato-crab cake and a tomato-chili jam, the crisp, seared foie gras with a trembling, pudding-like centre is superb. Believe it or not, the seared striped bass is even better. Assembled, architectural style, atop a dried tomato, black olive, and almond pesto, with a miniature charred duck brochette propped on the side, the fish is moist and delicate, the skin crisp and salty. The accompanying pesto provides a Mediterranean accent with strong flavours that blend together while remaining distinct—incredible.

Chef de Canck's cooking, like that of so many other modern chefs, better lends itself to the smaller starter format with fewer ideas on the plate than to the generous, full-blown flavour fest of the main course. You might want to stick with this kitchen's strength: fish. It's not that the meat selections aren't very good. It's that two of them—the blackened duck magret with shrimp, and veal liver with gnocchi and asparagus—offer thick cuts that, though flavourful and cooked rosé, are surprisingly tough. This is especially true of the duck. Far more successful are the veal sweetbreads matched with chorizo. The two flavours—elegant and buttery, robust and spicy—though worlds apart, complement each other exceedingly well. A further twist is provided by an intense veal jus enhanced with the sweetness of red pepper.

One of the house's best dishes is the delicately flavoured and textured panfried mahimahi, which is set on a pool of aromatic oils: curry, paprika, and, of all things, chlorophyll. Equally delicious is the grilled red tuna with homemade agnolotti pasta pockets filled with scallops and surrounded by a sauté of shiitake mushrooms, onions, and zucchini.

There are a few disappointments. The lobster can be a tad chewy. And I'm told that the marinated and lightly smoked Ouananich salmon is a delicate hit-or-miss affair. Sometimes it's melt-in-your-mouth tender, other times it's flaky and oversalted.

But these are quibbles. It's more productive to point out how much the desserts have improved of late. Memories of caramel swirls and too many tuiles of days past fade with each bite of a gently flavoured maple parfait glacé set on a crisp hazelnut butter cookie and served with berries and pink peppercorns. Another favourite is the pecan tartlet spiked with Jack Daniel's whisky and topped with luscious homemade walnut ice cream. Chocolate lovers will savour the fudgy "moelleux" cake served with a scoop of the best pineapple sorbet ever. And don't pass up the trio of crème brûlées: chocolate, coffee, and lemongrass-star-anise.

La Chronique's crowded room is manned by young waiters who appear to do everything right, with a large dose of personality and unaffectedness.

IN THE KITCHEN • Chef and owner Marc de Canck.

DECOR, DRESS, AMBIENCE • The setting is that of a fancy bistro: pale-yellow walls, a large grouping of black-and-white photographs (many of them taken by chef de Canck himself), elegant banquettes, sleek wooden chairs, and a small corner bar. Centred on one of the walls is a large clock whose time is fixed at 4:50 P.M. — the idea being to capture the moment of serenity before the night's dinner service begins.

WINE LIST • La Chronique has an exceptional wine list; its 280 selections provide fine drinking at every level. The bottles are well chosen and affordable, with many priced under $40. There are also ten fine red and white selections available by the glass.

DON'T MISS • The smoked and seared salmon, the hot foie gras, the panfried mahimahi, the grilled tuna, the veal sweetbreads, and the trio of crème brûlées.

WORDS TO THE WISE • There are certainly flashier, more ambitious restaurants in town, but most diners will be elated with Marc de Canck's fresh take on market cuisine. There's plenty to discover here — and many bites to be relished.

LA CHRONIQUE
99 Avenue Laurier West (near St. Urbain)
Telephone: (514) 271- 3095
Open: Lunch, 11:30 A.M.-2:30 P.M., Tuesday to Friday;
dinner, 6 P.M.-10:30 P.M., Tuesday to Friday, and 6 P.M.-10:30 P.M., Saturday
Wheelchair access: Yes
Reservations: Recommended; nonsmoking environment
Cards: All major cards
Price range: Starters, $11-$14; main courses, $22-$30; desserts, $8; lunch menu, $16-$24; Friday and Saturday four-course table d'hôte menu, $55

| ★★1/2 | $ $ | REVIEWED 02/00 |

LA COLOMBE

SNAPSHOT · Now celebrating its twelfth anniversary and reaching new heights every year, this bring-your-own-wine restaurant offers serious gourmet food at more-than-reasonable prices. The award-winning decor perfectly captures the sophisticated funkiness of the surrounding neighbourhood—the Plateau Mont Royal. This is one of Avenue Duluth's most popular restaurants, so be sure to make reservations several days in advance, and be prepared to search for one of the area's few parking spots (especially in winter).

THE BIG PICTURE · La Colombe is located in the Plateau Mont Royal, on the corner of Duluth and St. Hubert—BYOW central. Fine dining amid the pasta palaces and brochetteries on Duluth? Yes. Fresh fish, duck, game, and raw-milk cheeses are on the menu at La Colombe, and the desserts are made with that ne-plus-ultra chocolate, Valrhona. The style here is cuisine du marché, and everything—from stocks to desserts—is not only made from scratch but also presented with flair. Ask around. You'll hear nothing but raves about two points: the high quality and the low prices.

The clean, contemporary cuisine suits the simple yet stylish room to a T. Take, for instance, the smoked salmon. Instead of the standard diagonally cut, paper-thin slices with lemon, capers, and sliced onion, chef Moustafa Rougaibi slices the filets straight, a tad thicker, and wraps them in a circle around a julienned carrot and bean sprout salad dressed with Szechwan vinaigrette. The deep-orange strips of salmon are lush and smoky, and the sesame oil, soy sauce, and rice wine vinaigrette, studded with black sesame seeds, gives an exotic boost to every bite.

The cream of cauliflower soup has a gentle flavour that cauliflower haters would enjoy but aficionados might find a bit too subtle. A cold-weather favourite is the hot salmon and Arctic char mousse, which is finely textured and strongly flavoured. The accompanying beurre blanc is rich and velvety—the real McCoy—

with a hint of sweetness provided by a shot of maple vinegar.

The deer and apple salad is made with braised tongue. It's served cold, julienned, and paired with apple matchsticks and assorted baby lettuces. Unfortunately, like most tongue, the meat is bland and could use a stronger, more acidic dressing than the one provided.

Lamb lovers are sure to enjoy the restaurant's braised lamb shank. The meat is rich, tender, evenly braised, and sauced with an intensely flavoured garlic, rosemary, and reduced lamb jus. This hearty dish, served with Puy lentils and carrots, is far superior to many in town. Also on a par with the city's best is the grilled veal chop. The thick, juicy chop is presented on a deep square plate atop a mound of grilled peppers and surrounded by sautéed hedgehog mushrooms. Its herb-laden sauce includes tarragon, thyme, rosemary, parsley, and, interestingly enough, wild ginger. Expect to pay five dollars more for the chop, but considering the size of portion, the quality of the meat, and the fresh wild mushrooms, it's worth it.

The main-course repertoire often includes meaty duck magrets (breast) and tender confits (leg) served with delicious fruit sauces, such as cherry. There's always fresh fish available, and one of the best is a generous portion of Arctic char, perfectly prepared, moist, and delicate.

Those willing to splurge may also enjoy the selection of raw-milk cheeses from one of Montreal's top cheesemongers, Pierre-Yves Chaput—generous servings of St. Nectaire, Pierre Robert Triple Crème, Fourme D'Ambert, and Briquette Livradoise.

Chocolate desserts are a passion of the chef's. One of his best is a hazelnut dacquoise cake spread with marmalade and topped with a seriously rich, creamy mousse made with Valrhona chocolate. Every bite provides the perfect match of bitter and sweet enhanced with a splash of raspberry coulis. Even the simple custard-filled crêpes are served with a milk chocolate sauce made with the best couverture-quality chocolate.

Service at La Colombe is friendly, courteous, and prompt. Just don't expect the waiters to pour the wine: you brought it, you pour it.

IN THE KITCHEN • Chef Moustafa Rougaibi.

DECOR, DRESS, AMBIENCE • The long narrow room of this unpretentious neighbourhood eatery features a small open kitchen, raw-wood siding, wine-bottle spotlights, and rubber-tire rugs. Renovated two years ago using mainly recycled materials, this funky little restaurant was awarded the Jury Prize at the 1999 Design Montreal competition. For a place that's small and usually packed with a loose-lipped BYOW crowd, the noise levels are surprisingly low.

WINE LIST • None. At La Colombe, you bring your own. Take note: only wine is allowed on the premises, so leave the beer and spirits at home.

DON'T MISS • The lamb shank, the Arctic char, the cheese course, and the Valrhona chocolate desserts.

WORDS TO THE WISE • You might want to leave your car at home, especially on weekends, as parking anywhere in this area is a nightmare. Reservations can also be problematic. La Colombe already has a strong local customer base that latches onto tables like piranhas. With only 40 seats available, your best bet is to make a reservation (for no more than six people) several days in advance.

LA COLOMBE
554 Avenue Duluth East (near Berri)
Telephone: (514) 849-8844
Open: 5 P.M.-10 P.M., Tuesday and Sunday, and 5 P.M.-11 P.M., Wednesday to Saturday (6 P.M. and 9 P.M. sittings on Thursday, Friday, and Saturday)
Wheelchair access: Yes
Reservations: Essential; no reservations for groups of more than six; nonsmoking environment
Cards: All major cards
Price range: Daily prix fixe menu, $30 (plus a few à la carte extras)

★★1/2	$ $	REVIEWED 09/00

LA GAUDRIOLE

SNAPSHOT · This neighbourhood bistro is the ideal spot for budget-concious gourmets. Here, the excitement is on the plate. The ingredients are exotic, the plate presentations are decorative, and some of the flavour combinations are downright adventurous. When was the last time you were served wild rice with cinnamon? The setting is unpretentious, and the service is casual. Two added bonuses: an affordable wine list and a lunchtime table d'hôte.

THE BIG PICTURE · La Gaudriole draws neither the crowd-loving trendies nor the decor-needy fashion plates. This neigh-bourhood bistro is *the* place for gourmets with an eye on the bottom line. Its location — between the chic boutiques and restaurants of Laurier West, and the specialty food stores and branché restaurants of Laurier East — could not be more appro-priate. Why? Because La Gaudriole offers the best of both worlds: the stylishness of the West and the lack of pretension of the East.

The menu offers the popular abridged table d'hôte format, with a choice of starters included in the main-course price. Top-ping an intriguing list of starters is a cream of vegetable soup with sorrel, which is ideally seasoned and full-bodied. Another offers three paper-thin croutons topped with generous mounds of tangy creamed goat's cheese and sun-dried tomatoes. Instead of the predictable mesclun mix, the dish is served with a lightly dressed salad of potent baby mustard greens and gentle pea shoots.

For a mere nine-dollar supplement, La Gaudriole offers a hot foie gras starter with roasted apple and cherry wine. The thick slices of pan-seared duck foie gras are placed atop a round of roasted apple topped with macerated cherries and set on a pool of reduced cherry-wine sauce. It's a generous portion that could eas-ily set one back $25 elsewhere. Yet there are three elements lacking for this dish to meet its full potential: a crisp crust to contrast with the soft interior, a hint of sweetness or acidity to offset the dish's richness, and more salt to enliven the taste.

After reaching for the salt mill time and time again, you might come to the conclusion that this kitchen may be a little tentative in the seasoning department. An example of this would be the wild game and port pâté. The two triangles of terrine, served with smoked duck breast and candied ground cherries, are so bland that there's no discernible taste of game, let alone wild game. Even the duck lacks any smoked flavour.

Fortunately, flavours come alive again with the main courses. Tilapia is a firm-fleshed white fish rarely seen on Montreal restaurant menus, as its delicate flavour presents a challenge to most chefs. The solution at La Gaudriole is to boost its flavour with a celery, bell pepper, and orange-zest salsa, further enhanced with a mango-mustard sauce. In this combination, the tilapia provides the base texture, while the salsa gets the party going, so to speak.

Grilled marlin is perfectly cooked — crusted on the outside and translucent on the inside. On this plate, the sauce, a black bean and citrus coulis, seems superfluous. Puréed black beans have a thick consistency and an earthy taste that adds little to the fish. A squirt of lemon may have sufficed.

Two meat dishes turn up toothsome cuts and full flavours. The medallions of deer are served with a black chanterelle essence (sauce), grilled fennel, and duchesse potatoes. The chanterelle essence has the look and consistency of chocolate sauce and a taste so rich that you'd swear there's chocolate in there somewhere.

Considering the exorbitant cost of lamb tenderloin, La Gaudriole's offering of six small filets nestled between thin strips of vegetables, steamed potatoes, and refried flageolet beans is a steal. The surrounding sauce is a light infusion of purple basil flowers. But here the side dishes disappoint. The fried flageolets, though interesting in concept, are dry and heavy, and the steamed potatoes, another starch, are undercooked and underseasoned.

The cheese course is another bargain. Among the Quebec and French cheeses, don't miss the aged Perron Cheddar, the Victor et Berthold, and the St. Maure goat's cheese.

Desserts are given their due at La Gaudriole; presentations are glamorous and flavour combinations intriguing. The best is the "caprice de Patrice." This showstopper consists of a delicious chocolate mousse filled with a smooth ginger cream. The mousse is set atop a round of spicy carrot cake that's surrounded on three sides by twisted carrot chips, making for one of the best restaurant desserts around.

IN THE KITCHEN • Chef and owner Marc Vézina.

DECOR, DRESS, AMBIENCE • The decor is simple, with a long mirror down one side, grey-and-burgundy walls, and about 15 tables surrounded by modern wicker chairs and covered with white-and-baby-blue tablecloths. The atmosphere is subdued, the antithesis of a trendy Plateau bistro.

WINE LIST • Wine prices are reasonable. Unlike many restaurants which double or triple the wine's retail price, La Gaudriole marks up its offerings only one and a half times. I know of no other Montreal establishment where patrons can order Chablis for $26, Sancerre for $36, or a first-rate wine such as a Cahors Château Lagrezette for only $33.

DON'T MISS • The soups, the grilled marlin, the lamb tenderloin, the deer, the cheese course, and the "caprice de Patrice" for dessert.

WORDS TO THE WISE • Despite some ups and downs with the food, a meal at La Gaudriole is pleasurable. I wouldn't hesitate to recommend this neighbourhood restaurant to young gourmets eager to sample artfully arranged, luxurious ingredients in an unpretentious setting. Service is so friendly that you get the feeling you're eating dinner at a friend's house.

LA GAUDRIOLE
825 Avenue Laurier East (near St. Hubert)
Telephone: (514) 276-1580
Open: Lunch, 11:30 A.M.-2 P.M., Tuesday to Friday;
dinner, 5:30 P.M.-10 P.M., daily
Wheelchair access: Yes
Reservations: Recommended
Cards: All major cards
Price range: Main courses (with starters included), $18-$29;
desserts, $4-$12

★★1/2	$ $ $	REVIEWED 07/00

LALOUX

SNAPSHOT · For just over a decade now, this "bistro de luxe" has been the haunt of the smart set: literati, politicos, and the odd Québécois vedette. It's also been the ideal setting for the nouvelle cuisine of chef André Besson. Laloux's customers come not only for the terrific soups, sauces, fish, and seafood, but also for the impressive variety of affordable wines. Despite the good food and chic setting, service can sometimes be a bit distant.

THE BIG PICTURE · Say the word "Laloux" to any restaurant-going Montrealer, and you're bound to get a smile. Not the ready grin of a flirtatious schoolgirl, but a warm smile—the kind that appears when one recalls an old flame. The word itself is luxurious, for it sounds more like a French cheese or a meringue confection than the name of the restaurant's original chef, Philippe Laloux.

Back in the restaurant's heyday, discoveries were always to be made here: hot foie gras, sweetbreads, and raw-milk cheeses. Laloux's in-house sommeliers introduced many to the glories of wines like Chorey-les-Beaune and Pouilly-Fumé. Service was always the ideal combination of friendly, discreet, and professional. One couldn't have asked for more. Although these days the restaurant still appears crowded every night, some complain that the menu hasn't budged over the years. Others say the food is uneven. Sadly, there are even complaints that the service is no longer up to snuff.

Diners are still treated to the traditional ramekin of pâté de foie, which is as smooth and delicious as ever. Indeed, the menu hasn't changed much. The cuisine is still as elegant and understated as the decor — nouvelle French, with an emphasis on seafood. Many of chef André Besson's signature dishes remain: tourte de gibier, red snapper supremes, seared scallops, crab ravioli, and assorted bisques.

Soups are one of this kitchen's strengths. Both a full flavoured and piping hot lobster bisque, and a perfectly salted cream of mussel soup, garnished with plump, tender mussels and a julienne of carrot and leek, are sensational. Equally successful is the salmon and scallop ceviche served with a dill, avocado, and tomato salsa.

Other standouts include sweet and sour ginger dim sum, which offers wonton-wrapped dumplings filled with crab, pork, veal, carrot, and ginger. The creamy sauce is the ideal accompaniment — the French alternative to the traditional Asian pairing of soy.

Sauces at Laloux are consistently excellent; they are certainly one of Besson's fortes. They're so good, in fact, that they occasionally outshine the dishes themselves. Take, for example, the tourte de gibier. The pie's two poivrade sauces — one made with chicken stock and cream, the other with a veal demi-glace — are lush and flavourful, adding richness to the gamy and spicy taste of the dry wild-meat filling while obscuring a crust that is more soggy than flaky. You'd think the chunky pie's only role was to soak up those wicked sauces.

Equally successful are the lighter jus sauces. A main course of calf's liver needs no more enhancement than its own pan juices deglazed with a splash of raspberry vinegar. The meat's texture is velvety, and the raspberry adds a fruity zing. Who'd have suspected liver could be such a treat?

Besson's menu favours fish and seafood. Seared scallops served on a mound of zucchini and tomato cubes are tinged with just a hint of coconut. It's a lovely dish, perfectly prepared, especially the pan-seared scallops, which are buttery and meltingly tender. The red snapper is also outstanding. Expertly cooked and topped with a sauce tinged with sherry, this simple dish, served with a thin tomato tart, holds its own next to many flashier concoctions.

Only a few dishes disappoint. The grilled lamb tenderloin with mango chutney and licorice sauce scores low on flavour and seasoning. The other clinker is a dessert listed as "surprise de fraises au citron." This pairing of lemon mousseline cream and sliced strawberries is "surprisingly" awful. The lemon cream is overly rich and tastes as though it was made with bottled lemon juice.

The other desserts, all made in-house, turn in a better performance. The bistro favourite, oeuf à la neige, is light, sweet, and reassuringly gooey. "Le Grand Dessert" offers a large sampling of Besson's best: vanilla and caramel ice cream, pistachio and cherry iced parfait, gianduja mousse, and a gâteau Mont Royal filled with raspberry ganache.

That the food at Laloux is still good is no surprise. That the service has fallen from friendly and top-notch to confused and perfunctory is a bit of a mystery. There is often no maître d' on hand to orchestrate the goings-on, waits between courses are far too long, and the sommelier is aloof enough to make you consider drinking water with your meal. Sullen expressions are everywhere. Faced with the indifference of the staff, you might end up pouring your own wine. Try not to take it personally.

IN THE KITCHEN • Chef André Besson.

DECOR, DRESS, AMBIENCE • This is one of Montreal's most beautiful dining rooms: yellow walls hung with large, dark-green-framed mirrors, black bistro chairs, crisp white-linen-covered tables, and jazzy background music. The overall effect is chic yet soothing.

WINE LIST • Complementing the food is a wine list offering an incredible choice of fairly priced, interesting bottles, many privately imported.

DON'T MISS · The hot foie gras, the fish and seafood, the calf's liver, and the "Grand Dessert."

WORDS TO THE WISE · Laloux retains a perfume of French sophistication. The quality of the food has not waned, and the setting is as chic as it gets. The tourist literature offered at the door describes Laloux as a bit of "Paris on Pine." Perhaps the staff takes this catchphrase, and themselves, a bit too seriously.

LALOUX
250 Avenue des Pins East (near Laval)
Telephone: (514) 287-9127
Open: Lunch, noon-3 P.M., Monday to Friday;
dinner, 5:30 P.M.-10:30 P.M., Sunday to Wednesday, and
5:30 P.M.-11:30 P.M., Thursday to Saturday
Wheelchair access: Yes
Reservations: Essential
Cards: Major cards
Price range: Starters, $3.95-$35 (caviar); main courses, $14.75-$35; desserts, $5-$12.75

★★	$ $ $	REVIEWED 04/01

LA MAÎTRESSE

SNAPSHOT · In a city where hotel dining rooms usually have little to offer, La Maîtresse stands out for its Mediterranean-style cuisine with a strong emphasis on fish and seafood. If you're on the tony stretch of Rue Sherbrooke at lunchtime, consider popping by for a bowl of soup and one of chef José Rodriguez's creative salads. The decor is jazzy and modern, and the well-chosen wine list is priced to sell. The overly enthusiastic service can sometimes be shaky.

THE BIG PICTURE · I arrived at La Maîtresse on a sleepy Wednesday night, pulled on the door handle, and, to my surprise, found it wouldn't budge. I tried the second entrance through the lobby of the adjacent Hôtel Versailles, and there I came upon a smiling waiter. Yes, the restaurant is open for dinner, he assured me, it's just that the front door sticks from time to time. Hmm, not the most auspicious start to the evening.

He and his cohorts then sprang into action. With the enthusiasm of Boy Scouts looking to score a few badges, the troop of good-looking young waiters swarmed, offering to take my coat, escort me to a table, and serve me a drink (I was tempted to ask for a foot massage). Before anything significant happened, the ever-smiling maître d' arrived to inquire whether everything was all right. I was charmed but also disconcerted; this hovering pack of charmers was trying too hard.

Fortunately, the kitchen shows a higher level of professionalism. Chef José Rodriguez's cuisine du marché follows the wave of Mediterranean cooking that favours fish, greens, olive oils, and emulsions. Like many of today's best chefs, Rodriguez has a delicate, almost feminine hand; his plate presentations are simple and assembled with style.

As is often seen in this school of cuisine, starters prove the most successful. The salads are out of this world. A Mediterranean salad consisting of a potent combination of greens— Niçoise lettuce, celery leaves, dill, flat-leaf parsley, and endive—is dressed with a piquant lime vinaigrette. Add to this tender warm scallops, moist mussels, lobster bits, squid, and sliced Kalamata olives, and you're looking at one of the best seafood salads around.

Smoked-salmon lovers should try the smoked salmon with ribbons of cucumber, red onion, sour cream, and chives. The fish, smoked in-house, has a delicate smoky flavour and a lovely silky texture. A mound of cucumber ribbons provides a fresh note— the ideal cleansing bite between melting morsels of salmon.

Also delicious is the fennel, parsley, and Parmesan salad— everything sliced a millimeter thin. The flavours are alive, enhanced only with lemon and extra-virgin olive oil. The fourth salad, made with apple matchsticks, cranberries, and watercress, is served with a phyllo beggar's purse filled with herbed goat's cheese. The salad mixture is the high point here, for the cheese selected is ho-hum—too bland for most chèvre lovers' taste buds.

If you're craving soup as opposed to salad, try the velouté of green pea with croutons and crispy lardons. The perfectly seasoned, bright-green potage provides a welcome taste of spring, enhanced so perfectly by the earthy fried lardons and garlic croutons.

Main courses are, for the most part, successful. You won't go wrong with the marinated grilled shrimp with Basmati rice, brunoise of vegetables, and curry emulsion. The shrimp are firm, gently spiced, and well matched with the light, coconut-tinged, Thai-style curry. Continuing on the salad theme, there's a melt-in-the-mouth tender grilled turkey paillard served on a bed of arugula and watercress, dressed with a lemon-thyme vinaigrette. Though it sounds like diet food, every bite is an indulgence.

Equally spa-worthy were the pan-seared scallops with sautéed leek enhanced with a ginger-citrus essence. My complaint here concerns the scallops: their texture is on the stringy side and the flavour is a bit dull. With such faint flavours in play, this dish loses its excitement after the first few bites.

Meat lovers will enjoy the pan-seared filet mignon with Cabernet Sauvignon sauce, sweet dauphinoise potatoes, grilled scallions, and grilled asparagus. It's a heavy dish after the light starters, but the beef is delicious and perfectly cooked to the ideal medium-rare. The vegetable accompaniments are interesting, though I wonder how many patrons enjoy (or can stomach) grilled scallions. Flank steak with a shallot sauce mysteriously arrives sans sauce. This usually tough cut of steak is tender, and the homemade skin-on fries are addictive.

After sampling most of La Maîtresse's desserts, I have no doubt that this kitchen's talents lie in the savoury, not the sweet. A cold tarte Tatin topped with vanilla ice cream is marred by a soggy, undercooked crust. The chocolat La Maîtresse appears to be no more than a thick round of cloying ganache with raspberry-passion-fruit coulis.

Service here can be a problem. Shaky hands and butter fingers abound. The last time I dined here, our waiter brought an incorrect appetizer, cleared wine glasses before they were empty, served water to only two of the three of us, and lingered around our table like a lost puppy.

IN THE KITCHEN • Chef José Rodriguez.

DECOR, DRESS, AMBIENCE • Aubergine-and-cream-coloured walls frame the long dining room, and a line of recessed ceiling fans turn slowly in time to the rhythm of the jazzy background tunes. Obviously designed — by acclaimed Montreal designer Michael Joannidis — with the after-hours crowd in mind, much of the space has been dedicated to an elongated, luminescent, glass-topped bar and a small lounge near the front door. Off to the right, a grand piano sits on a raised platform. In keeping with the nouveau cool surroundings, the ambience is subdued, almost sleepy.

WINE LIST • La Maîtresse's wine list is another of its strong points. The selection is well thought out and priced to sell. A bottle of Sancerre will cost you a mere $42 — a rarity in any downtown restaurant, and unheard of in a hotel restaurant.

DON'T MISS • The pea soup, the salads, the filet mignon, the grilled shrimp, and the flank steak.

WORDS TO THE WISE • La Maîtresse is a restaurant that shows promise. But with a cramped dining room and less than stellar service, the only wow factor at present comes courtesy of the kitchen.

LA MAÎTRESSE
1800 Rue Sherbrooke West (near St. Mathieu in the Hôtel Versailles)
Telephone: (514) 939-1212
Open: 7 A.M.-midnight, daily
Wheelchair access: Yes
Reservations: Recommended
Cards: Major cards
Price range: Starters, $4.95-$12.50; main courses, $8.75-$24; desserts, $3.95-$9

| ★★★ | $ $ $ | REVIEWED 11/99 |

LA RAPIÈRE

SNAPSHOT · With traditional dishes from the southwestern French province of Gascogne, a dining room that could be described as the epitome of understated elegance, and formal, friendly service, La Rapière remains, after close to 30 years in business, one of Montreal's best French restaurants, an "haute temple de gastronomie." This is the place for subdued celebratory meals and romantic anniversary dinners, as well as for entertaining out-of-town guests eager to experience the glories of a civilized meal.

THE BIG PICTURE · The past decade has been rough for classical French cuisine. There are many misconceptions about French restaurants that may have turned customers, especially younger ones, away. First, the idea that French restaurants are expensive. True — a meal laced with foie gras, tournedos, and various forms of duck can be costly. Yet many of the city's newer restaurants have been quietly raising their à la carte prices while French restaurant prices have hardly budged. Second, the notion that French food is intimidating. False. Classical French cuisine, which may have once seemed complicated and fussy, is tame compared to many of today's elaborate fusion-style concoctions. Third, the perception that French restaurants are formal and stuffy. Possibly. Today's French restaurants have retained their sense of pride and professionalism, qualities sorely lacking in many of the city's popular high-end restaurants. But French restaurants have adapted to the times by becoming more accommodating, often spicing up their classic menus and succumbing to casual dress codes to draw the modern diner.

La Rapière's menu features traditional dishes from the southwestern province of Gascogne, known for its potted meats, pâtés, cep mushrooms, Bayonne ham, and duck and goose specialties, including smoked magret (breast), confit (leg), and foie gras. Incidentally, Gascogne is the homeland of D'Artagnan, the dashing musketeer, often depicted with a long, slender "rapière" in his hand—hence the name of the restaurant.

What more appropriate way could there be to start off a meal in this house than with an appetizer of smoked goose breast? The strong-flavoured goose meat (smoked on the premises) is served fanned out in a dozen paper-thin slices with a salad so perfectly dressed you'll wish there was twice as much.

A portion of duck foie gras terrine is delicate, just a bit rosé, though the surrounding port aspic has no discernible port flavour. A freshly baked puff-pastry cushion filled with snails and thin strips of Bayonne ham sounds tempting, but the dish turns out to be bland and underseasoned. The accompanying sauce is served lukewarm and only tastes creamy.

Main courses are superb. A Dover sole meunière is expertly filleted by the waiter at a side table. The lightly fried fish is served with a rich brown-butter sauce, a turned boiled potato, carrot slices, fanned zucchini, and a velvety turnip flan. The sole is perfectly cooked—delicate and firm—and it has a delectable buttery flavour.

Equally delicious is the "magret et confit de canard à l'aigre-doux." The dark-brown, glistening confit falls away from the bone at the slightest touch of a fork. The sliced magret comes from the same bird, but it tastes completely different. It has crisp skin and rosy flesh, and it's accompanied by a tangy sweet and sour sauce —another southwestern duck favourite served to perfection.

One of La Rapière's specialties is cassoulet. Skilfully served by the waiter from a small earthenware pot (a "cassole," from which the dish's name is derived), this delicious pile of tender white haricot beans, cooked preserved pork rind, duck confit, and garlic and Toulouse sausages is bursting with rich and intense flavour. Since it contains no mutton, aficionados would consider this the Castelnaudary, as opposed to the Carcassone or the Toulouse, variety. Whatever its lineage, the taste is sublime.

Who can resist the cheese course, especially when it's presented by someone as charming as the patronne of this establishment, Madame Lise Naud? Among the imported raw-milk cheeses that arrive at our table are Munster, Petit Livarot, Double Crème, and a goat's cheese. The topper is a small but decidedly potent piece of blue made from raw sheep's milk—a cheese for cheese lovers only!

Desserts here are classic French. A small, cake-shaped nougat glacé is filled with a generous handful of candied fruit and served with a ladle of custard cream that is decoratively swirled with raspberry coulis. Surprisingly, the crème brûlée is served hot. Crème brûlée should be served cold — that's the rule — nonetheless, this version is so scrumptious, you'll hardly care.

Service at La Rapière is outstanding. From the skilful boning of the Dover sole to the knowledgeable wine service (even to the way the bill is presented — discreetly, at the elbow of the only man at the table), the excellent waiters stand as shining examples of what the service aspect of a fine dining experience should be.

IN THE KITCHEN · Chef Denis Periau.

DECOR, DRESS, AMBIENCE · Tucked away in a corner of the Sun Life Building since moving from its original location on Rue Stanley several years ago, this elegant room, with its tasselled hanging lamps, terra-cotta-coloured walls, large stained glass windows, ornate tapestry, and proper dining chairs, is the epitome of understated French style. The bar sparkles like a jewel; one can imagine F. Scott Fitzgerald and the Smart Set there, sipping gimlets and sidecars.

WINE LIST · The list includes a wide selection of mid-to-high-priced French wines and a small, but good, choice of half bottles.

DON'T MISS · The duck (foie gras, confit, or magret), the sole meunière, the cassoulet, and the cheese course.

WORDS TO THE WISE · At a time when the designer-clad masses pile into loud restaurants serving exotic cuisine and the fickle foodies seek out the newest chefs, many of the city's gourmets quietly continue to frequent Montreal's formal French restaurants. La Rapière has been an outstanding example of this genre since it opened its doors in 1974. As you watch the tuxedoed waiters quietly go about their duties, you'll realize that this is one of the most civilized dining rooms around.

LA RAPIÈRE
1155 Rue Metcalfe (in the Sun Life Building)
Telephone: (514) 871-8920
Open: Lunch, noon-3 P.M., Monday to Friday; dinner, 5:30 P.M.-
10 P.M., Monday to Friday, and 5:30 P.M.-10 P.M., Saturday
Reservations: Recommended
Wheelchair access: Yes
Credit cards: All major cards
Price range: Starters, $4.50-$12.75; main courses, $22.75-$29.75;
desserts, $3.75-$6.25; three-course table d'hôte menu, $20.75-
$32.25

★★★1/2	$$$$	REVIEWED 08/00

L'EAU À LA BOUCHE

SNAPSHOT • It is at this lovely hotel/restaurant in the Laurentian
Mountains that renowned Quebec chef Anne Desjardins has de-
veloped her signature brand of regional cuisine using the best local
produce. The simple country setting includes a beautiful garden
next to the restaurant that supplies the kitchen with fresh herbs
and vegetables. As with all Relais & Château properties, here you
can expect fabulous food, solicitous service, and an extensive wine
list—all at a price, of course.

THE BIG PICTURE • There are but a handful of Quebec chefs
whom restaurant-goers know by name, and only one of them is a
woman: Anne Desjardins. Quebec foodies are big fans of Desjardins's, having voted her restaurant, L'Eau à la Bouche, "Best in
Montreal and Vicinity" in a *Gourmet* magazine poll from 1996 to
1998. In that same magazine, chef Desjardins has been described
as "a passionate advocate of regionality," and "an innovator with
an allegiance to regional cooking." Such heady acclaim, bolstered
by the establishment's membership in the luxury Relais &
Châteaux hotel and restaurant chain, ensure that expectations for
a meal at L'Eau à la Bouche are high.

One look at the menu confirms chef Desjardins's profile. Her market cuisine includes Quebec's finest: squab from Bellechasse, red deer from Boileau, hydromel honey wine, as well as locally produced foie gras and raw-milk cheeses. Also prominently featured are fresh herbs and edible flowers from a garden a few steps from the kitchen. Look no further than a summertime amuse-bouche of homegrown zucchini blossoms filled with local goat's cheese for your first glimpse of her simple, ingredient-based style.

Starters include salmon tartare, sautéed wild mushrooms, and roasted breast of squab. All three are superb. The tartare consists of cubes of ultrafresh raw salmon seasoned with wild ginger and mustard. The mix is shaped into three large, perfectly formed quenelles and placed beside squiggles of seedy mustard dressing and a salad of salty marsh greens (samfire) and purslane. The sautéed mushrooms include chanterelles and shiitakes served with a cream-based sherry sauce; the whole is topped with a single goat's cheese ravioli. The roasted breast of squab is set on a row of green beans and surrounded by a full-flavoured reduction sauce. The meat is heavenly, both crisp-skinned and medium-rare. My only complaint is that the portion is small for its $22 price. Take off a few green beans, and you'd be looking at an amuse-bouche.

Two of the main courses, scallops pan-seared "à l'unilatéral" (on one side) and Lower St. Laurent lamb cooked in two ways, are outstanding—fine examples of the talent of this kitchen. Seven medium-sized scallops are perfectly caramelized on one side and placed around a mound of sautéed chanterelles. The dish is topped with marsh samfire and enhanced with a ginger-mushroom emulsion. The scallops and mushrooms have the same tender consistency. The sea, the earth, and the exotic flavours coalesce, and every bite offers unique tastes—a mouth-watering dish if ever there was one.

The lamb is equally divine. Served with baby squash and a miniature ratatouille, the two roasted rack chops are toothsome and full flavoured (a real treat, given that Quebec lamb is so often bland). The braised leg is a revelation. Here is meat as tender and melting as a confit of duck. And it's not only perfectly seasoned but also ideally enhanced with a garlic-rosemary sauce.

A dish of roasted Boileau venison includes two slices cut from the loin and accompanied by a single yellow carrot, wild rice mixed with corn, sautéed sour red cherries, and a sauce made with hydromel Cuvée du Diable. This dish plays right into the restaurant's style, as every ingredient reflects Desjardins's commitment to regional cuisine. Yet, once again, the portion is inadequate. The two venison medallions are small, and the meat itself is no more exciting than your standard roast beef.

Those up for cheese should be warned that it's offered on the set menu in lieu of dessert (or à la carte for an extra $12.50). The cheese selection is small—only three Quebec cheeses and three French—but the Laracam and a cinder-coated goat's cheese are hard to pass up, especially as they're served in generous, room temperature slices with a stack of croutons and a few scattered nuts.

As for the desserts, there's an hydromel crème brûlée with a perfectly caramelized topping and a small assortment of summer berries. Once again, the portion is skimpy, and the flavouring—the honey wine—while well suited to many recipes, gives the cream a peculiar taste. A marzipan tart is far more satisfying. It's lined with rhubarb pulp and topped with a golden puff of baked almond cream. Alongside is a scoop of sour, milk-based rhubarb sorbet and a sweet white-chocolate mousse.

L'Eau à la Bouche's wait staff is both gracious and solicitous. The sommelière is especially helpful, pointing out excellent bottles within one's budget or recommending wines by the glass.

IN THE KITCHEN • Chef and co-owner Anne Desjardins.

DECOR, DRESS, AMBIENCE • The main dining room has large windows, wood panelling, and Dijon-mustard-coloured walls. The ceiling is covered in panels of burgundy-flowered fabric. The setting is country quaint, with appropriately casual decor. High-backed green-and-black chairs add a odd touch of modernity.

WINE LIST • Wine lovers are well served at L'Eau à la Bouche. Not only does the wine list offer an impressive selection of the finest French, Italian, and Californian wines (among others), but also the wait staff is adept at pairing food and wine. There's also the "menu découverte," a multicourse tasting menu featuring wines from a given region, such as Bordeaux or the Napa Valley.

DON'T MISS · The salmon tartare, the sautéed wild mushrooms, the roasted squab, the seared scallops, the lamb, and the marzipan tart.

WORDS TO THE WISE · L'Eau à la Bouche's rave reviews are merited. Anne Desjardins is obviously passionate about her ingredients, which she uses most thoughtfully. Not all is perfect, however. There's a problem with the price-to-portion ratio, and there are occasional lapses in service. Nonetheless, this kitchen hits many high notes, and in today's competitive world of upscale restaurants, that's worth applauding.

L'EAU À LA BOUCHE

3003 Boulevard Ste. Adèle, Ste. Adèle
Telephone: (450) 229-2991
Open: 6 P.M.-9 P.M., daily
Wheelchair access: Yes
Reservations: Essential
Cards: All major cards
Price range: Starters, $21-$32; main courses, $36-$46; desserts, $12.50; tasting menus, $57, $67, and $77; six-course food and wine "découverte" menu, $125

★★1/2	$ $ $	REVIEWED 11/00

LE CAVEAU

SNAPSHOT • A Montreal institution since 1949, this three-story restaurant, popular with the conservative downtown crowd and local university professors, offers cuisine bourgeoise in a charming French-parlour setting. The menu includes traditional dishes like lobster bisque, sole meunière, and entrecôte bordelaise. Though service tends to be brisk, it is unfailingly courteous.

THE BIG PICTURE • The humble restaurant appears to carry a stigma these days. Increasingly, fashionable eating spaces bill themselves as bistros, brasseries, grills, eateries, wine bars, or cafés; many favour the cool look of art galleries, decorator boutiques, and clothing stores. Of course, one understands the public's hunger for all things new and exciting. Yet so quickly has the restaurant concept changed in the past decade that when you enter the dining room of Le Caveau, you won't believe your eyes. Here's the real deal: an enchanting, old-fashioned French restaurant, almost a parody of the genre, uncommon enough on today's dining-out landscape to look new—even bold.

In business for over 50 years, Le Caveau is one of those downtown restaurants often referred to as an institution. Besides the fact that it creates an authentic French atmosphere, the secret of its success appears to lie in a style of French cooking known as "cuisine bourgeoise," which includes traditional dishes such as cassoulet, rack of lamb, and escargots. After seeing countless culinary concoctions served with quirky sauces, oven-dried vegetables, and mashed potatoes enhanced with everything but the kitchen sink, it's refreshing to see a piece of meat garnished with nothing more than a bouquet of watercress.

A fine start to a meal at Le Caveau is one of the many soups. A steaming bowl of cream of cauliflower soup is perfectly seasoned and offers a pronounced cauliflower flavour (cauliflower soup is so often creamy and insipid). The gratinéed onion soup has a tangy Gruyère topping, deeply caramelized onions, and a generous dose of thyme. A vegetable soup, loaded with lentils, carrots, and celery, is heartier than most Italian minestrones. Only an excessively salty duck consommé falls short, though its two large duck ravioles are meaty and delicious.

Simple salad starters are equally appealing. An endive and Roquefort duo combines pungent, salty cheese and refreshing bitter leaves—ideally matched with a glass of fruity Chardonnay. The classic chèvre chaud consists of a large crouton topped with mild goat's cheese and toasted slivered almonds surrounded by a mixed salad. The most adventurous salad offers tender strips of intensely flavoured, medium-rare hare meat and sautéed chanterelle mushrooms on a bed of crisp greens.

Main courses arrive in minutes. A small lidded pot is uncovered to reveal a golden crumb crust atop what turns out to be a pasty—as opposed to creamy—cassoulet. The overcooked haricot beans on the top have formed a kind of porridge, encasing pieces of garlic sausage, Toulouse sausage, and duck. Thankfully, the beans at the bottom of the dish are less mushy. But what's lacking here is a richness of flavour—more herbs, garlic, a touch of tomato are needed before one could include this version in one's personal pantheon of memorable cassoulets.

Two meat dishes—carré d'agneau and tournedos bordelaise —will take you back in time, straight to the pages of Jacques Pépin's and Julia Child's first cookbooks. The rack of lamb, served whole and coated in a herbed crumb crust, is succulent and cooked to the ideal rosé. A single large tournedos accompanied by slices of garlic toast is a bit on the dry side, and it's served with a bordelaise sauce better described as "bordelaise light." Both meat dishes come with a side dish of seasonal vegetables: al dente brussels sprouts, buttery spaghetti squash, and sautéed sliced potatoes.

This kitchen does occasionally take a walk on the wild side. A generous portion of scallops and shrimp is served in and around a tulip-shaped tuile set on a mound of linguini and topped with a handful of deep-fried rice noodles. Although the seafood is fresh and tender, the tomato sauce, enhanced with fennel and pastis, has a thin consistency and an underlying sweet flavour—not bad, just different. Better still is the delicate panfried halibut, which has a delicious spicy paprika crust and is served with rice, sautéed onions, spinach, and a slice of eggplant.

Desserts come up short. A homey-looking slice of sugar pie is alarmingly sweet, as is the meringue topping on a slice of lemon meringue pie. An orange crème brûlée is a total failure, for it has an unappealing curdled consistency and lacks a firm caramel topping. Unless you insist on a sugar fix at the end of a meal, stick to the excellent coffee and the cassis-liqueur-filled chocolate hearts offered on the house.

Service is smooth and efficient. Though speedy service has its benefits (all the dishes arrive piping hot), the rush leaves little time for wine and water glasses to be refilled and cutlery to be replaced.

IN THE KITCHEN · Chef Frank Laroche.

DECOR, DRESS, AMBIENCE · The setting resembles a French family-run hotel dining room. The waiters are decked out in black vests, bow ties, and floor-length aprons. White-linen-covered tables, adorned with small lamps with pleated shades askew, fill a square parlour decorated with flowered wallpaper, gold-framed oil paintings, and a grandfather clock. The crowd is mixed: couples young and old, large families, groups of friends, and tweedy university types. As the evening progresses, conversation levels pick up considerably, briging a welcome buzz to this romantic, low-lit room.

WINE LIST · The wine list is short and French, with interesting, well-priced selections at many price points. Only two wines are available by the glass, but both are of high quality and relatively inexpensive (under seven dollars).

DON'T MISS · The soups, the salads, the rack of lamb, and the panfried halibut.

WORDS TO THE WISE • Dwarfed by the surrounding chrome-and-glass towers of downtown Montreal, Le Caveau has a comfortable atmosphere well suited to occasions such as the intimate tête-à-tête, the two-couple thing, or the let's-impress-the-client lunch. If you're a traditionalist who pines for the Gallic way of life and rhapsodizes about unpretentious cuisine, this charming establishment will be hard to beat.

LE CAVEAU
2063 Rue Victoria (near Président Kennedy)
Telephone: (514) 844-1624
Open: 11:30 A.M.-11 P.M., Monday to Friday;
4:30 P.M.-11 P.M., Saturday and Sunday
Wheelchair access: No
Reservations: Recommended
Cards: All major cards
Price range: Starters, $3.95-$17.95; main courses, $14.50-$39.95; desserts, $4.75-$6.50

★★1/2	$ $	REVIEWED 12/01

LE CHRYSANTHÈME

SNAPSHOT • The high quality of the fare at Le Chrysanthème should come as no surprise, as this is the sister restaurant of the city's best Chinese establishment, L'Orchidée de Chine. The Szechwan and Cantonese dishes here are utterly delicious, prepared with first-rate ingredients, and beautifully presented. The only shortcoming is the heat factor: food rated spicy on the menu may be a bit tame for adventurous palates. Though there's an air of sophistication about this restaurant, the ambience and service can be a bit cold.

THE BIG PICTURE • "Restaurant food used to be so elaborate," opined a chef friend between mouthfuls of his scallop and sweet corn soup. "What most restaurants are serving today is no more than gussied-up comfort food, not all that different from what we usually eat at home."

He's right, of course, and his wife and I nodded in approval as we downed our own bowls of soup: classic hot-and-sour, laden with strips of chicken, mushrooms, and tofu suspended in a thick, spicy broth; and crab-and-asparagus, chock-full of white asparagus and sweet crab. But how many of us, I asked, are making soups like this at home? Not many, we concluded; probably just those of Chinese heritage who were fortunate enough to have inherited the family recipes, or skilled amateur cooks with a particular interest in Chinese or Szechwan cuisine.

All this soup (and foodie talk) was the prelude to a recent meal at Le Chrysanthème. The soups, which were hot, made with fine ingredients, and richly flavoured, turned out to be as satisfying as the other appetizers sampled: lamb dumplings, pork wontons, vegetable spring rolls, and five-flavoured spareribs.

Bathed in a spicy garlic sauce, the thin-skinned dumplings were wrapped around lamb forcemeat that had distinct texture and flavour, a welcome change from the usual dull and pasty meat fillings. The delicate pork wonton ravioli arrived in a pool of ginger soy sauce with a peppery taste that lingered on the lips. The spring rolls, as skilfully rolled as Cuban cigars, came packed with a julienne of fresh vegetables, and they were not in the least bit greasy. Also delicious were the crispy five-flavoured spareribs. Though the boned meat was a bit stringy—more dry than succulent—every chewy morsel was enlivened with aromatic spices (anise, cinnamon, fennel seeds, cloves, and Szechwan pepper), and the crisp skin crackled under the teeth. Indeed, few of us are preparing such complex dishes at home.

In keeping with the excellence of the appetizers, main courses also scored high. We devoured a generous bowl of toothsome shrimp served in a light soy sauce strewn with basil leaves and snow peas. Another predictable winner was the General Tao's chicken. The large pieces of breast meat were moist, crisp, and ever-so-lightly breaded, and the sauce was tangy without being gooey or overly sweet, like so many inferior versions.

Far more fulfilling in the spice department were the Singapore-style noodles and the crispy duck with five-flavoured salt. The dish, a mixture of chicken strips, shrimp, short vermicelli noodles, bean sprouts, and julienned carrots, was fragrant and laced with a subtle curry flavour.

The duck was the highlight of the meal. Every bite of the crisp, spicy, and pleasantly salty breast meat melted in the mouth. Surprisingly, it wasn't at all fatty—a coup for this kitchen. Before the dishes were cleared, I couldn't resist scooping up the last few slices of duck, which turned out to be just as delicious cold. The steamed rice—light and not at all gummy—was also first-rate.

Though it was recommended by our waiter, the spicy beef with Chinese pancakes was a disappointment. The thin strands of beef, fried beyond recognition, tasted oily and bitter, not spicy; and the bland pancakes offered little in the way of support.

Desserts appear to be an afterthought at Le Chrysanthème, as there are none listed on the menu. After an unenthusiastic listing by our waiter, we settled for a tutti-frutti-tasting orange sorbet and a few cups of weak Chinese tea.

Halfway through our meal, I noted that not a single staff member—including the hostess at the door—had offered a welcoming word or even cracked a smile. When I asked our waiter for menu recommendations, he actually looked surprised. To be fair, plates arrived like clockwork, water and wine glasses were refilled promptly, and dishes were served with care. But with such a cold shoulder coming from the staff, I felt a bit like someone caught crashing a wedding.

IN THE KITCHEN • Chef Peter Ng.

DECOR, DRESS, AMBIENCE • Located in a townhouse on the sleepy section of Rue Crescent below Ste. Catherine, this elegant space features a contemporary decor with dark-grey-and-old-rose-painted walls, and Chinese screens and prints. A second, small room includes a whimsical arrangement of large decorative fans (a creative, not so subtle way to delineate the smoking section).

WINE LIST • Le Chrysanthème maintains a small but affordable selection of wines. A bottle of Gewurztraminer offers a welcome fruitiness that marries well with sweet and spicy food.

DON'T MISS • The soups, the lamb dumplings, the pork wonton ravioli in ginger sauce, the spring rolls, the five-flavoured spareribs, the shrimp with basil and snow peas, the General Tao's chicken, and the crispy duck with five-flavoured salt.

WORDS TO THE WISE • Service problems aside, this Chinese restaurant is one of the city's finest. True, there are no chopsticks on the table (they are available upon request), and nothing is as spicy as authentic Szechwan should be, but there's no denying that this is a top choice for anyone with an urge to try something out of the ordinary.

Le Chrysanthème
1208 Rue Crescent (near Ste. Catherine)
Telephone: (514) 397-1408
Open: Lunch, noon-2:30 P.M., Tuesday to Friday;
dinner, 5:30 P.M.-11 P.M., Tuesday to Saturday, and 5:30 P.M.-
10 P.M., Sunday
Wheelchair access: No
Reservations: Recommended
Credit cards: All major cards
Price range: Starters, $3-$7.50; main courses, $8.50-$16.50;
desserts, $3.50

★★★	$ $ $	REVIEWED 10/01

LE CLUB DES PINS

SNAPSHOT • Fashionable Avenue Laurier has its share of popular restaurants, and the Le Club des Pins is one of the most impressive. Chef Jean-François Vachon's style is Quebec nouvelle cuisine, and his plates feature many of the best local ingredients. Owner Carl Chevalier has kept the wine list stocked with well-chosen, affordable bottles, many of them privately imported. All this and more in a quaint Provençal setting.

THE BIG PICTURE • Strolling down Avenue Laurier, I stopped to look inside a restaurant I had last reviewed two years previously: Le Club des Pins. It was all still there: the patterned tablecloths, the bright-yellow walls, and the amusing mural of an imaginary St. Tropez café called "La Pétanque." Yet, as familiar as it all seemed, I knew that much had changed. The charming owner of Le Club des Pins, Danielle Matte, had sold the restaurant over a year ago, and its enfant-terrible chef, Martin Picard, had also moved on. I asked around, but no one seemed to know more than that.

The good news is that Le Club des Pins is once again going strong. Two young men—owner Carl Chevalier, 25; and chef Jean-François Vachon, 28—are now in charge. Not only have they retained the restaurant's assets, but they've also improved upon them, turning what was once a creative little bistro into a restaurant on a par with Montreal's best.

There's much to like about the revamped establishment. Besides the sunny decor, there's the menu, which is ideal in length and smartly put together. Diners are given numerous options, including à la carte offerings and various menus: three courses ($30), four courses ($45), and an elaborate eight-course "menu de dégustation" ($75 or $110, with six wines by the glass).

The most welcome—and obvious—improvement is the food. Having worked in the kitchens of both Les Caprices de

Nicolas and Globe, Vachon is familiar with Montreal's fine-dining terrain. Scattered throughout the menu are sublime local ingredients, such as Quebec foie gras, guinea hen, Boileau venison, Tournevent goat's cheese, and vegetables from Quebec organic farmer Pierré-André Daignault. As opposed to a cuisine based on specialties from Provence or the Languedoc, the style is now more Quebec nouvelle cuisine, which makes sense, as Vachon hails not from Carcasonne, but from Chicoutimi.

Dinner begins with three different amuse-bouches: a velvety velouté de volaille, an ethereal blini with smoked salmon, and a meaty Malpeque oyster topped with a spicy cold tomato soup and served as a shooter—a serious palate jolter.

Following that bit of fun is a lovely starter consisting of raw, thinly sliced yellow beets (listed as "carpaccio") topped with matchsticks of Granny Smith apple and shavings of Ossau-Iraty sheep's milk cheese from the Midi-Pyrénées. Also delicious is a potato galette wrapped in pancetta with goat's milk Cheddar (Chèvre Noir) and caramelized pears for a perfect interplay of sweet, salty, tangy, and earthy.

The star of the starters is the foie gras. Ideally seared on the outside and trembling within, the thick pieces of liver are sandwiched between slices of chocolate bread and served with fresh figs and a fig-caramel sauce enhanced with more chocolate. Surprised by the chocolate and foie gras combination? Don't be. It works, as the Manjari chocolate used is fruity and bitter and just sweet enough to enhance without overwhelming.

Main courses are uniformly delicious. The breast of guinea hen offers moist white meat beneath crisp brown skin. So crisp is the coating that I hear it crackle under my knife and pop in my mouth. Served alongside are glistening fingerling potato halves and sautéed Savoy cabbage with Morteau sausage. The panfried Mediterranean sea bass is ideally cooked and has a flavour as fresh as sea air. The smooth mashed potatoes bring it all down to earth, and a few baby clams add a welcome bit of texture.

My favourite of the three dishes is the roasted Boileau venison loin with braised shoulder meat and sautéed spaghetti squash. While the sliced loin is tender and intensely flavoured, the braised shoulder meat is even more so, especially as it is enhanced by a shot of truffle oil. The taste is heavenly, lacking only a sprinkling of salt. When you ask for salt in this restaurant, you're handed that luxurious French salt, sel de Guérande—proof that these boys are commited to quality.

Desserts are good, though not quite on a par with the rest of the meal. I'd avoid the lavender crème brûlée, which tastes more of the propane gas used to caramelize the top than of lavender. Try instead the poached pear with cinnamon ice cream or the warm chocolate cake with homemade vanilla ice cream.

Service starts out strong, but it tends to lag as the restaurant fills up.

IN THE KITCHEN · Chef Jean-François Vachon.

DECOR, DRESS, AMBIENCE · The deep, narrow dining room is painted in rich tones of sunflower yellow and burnt sienna. Stencils of aubergines, peppers, olive oil, fish, and an amusing mural of a café called "La Pétanque" set the scene somewhere in mythical Provence.

WINE LIST · As was always the case here, the wine list includes an interesting selection of fairly priced, predominantly southern French wines, many of them privately imported. And, with only a dozen bottles priced over $100 and more than twice as many priced under $50, this list favours customers with an eye on the bottom line.

DON'T MISS · The amuse-bouches, the foie gras, the guinea hen, the venison, the sea bass, and the chocolate moelleux cake.

WORDS TO THE WISE · Good news or bad news: At Le Club des Pins, smoking is only permitted at the bar in the back of the restaurant.

LE CLUB DES PINS

156 Avenue Laurier West (corner St. Urbain)

Telephone: (514) 272-9484

Open: Lunch, 11:30 A.M.-2:30 P.M., Tuesday to Friday;
dinner, 6 P.M.-10:30 P.M., daily

Wheelchair access: Yes

Reservations: Essential; nonsmoking environment
(except in the bar)

Cards: All major cards

Price range: Starters, $7-$23; main courses, $24-$30;
desserts, $5-$7; prix fixe menus, $30-$75 ($110 with wine)

★★	$ $ $	REVIEWED 07/99

LE GOURMAND

SNAPSHOT • With its French/Cajun menu, artistic plate presentations, and friendly atmosphere, this popular Pointe Claire restaurant has everything to keep suburban gourmets happy. In summer, the large flowered terrace is a great place for people-watching while feasting on terrific grilled meats and home-style desserts. Reservations are essential.

THE BIG PICTURE • How does a restaurant that doesn't have a prime downtown location attract an urban clientele? In the case of Le Gourmand, it does so by combining a casual atmosphere with sophisticated cuisine. The combination justifies the detour. Those who live nearby, of course, have been in the know for quite some time.

Some of Le Gourmand's menu items are strictly French, while others, heavy on the spices and garnished with salsa, have a Southwestern accent. Starters include chicken liver quenelles, beef and lentil soup, and avocado salsa with goat's cheese au gratin. The three quenelles of chicken liver pâté have a slightly bitter flavour that contrasts perfectly with the accompanying sweet onion confit. The soup, backed by a rich beef broth, is hearty and delicious. The salsa, with a strong Paillot goat's cheese melted over the top, is seasoned with a potent mix of Cajun spices (which might be a bit hot for the average palate).

Main courses—a filet mignon with roasted corn and black bean salsa, and a loin of Charlevoix veal with Cognac sauce—are highlights of this menu. The grilled filet mignon is both toothsome and flavourful. Its marchand à vin sauce—a reduction of beef glaze, red wine, and shallots enriched with butter, lemon juice, and parsley—is a perfect match for the meat.

The veal loin is served with fanned yellow zucchini, fresh green beans, roasted onions, and carrots—all garnished with Yukon Gold potato chips and deep-fried parsley. The Cognac cream sauce is the ideal enhancement for the gentle flavour of the veal. Thumbs up to the chef, whose main courses are presented in a contemporary style, with food layered in the centre of the plate, rather than in the traditional clockwise arrangement.

Of the desserts, the best is a warm chocolate pecan pie with a brownie-like texture that's served with sweetened whipped cream and apricot sauce. A thin apple tart with caramel sauce and vanilla ice cream could have used a few more minutes in the oven, as the crust is almost raw and the apples are still crunchy.

Though friendly and courteous, the service here lacks polish. At a recent meal, when asked about a particular wine, the waitress responded, "I hear it's good." Not surprisingly, it turned out to be ordinary. Such indifference doesn't cut it in a restaurant serving food as good as this.

IN THE KITCHEN · Chef and owner Michael Oliphant.

DECOR, DRESS, AMBIENCE · There's definite air of conviviality at Le Gourmand. The restaurant is set in an old stone house with an adjoining flower-laden outdoor terrace. The crowd is made up of sophisticated suburbanites, young and old. Look into the kitchen, and you'll see baseball-capped chefs turning out plates of funky-looking food. Many customers appear to be regulars, as they address the restaurant's young waitresses by name.

WINE LIST · The wine list is short, primarily French, with no half bottles and a few offerings by the glass.

DON'T MISS · The soups, the grilled meats (filet mignon and veal loin), and the chocolate pecan tart.

WORDS TO THE WISE · At more than $60 a head with wine and service, Le Gourmand is too expensive to fall into the category of local canteen. These are restaurant prices. Yet for all the hard work and good intentions, there are still a few obvious wrinkles that need ironing out. The food is Le Gourmand's strongest asset. But with greater emphasis placed on professional service, this restaurant could soon become *the* West Island favourite.

LE GOURMAND
42 Avenue Ste. Anne (near Lakeshore), Pointe Claire
Telephone: (514) 695-9077
Open: Lunch, 11:30 A.M.-3 P.M., Monday to Friday;
dinner, 5:30 P.M.-10 P.M., daily
Wheelchair access: Yes
Reservations: Essential
Cards: Major cards
Price range: Starters, $3.25-$8.95; main courses, $14-$36;
desserts, $4.25-$6; table d'hôte menu, $26-$39

★★	$ $ $	REVIEWED 04/00

LE GRAND CAFÉ

SNAPSHOT · Le Grand Café's name is somewhat misleading. It's really a bistro, and a small one at that. The menu includes many high-flying modern dishes peppered with exotic ingredients. Best of all may be the ambience, enhanced by the café's high-spirited clientele, and the wine list, which is both interesting and priced to sell.

THE BIG PICTURE · The best cafés are places where people are happy just to hang out. At the end of two meals at downtown's Le Grand Café, I found myself doing just that. In this sense, Le Grand Café is a café where "grand confort" wins out over "grande gastronomie." It has a laid-back ambience and certainly one of the friendliest wait staffs, headed by mâitre d' and co-owner Claude Glavier. The attempt to please is obviously successful, as the place is usually packed with contented diners.

Alas, all is not perfect. The onion soup is served with the croutons and grated cheese on the side. This is a shame, as the soup, made with a delicious beef stock packed with tender onions, loses all its charm without its gratinéed croutons. Another bistro/café classic, frisée aux lardons, could also use a bit of attention. Although the egg is perfectly poached, it's set atop a bed of soggy lettuce (frisée, not the classic Niçoise) and the meaty fried lardons are cold.

A serving of pâté (incorrectly described on the French menu as "rillettes") is fanned out in thin slices and garnished with leek sprouts, gherkin halves, and a sprinkling of rice noodles. The pâté is smooth and well seasoned, but the presentation is over the top. The asparagus salad substitutes overdone with dull. It's just a bowl full of mesclun mix with a few watery asparagus spears, all smothered with a sweet soy-sauce vinaigrette. Where were all those creative instincts when this plate was put together?

Main courses fare better. The Grand Café is at its best with meat dishes. The pepper steak offers a modern rendition of the classic bistro favourite. Stacked on a bed of caramelized endive and topped with a cloud of mashed potatoes, the entrecôte is coated in a rich green-peppercorn sauce. The house veal chop is equally impressive, for the meat is rosé, tender, and flavourful. A duck filet covered in Cajun spices has the robust flavour of barbecue, though the meat itself is rather tough. The accompanying barley risotto has a pleasant nutty taste and a texture as comforting as breakfast porridge.

Fish lovers are in for a treat. The panfried filet of sole is an impressive dish: the fish has a delicate flavour and a moist, melting texture. It's served with sautéed red cabbage, sliced green beans, and chayote, which, with its lovely squash flavour, delivers a delicious creative touch.

Desserts are homemade and in keeping with the decorative style. Though the waiter claims the Key lime pie is "the best in the city," it has none of the traits of the real thing—graham crust, cream or meringue topping, or Key lime juice. He should redirect his sales pitch to the creamy white chocolate mousse served with raspberry coulis and strawberries. Profiteroles would be another good choice if the chocolate sauce wasn't so thick and gloopy. The intensely flavoured mango and raspberry sorbets offer the most refreshing end to the meal.

Though the food at Le Grand Café is uneven, the personal touch will win you over. Service is casual and so friendly that you shouldn't be surprised if the waiter gives you the classic French/Québécois two-cheek kiss on your way out.

IN THE KITCHEN • Chef Jean-Yves Naud.

DECOR, DRESS, AMBIENCE • With its low lights, checkered floor, wood panels, and welcoming ambience, this downtown bistro is more than just another steak-frites-eater's paradise. The crowd appears to be made up of either local business types or tourists. The relaxed ambience creates the impression of a branché dinner party with background music ranging from frantic accordion to mellow Motown.

WINE LIST · Skip the wine list and talk to your waiter, who will be more than pleased to suggest a few of his recent favourites within your budget.

DON'T MISS · The meat and fish entrées, and the white chocolate mousse.

WORDS TO THE WISE · Le Grand Café has attracted a loyal local clientele—the kind of patrons who feel at home in convivial surroundings and who tend to overlook the offbeat, hit-or-miss nature of the food. Sure, there's creative license going on with the "Grand" part of the name. But the spirit here is that of a true café.

LE GRAND CAFÉ
1181 Avenue Union (near Cathcart)
Telephone: (514) 866-1303
Open: 11:30 A.M.-10 P.M., Monday to Wednesday;
11:30 A.M.-11 P.M., Thursday to Saturday
Wheelchair access: Yes
Reservations: Recommended
Cards: Major cards (and Interac)
Price range: Starters, $3-$9; main courses, $12-$28;
desserts, $4-$6

★★1/2	$ $ $ $	REVIEWED 10/00

LE LATINI

SNAPSHOT · If it's high-quality Italian food you're after, you can't do much better than Le Latini. In this eclectic modern/traditional setting, one can feast on authentic Italian cuisine meticulously prepared with only the best local and imported ingredients. There's an ever-evolving and impressive wine list, but considering the high prices charged for a meal here, service sometimes comes up short. Le Latini has been a Montreal institution popular with the upscale business crowd for many years.

THE BIG PICTURE · The Italian word that best describes my first visit to Le Latini is "fantastico!" My companion and I were shown to a table in the elegant second-floor dining room. While sipping Moscato, we soaked up the fabulous view of the illuminated downtown core from the floor-to-ceiling windows before tucking into a true Italian feast.

The fruity, emerald green, extra-virgin Venetian olive oil found on every table sets a high tone for the meal. The classic prosciutto and melon starter is comprised of delicate and ultralean slices of cured ham draped into mounds and set around two thick slices of pristine melon. That old Italian standby, tomato with Mozzarella, is made with Mozzarella di bufala, and the tomatoes, dressed with a simple balsamic vinegar and olive oil vinaigrette, are ripe, flavourful, and firm.

Other starters include crisp and tender fried calamari, a chunky and satisfying minestrone, and an arugula salad dressed with only olive oil and freshly shaved Parmesan. The mussels with marinara sauce, and the deep-fried soft-shell crab served with a raisin and onion marmalade are also both delicious.

Main courses—veal and tomato risotto and mushroom ravioli—live up to their press clippings. The risotto, rumoured to be one of the only ones in Montreal made from scratch, is a triumph. The rice is firm yet creamy, the veal is tender, and the tomato flavour is rich; the dish is perfectly seasoned. The ravioli is also a winner. The homemade al dente pockets are filled with a highly perfumed mushroom filling, and the buttery cheese sauce tastes of the finest Parmigiano-Reggiano.

The seafood linguini is also excellent. It's served with toothsome shrimp and tender mussels and baby clams, all enveloped in a tomato-basil sauce. Though authentic, the many-layered lasagna, by contrast, is made with a veal-and-cream-enhanced tomato sauce that's bland—nothing to write home about.

Le Latini's scampi and veal chop don't disappoint. The generous portion of scampi—about ten halves baked in the shell with white wine and basil—are sweet and tender, almost soft, and they aren't in the least bit mushy. The accompanying tomato and basil linguini is also first-rate. The veal chop is near perfect in every way: ideally grilled, with a caramelized crust and ever-so-slightly rosé in the centre.

Recommended desserts include an Amaretto-enhanced tiramisu, and that multilayered ice cream bombe, cassata. Steer clear of the acidic lemon tart and the bitter, spongy, and over-cooked crème caramel.

Service at Le Latini is professional and efficient but inconsistent. There's a divide here between regulars, who are always treated solicitously, and first-timers, who can be treated like noncharter members of an exclusive club. Depending on which camp you fall into, this can make for very different experiences.

IN THE KITCHEN · Chef and owner Moreno DiMarchi.

DECOR, DRESS, AMBIENCE · On the main floor there's a large open kitchen fronted by impressive displays of fresh fruit and seafood. At dinnertime, the second floor is the place to take in the exciting views of the south-central downtown core. Le Latini's patrons are, for the most part, sophisticated and affluent — businesspeople come here to put major dents in the old expense account.

WINE LIST · Le Latini's wine list offers an impressive selection of fine Italian wines. As they do at most of the city's Italian restaurants, expect prices here to skyrocket as the quality rises. Be sure to check out the daily wine specials listed at the bottom of the menu, where there are many affordable discoveries to be made.

DON'T MISS · The calamari, the prosciutto and melon, the risotto, the pasta, and the cassata.

WORDS TO THE WISE · The big problem nonregulars run into here is the lack of pampering. The owners, seemingly happy to fawn over regulars and recognizable faces, sometimes treat new-comers with indifference. You may want to overlook the offhand treatment, however, just to experience the best of the food.

LE LATINI
1130 Rue Jeanne Mance (near René Lévesque)
Telephone: (514) 861-3166
Open: Lunch, 11:30 A.M.-3 P.M., Monday to Friday;
dinner, 5 P.M.-11:45 P.M., Saturday, and 4 P.M.-10 P.M., Sunday
Wheelchair access: Yes
Reservations: Essential
Cards: All major cards
Price range: Starters, $7.25-$19.25; main courses, $20.50-$49;
desserts, $6.75-$9.50

★★1/2	$ $ $	REVIEWED 11/01

LE LUTÉTIA

SNAPSHOT • Few hotel restaurants in Montreal are packing them in these days. Many are dull to a fault. That's hardly a problem at Hôtel de la Montagne's Le Lutétia. With its elaborate rococo setting reminiscent of a lavish eighteenth-century salon, Le Lutétia stands out as the most elaborate of the city's hotel dining rooms. The restaurant's new chef, Eric Gonzalez, presents a sumptuous nouvelle cuisine menu full of American accents. Though the wine list is exemplary, service can be uneven and noise levels are high. Call in advance for the house specialty: pressed duck.

THE BIG PICTURE • Le Lutétia's menu has always been extravagant, perhaps now more than ever. Lobster, foie gras, and caviar abound. Unlike many Montreal chefs, who let the ingredients do the talking, Le Lutétia's Eric Gonzalez puts equal emphasis on cooking techniques. There are consommés, confits, veloutés, parmentiers, and brandades. This is fancy food, ideal for celebrations. Gonzalez's style may be luxurious, but there's nothing stodgy about it. Reflecting his French training (he hails from Provence) and his three years in New York, his jazzy nouvelle cuisine is peppered with American influences. Flavour enhancers range from

pesto, mushroom marmalade, and fruit ketchup to truffle vinaigrette, Champagne sabayon, and sea urchin cappuccino. He's
lifted the best of both worlds, no matter what the pedigree.

The amuse-bouche, a single meaty jumbo shrimp served with
a spoonful of mango-green-pepper marmalade and a dribble of
passion fruit sauce, is an enticing introduction to Gonzalez's style.

Starters are also impressive. A shallow bowl containing an
arrangement of lobster and glazed scampi cradling a quenelle of
mushroom-chervil cream arrives covered by one of Le Lutétia's
dramatic silver cloches. The bowl is uncovered, and a waiter arrives to add the soup, a velouté de crustacés. This cream of
seafood is velvety and deeply flavoured. The lobster and scampi
are tender, and the quenelle of cream adds a wonderful earthy
flavour, a frothy texture, and a cool temperature. Wow.

Another starter, pumpkin ravioli, is a tasty second. The thin-
skinned ravioli are filled with a light pumpkin-mascarpone
purée, arranged on a bed of caramelized onions, and topped with
a sprinkling of thyme, diced tomato, and preserved lemons.

Though main-course expectations (and prices) run high, you
will not be disappointed. Chilean sea bass served with sautéed
spinach and a skewer of grilled shrimp, clams, and pesto is pure
perfection. The fish is moist and offers the most subtle flavour on
the plate—simply the pure taste of the sea. The accompaniments
all fall into order, from the shrimp and clams to the stronger
spinach and pesto. The side dish of lemon and mascarpone pasta,
however, is superfluous.

The squab with veal and mushroom stuffing is another showstopper. The pudgy bird is boned, deep mahogany in colour, and
glistening; what a shame the skin has been steamed under the
cloche and has lost all its desirable crispness. The meat, however,
is heavenly: medium-rare, gamy in flavour, and oh so rich. The
soft polenta with olives and lima beans served alongside provides
a neutral background, and the reduced jus around it reflects the
chef's preference for light sauces.

The cheese course is not to be missed. There is a wide variety
of cheeses—both local and imported—and they're served with
three original condiments: puréed pear, pistou, and an onion-

orange marmalade. Before the arrival of the desserts proper comes a delicious predessert: spiced jelly with grapes, pecans, and candied orange zest.

Desserts also reflect the chef's French/American approach. The first, a variation on the classic Black Forest cake, is made with thin layers of soft chocolate cake filled with an intense chocolate cream and topped with almond-flavoured whipped cream and cherries. Only serious chocoholics need apply. Less aggressive and far more elegant is a frozen vanilla parfait filled with diced pineapple, topped with gold leaf, and served with pineapple tempura bâtonnets on the side.

Service is one of Le Lutétia's only drawbacks. Though some of the waiters are friendly and professional, others appear indifferent and ill-informed about the menu and the wine list.

Note: A specialty of Le Lutétia is canard pressé, a dish rarely served outside its house of origin—the famed Parisian restaurant Le Tour d'Argent. The tableside service of this dish begins with the waiter removing the magrets from the breastbone, then chopping the carcass into small pieces and placing them in an elaborate silver screw-top press designed to extract the blood and juices from the bones for later use in enriching the sauce. Though not recommended for the squeamish, duck lovers are sure to lick their lips after every bite.

IN THE KITCHEN · Chef Eric Gonzalez.

DECOR, DRESS, AMBIENCE · Exiting the elevator on the hotel's second floor, one is quickly enveloped in the lavish decor. It's a real amalgam of styles: Baroque, Belle Époque, rococo. Plaster cherubs circle colourful ceiling frescoes, gossamer drapes line the windows and balcony, and the Louis XIV armchairs are upholstered in elaborate tapestries. Sparkling chandeliers abound. Surprisingly, the mix of styles works, creating an atmosphere of a movie set depicting a lavish eighteenth-century salon.

WINE LIST · The wine list, with its many colourful maps and wide selection of well-priced international bottles, is exemplary.

DON'T MISS · The seafood bisque, the ravioli, the Chilean sea bass, the cheese course, and the pineapple dessert.

WORDS TO THE WISE · As garish as the decor may sound, there's no denying that this "Let them eat cake" setting puts one in the mood for an extravagant night of fine dining. However, there's no avoiding the loud music, which emanates from the noisy bar below the restaurant (late in the evening, noise levels can be intolerable).

LE LUTÉTIA
1430 Rue de la Montagne (near de Maisonneuve, in the Hôtel de la Montagne)
Telephone: (514) 288-5656
Open: Lunch, noon-2:30 P.M., Monday to Saturday;
dinner, 6 P.M.-10:30 P.M., Tuesday to Saturday
Wheelchair access: Yes
Reservations: Recommended
Cards: Major cards
Price range: Starters, $7.50-$51 (caviar); main courses, $22-$32; desserts, $6.50-$10.75

★★1/2	$ $ $	REVIEWED 01/01

LE MAS DES OLIVIERS

SNAPSHOT · Though the setting may not be the most glamorous, this downtown institution, still going strong after 29 years, continues to pack in local businesspeople and politicos, who come here to feast on French fries, grilled meats, fish soup, and serious red wines. But good food alone isn't enough to draw such a high-powered crowd. The friendly, confident wait staff who greet regulars by name might have something to do with it as well.

THE BIG PICTURE • Le Mas des Oliviers . . . sounds romantic, no? One imagines a picturesque old farmhouse restaurant surrounded by groves of silvery olive trees, where grilled fish arrive on glazed ceramic platters along with such side dishes as pissaladière, vegetable tian, aïoli garni, ratatouille, and—for spreading on crusty baguettes—plenty of that lusty olive and anchovy spread, tapenade. Visions of Peter Mayle's Provençal fantasy world dance through one's head. Think cloudy pastis, sunny afternoons, garlic-laden food, colourful locals with berets askew, and bottle after bottle of chilled rosé.

But hold on here. Montreal's Le Mas des Oliviers hardly fits that description. On most nights, the place is packed with rumpled businessmen and bottle-blond women feasting off plates mounded with French fries and indulging in plenty of red wine. Wonderful smells emanate from behind the kichen door. If ever there was a restaurant that brings out the appetite, it would have to be Le Mas des Oliviers.

In this establishment, things are kept simple. The food is classic French, neither bistro fare nor nouvelle cuisine. The relatively short menu features—among other classics—duck and beef filets with pepper sauce, onion soup, crème caramel, and profiteroles.

With so many of the city's restaurants vying for the upscale clientele who frequent Le Mas des Oliviers, one wonders what has kept this decidedly unglamorous Rue Bishop haunt going strong for the past 29 years. My guess would be the most endearing wait staff around. The waiters at Le Mas des Oliviers are charming, confident, and—most impressive in a room this crowded—ever-present. Like a general leading his troops, the elegant French maître d' has everything under control. Especially appreciated are his wine suggestions, which often include Californian bottles.

Starters include a charcuterie plate comprised of a chunky, garlicky pâté de campagne, melting thin slices of Bayonne ham, and a quenelle of rillettes that is just a tad dry. A shallow bowl of sautéed shrimp is served Basquaise style, which turns out to include spicy onion, pepper, garlic, and tomato sauce. The portion is generous and the shrimp, though firm, are neither dry nor rubbery.

The "pescadou et sa rouquine" is a long-standing house favourite. The pescadou is a fish soup, and the rouquine (which translates as "the redhead") is the name for its accompaniments: bright-orange rouille, peeled garlic cloves, and Gruyère cheese. Ask the waiter to explain the procedure, and—with much enthusiasm—he'll direct you to take a crouton, rub it with a clove of garlic, add a generous smear of rouille, cover it with cheese and set it atop the soup. When the crouton sinks to the bottom, the soup is ready for slurping. And what wonderful soup it is: full flavoured, tinged with lobster and pastis, and loaded with flakes of white fish.

Main courses include three excellent choices: panfried perch, rabbit with herbs, and an entrecôte à la moelle (with marrow). The perch is especially lovely, with its crisp skin and delicate alabaster flesh. The accompaniments include rice pilaf and a sauce similar to the Basquaise pepper, onion, and tomato mélange served with the shrimp.

The rabbit dish can be found in any region of France. This roasted lapin aux herbes is served in two parts: leg and sliced saddle. The meat is tender and flavourful (rabbit is so often dry and tasteless), and its accompanying thick brown jus has the pronounced flavour of fresh rosemary.

The medium-sized entrecôte is grilled to perfection: lightly charred on the outside, pink and juicy on the inside. Its bold red wine sauce provides a fine match. Only the marrow falls flat; the large pieces are flaccid, warm, and have little taste.

Not to be missed are the house French fries. You'll spot them at most tables, and after one taste you'll understand why. The fries are crisp on the outside, soft on the inside, and offer real potato flavour. The delicious homemade mayonnaise is perfect for dipping and worth every extra calorie.

Desserts include textbook profiteroles that are smothered in a chocolate sauce so delicious that the restaurant's owners should consider selling it commercially. Slices of chocolate terrine, set atop swirls of crème anglaise and coulis, are light and smooth.

IN THE KITCHEN · Chef Pierre Dominique.

DECOR, DRESS, AMBIENCE • The room is dark—grotto-like —with wide wood beams and low stucco ceilings. The only hint of olive trees is a plate of green olives and celery sticks in the middle of the table. The conservative crowd is made up of well-dressed women and bleary-eyed business types. Though the setting may be less than idyllic, the room is crackling with ambience.

WINE LIST • The wine list includes an impressive array of French offerings (from the $28 house wine to the Châteaux d'Yquems, Cheval-Blancs, and Lafites) and many fine international selections as well. In addition, there are ten daily specials priced between $50 and $70. Don't hesitate to ask the waiters for suggestions.

DON'T MISS • The fish soup, the roasted rabbit, the entrecôte, the French fries, and the profiteroles.

WORDS TO THE WISE • Though you won't get the ultimate Provençal experience at Le Mas des Oliviers, you'll probably have a wonderful time nonetheless. The party-hearty lawyer/accountant/politico/glamorous-dame crowd is tailor-made for serious people watching. The food is generally solid, and the courteous wait staff will make you feel like one of the regulars.

LE MAS DES OLIVIERS
1216 Rue Bishop (near Ste. Catherine)
Telephone: (514) 861-6733
Open: Lunch, noon-3 P.M., Monday to Friday;
dinner, 6:00 P.M.-11 P.M., Monday to Friday, 5:30 P.M.-11 P.M., Saturday, and 5:30 P.M.-10 P.M., Sunday
Wheelchair access: Yes
Reservations: Recommended
Cards: Major cards
Price range: Starters, $4-$12.50; main courses, $22.50-$32; desserts, $5-$6.50

★★★	$ $ $	REVIEWED 02/01

LE MITOYEN

SNAPSHOT · Only 30 minutes from downtown Montreal, this lovely old house is the ideal setting for a leisurely romantic dinner. Chef Richard Bastien uses only the best Quebec produce in his elegant and inventive cuisine du marché. Despite the long waits between courses, dinner at Le Mitoyen provides a gourmet experience at the highest level.

THE BIG PICTURE · Laval residents have a fabulous gourmet oasis in Richard Bastien's French restaurant, Le Mitoyen. After a drive less time-consuming than you'd expect (no more than 30 minutes from the city centre), you'll arrive in front of a lovely house, across from a church, in the middle of a quiet square in the village of Ste. Dorothée.

Unlike those of so many restaurants of this genre, Le Mitoyen's menu descriptions are simple one-liners. Though chef and owner Bastien is dedicated to using only the best Quebec produce, it's surprising to see that these ingredients are not specifically listed on the menu. Nonetheless, their high quality is apparent with every bite.

The roasted quail with caramelized wild cranberry sauce is the ideal introduction to Bastien's style. The small bird is prepared in two ways: the legs as a confit, and the breast sautéed to order. The pieces are then stacked on top of a lightly seared polenta cake and surrounded with a red pepper fondu, a few leaves of steamed spinach, and a potent cranberry sauce. Here's a dish with every ingredient exploited to its fullest: the quail's dark and white meats cooked separately, the polenta's creamy texture enhanced with a crust, and the cranberry and caramel sauce providing a sweet and sour enhancement. This isn't just good cooking, it's smart cooking.

Equally pleasing is the hot foie gras. Unlike so many restaurants, which skimp on foie gras, Le Mitoyen offers an ideal portion size (at $19.50, the price is ideal too). Three foie gras medallions are perfectly seared and placed on a poached pear half, the whole swirled with a reduced cider sauce.

The caribou-stuffed ravioli—not listed on the menu—provides an interesting surprise. The half-moon-shaped pasta pockets are served with a creamy caribou stock and curry sauce. Curry and caribou isn't a combination you'll come across every day—talk about strange bedfellows—but it works.

Although the couples dreamily looking into each other's eyes in this candlelit room don't seem aware of it, waits between courses can be long. Granted, a meal of this quality should be taken at a leisurely pace, but at this rate, even the most voluble conversationalist is likely to run out of material.

Three popular main courses are duck magret, veal filet, and ostrich medallion. The duck, with a honey-spice sauce, caramelized onions, and a rice mix (Basmati and wild, with almonds), definitely shows potential, were it not for the meat. Not only is the breast undercooked, but there's also a thick layer of white fat under the skin.

Tender enough to slice with a butter knife, the veal filet is obviously Quebec's finest. The accompaniments—barley risotto and sautéed black trumpet mushrooms—are elegant and well matched.

The ostrich filet is another winner. The rich red meat, which is served with a bold red wine sauce, has a flavour and texture somewhere between roast beef and venison. This is as far from chicken, or any other fowl, as you'll get. At its side are sautéed shiitake mushrooms and organic root vegetables: salsify, yellow carrots, and fingerling potatoes.

Come dessert time, try the soft chocolate cake. It will take an extra 15 minutes to prepare, but it's worth the wait. Despite its too-warm temperature and soupy consistency, the vanilla crème brûlée is rich and delicious. The chocolate tart, served with ginger and praline ice cream, is good, though hardly memorable. The fruit-stuffed crêpes provide an unwelcome surprise. They're rolled, sushi-style, with fruit and rice, and they come with a passion fruit sorbet and two fruit dipping sauces. It's nice, but a bit much.

Service is cordial and professional, even if a little lacking in warmth (there's a fine line between distant and warm, and the waiters here seem to err on the side of distant).

IN THE KITCHEN • Chef and owner Richard Bastien.

DECOR, DRESS, AMBIENCE • The elegant dining room, with its dark-orange walls, wood-beamed ceiling, and simple, country-style accoutrements—including an especially eye-catching straw rooster—offers the ideal combination of modern and classic comfort, a decor perfectly in line with Bastien's modern French cuisine.

WINE LIST • The wine list at Le Mitoyen is fairly priced, and though there are only a few half bottles, the in-house sommelier may recommend one of the six fine choices available by the glass.

DON'T MISS • The foie gras, the roasted quail, the caribou ravioli, the veal filet, the ostrich, and the vanilla crème brûlée.

WORDS TO THE WISE • Those weary of the downtown scene, with its lack of parking, crowds, and slushy streets in the winter, should add this Ste. Dorothée restaurant to their list (especially West Islanders, who live close by). With its intelligent cuisine du marché, top-notch regional products, and romantic setting, Le Mitoyen is certainly worth the trip.

LE MITOYEN
652 Place Publique, Ste. Dorothée, Laval
Telephone: (450) 689-2977
Open: 6 P.M.-10 P.M., Tuesday to Sunday
Wheelchair access: Yes
Reservations: Recommended
Cards: Major cards
Price range: Starters, $6.50-$19.50; main courses, $24.50-$29.50; desserts, $7.50; four-course table d'hôte menu, $34.50

★★1/2	$ $ $	REVIEWED 08/00

LE MUSCADIN

SNAPSHOT · With its candlelit setting framed in dark wood panelling and background sounds of Italian arias, Le Muscadin may appear to be nothing more than another restaurant of yesteryear. But you might be surprised to find as many locals here as tourists, enjoying a family celebration or a couple's night out. Good choice, as this Old Montreal favourite offers traditional Italian Canadian cuisine as well as a romantic ambience, friendly service, and a wide selection of fine Italian wines.

THE BIG PICTURE · A tuxedoed waiter drops an egg yolk into a pristine copper bowl. Another yolk follows. He then adds a few tablespoons of sugar, along with a splash of sweet Marsala. With a large copper whisk, he whips the mixture over a low flame, creating the glossy yellow froth known in Italian as "zabaglione," and in French as "sabayon."

The diners look on in anticipation as he pours the warm, thick cream into two stemmed glasses filled with fresh strawberries, topping each of them with a miniature cannoli. In a final decadent flourish, he caps the dessert with a shot of Grand Marnier and, with pinkie fingers raised, proudly presents his creation to two lucky diners seated at a table of six. Six spoons immediately come crashing into the glasses — the other diners, unable to resist temptation, dive in too. The waiter rolls his cart away with a smile, reassured by the spoon-wrestling scene at the table that his bit of theatre has been a hit. What a restaurant moment!

There are many memorable moments at Le Muscadin. Occasionally, groups of waiters arrive at tables, candle-adorned cakes in hand, serenading celebrants with an enthusiastic rendition of "Happy Birthday." One regular customer, eating alone, is fawned over by the staff. And he's not alone. Every diner — tourist, regular, or newcomer — is given the royal treatment.

Le Muscadin's menu lists Italian Canadian food as traditional and comforting as the setting: soups, pastas, antipasti, meats, seafood, and even that Old Montreal mainstay, Dover sole. The initial offering, a basket of garlic bread topped with herbs and fresh tomatoes, is crusty and oh-so-gently flavoured with garlic.

Starters are one of the fortes of this restaurant, especially the soups. Cappelletti in brodo consists of a rich homemade chicken broth filled with stuffed pasta dumplings. Although the dumplings turn out to be veal tortellini and not the promised cappelletti, they are delicious just the same. The stracciatella is also a winner. Again, it's a chicken-stock-based affair, this time with the addition of scrambled eggs.

The Caesar salad is another good choice, for the romaine is crisp and the dressing provides a subtle, creamy coating of garlic, anchovy, and cheese. Better still is the fried zucchini. Not only are the slices light, perfectly browned, and grease-free, but also the vegetable itself is not in the least bit bitter, a common drawback with zucchini.

Main courses are definitely old school. The filet mignon with Gorgonzola is prepared by the waiter tableside. In a large copper pan, he melts a spoonful of butter and stirs in a generous portion of Gorgonzola, followed by a dash of cream. He rolls the pregrilled filet mignon in the sauce, pours in some Cognac, and sets it aflame. The meat is then carved into thin slices, covered in the reduced sauce, and served with potatoes and a mound of sautéed red peppers and onions. It's an old-fashioned dish, not one to eat every day, but still quite good, despite its decadence.

Also delicious is the vitello à la Parma. Veal scaloppini is prepared in many guises at Le Muscadin, and this one offers thin panfried slices topped with capicolo, tomato, and melted Mozzarella. The veal is tender, but it's the flavour accents—the spicy capicolo and the white-wine-and-veal-stock-enhanced jus—that take this dish a step above standard Italian Canadian fare.

But just when you think this kitchen can do no wrong come a few disappointments. A portion of panfried veal liver is marbled with an off-putting number of veins and has a bitter aftertaste. The tortellini with peas, prosciutto, and a cream-based tomato sauce offers pasta cooked past the ideal al dente, little prosciutto, and no more than five wizened peas floating around in the mix.

The biggest letdown by far is the risotto with porcini mushrooms, as the rice is overcooked and the grains are drowned in a thin sauce. Though redolent of porcini, it lacks any of the richness and creaminess so essential to a risotto.

Besides the splendid sabayon, desserts include a tiramisu that might have benefited from either a bit more sugar or a stronger alcohol boost. Though the cannoli and the almond cake are not made in-house, both are very good. The almond cake, with its crunchy, chewy baked marzipan crust, is especially memorable.

IN THE KITCHEN • Chef and co-owner Leonardo Iacono.

DECOR, DRESS, AMBIENCE • The room is framed by dark wood panelling and enhanced with the background sounds of Italian romantic ballads. Young couples sit holding hands. Regular patrons are greeted at the door with gentle backslaps and firm handshakes. As the chafing dish makes the rounds, you'll see flashes of flambéed Cognac across the room through the glass-doored cabinets filled with prestigious wines and sparkling goblets.

WINE LIST • Le Muscadin's renowned 10,000-bottle wine list offers excellent choices at all price points, including many bottles in the $40 range. Wine connoisseurs are treated not only to exquisite stemware, but also to an elaborate decanting ceremony involving a decanting stand, a lit candle, and a silver-topped carafe. It's a rare bit of restaurant magic, a scene sure to impress even the snootiest oenophile. One problem is that there are only two wines available by the glass—one red and one white, both mediocre.

DON'T MISS • The soups, the fried zucchini, the Caesar salad, the veal, and the sabayon.

WORDS TO THE WISE • While there is the occasional faux pas at Le Muscadin, you'd never know it by looking at the customers, who couldn't appear happier to be here. From the rose-coloured parlour chairs to the waiter who, on a busy Saturday night, runs to the door to offer every woman a rose, this restaurant has charm to spare.

LE MUSCADIN
639 Notre Dame West (corner McGill)
Telephone: (514) 842-0588
Open: Lunch, noon-3 P.M., Monday to Friday;
dinner, 6 P.M.-10 P.M., Monday to Saturday
Wheelchair access: No
Reservations: Recommended
Cards: All major cards
Price range: Starters, $5.50-$11.50; main courses, $16.50-$36.50;
desserts, $4.50-$8.50

| ★★1/2 | $ $ | REVIEWED 04/01 |

LE PARIS BEURRE

SNAPSHOT · Disappointments are few at this authentic neighbourhood bistro, which specializes in cuisine bourgeoise, not haute gastronomie or conceptual cooking. It's honest fare—the kind of food you fantasize about when slicing through yet another pineapple-flavoured scallop. Start the evening at the bar, the ideal spot for soaking up the ambience while sipping a glass of Muscat de Beaumes-de-Venise.

THE BIG PICTURE · Tucked away on a nondescript block of Avenue Van Horne, with only a small blue neon sign as identification, Le Paris Beurre has been a popular destination for the past 16 years.

There are two menus at this Outremont eatery: the standard à la carte menu, and a weekly menu—"la formule"—that includes a soup with a starter and a main course. Poached leeks or steamed asparagus dressed with either a subtle curry or a balsamic vinaigrette provide a light start to the meal. Those up for something more filling should try the goat's cheese or gizzard (gésier) salad topped with ripe tomatoes, sliced red onion, and a generous dose of shallot vinaigrette.

The classic French pea soup, potage St. Germain, is thick, hearty, and perfectly seasoned. The fish soup is fishier than most, though pleasantly so, and its accompanying rouille is as spicy as it should be. Fish lovers may also enjoy the smoked herring. Served with sliced potatoes and dressed with a trickle of olive oil, this single herring filet has a delicate, melting texture and a gentle, smoky flavour.

Main courses are very good, simply and carefully presented, and certainly on a par with — if not superior to — the offerings at many Paris bistros. Lovers of red meat are well served at Le Paris Beurre, for both the skirt steak (onglet) and the filet mignon are a cut above. If you're out with a fellow carnivore, consider ordering the côte de boeuf for two. This large, thick rib steak is grilled, sliced, and presented in a copper pan; the slices range from well-done on the ends to medium-rare in the middle. The meat's flavour doesn't quite measure up to the aged and imported steak-house variety, but it certainly outshines the steaks served at many high-end restaurants.

Those not up for the rib steak might enjoy the duck. The confit is excellent: flavourful, not too greasy, and melting in texture. The pan-seared magret is ideally cooked with only a thin layer of fat topping flesh that is both pink and juicy. Delicious. Its sauce is simple: just deglazed pan juices enhanced with a few tangy cranberries. The accompanying vegetables include zucchini sautéed with tarragon, steamed potatoes, turnip, and carrots. Nothing jaw-dropping here, but satisfying just the same.

Yet not all is rosy. The roast rabbit, served with a rosemary and goat's cheese sauce, consists of an undercooked leg and an overcooked and dry saddle. Filet of tilapia, that increasingly popular white fish often described as a cross between turbot and sole, has a slightly metallic taste. It's correctly prepared and beautifully presented (covered with scalelike layers of sliced zucchini) but its pronounced flavour is off-putting — not one you'd be eager to try again.

It would be a sin to end a meal at Le Paris Beurre without dessert. There's a decadent poire Belle Hélène made with luscious vanilla ice cream and topped with a rich and thick chocolate sauce. The thin apple tart for two is worth the wait, as is the caramelized golden pineapple. A light chocolate mousse has the requisite frothy texture. And though the crème caramel is decidedly overcooked, the crème brûlée is the creamiest and most flavourful around.

Service is one of Le Paris Beurre's strong points. Every waiter or waitress here is well informed and friendly. Waits between courses are minimal, and you'll never pour your own wine—a small detail, perhaps, but in a restaurant this crowded, worth a mention.

IN THE KITCHEN • Chef Olivier Chaudet.

DECOR, DRESS, AMBIENCE • The L-shaped room, with its stained-wood floors, sponge-painted gold walls, paper-covered tables, and bistro chairs, appears to have been here for decades. Through a swinging door behind the bar and through small square windows in the dining room, one can see white-jacketed chefs busy at work. Past the bar and banquettes (the smoking section) nestled in the L, there's a reception room for private parties, and behind that, a 50-seat terrace—*the* place for warm-weather dining.

WINE LIST • The predominantly French wine list is simple and well priced. Two recent favourites include a $40 Cahors Clos Triguedina and a $48 Californian Kenwood Cabernet Sauvignon. The list also features a few prestigious bottles for those Outremont oenophiles who like to flaunt their wine knowledge.

DON'T MISS • The côte de boeuf, the duck, and the crème brûlée.

WORDS TO THE WISE • Le Paris Beurre is not Toqué!, La Chronique, or Les Halles, nor is a table here as sought-after as one at Montreal's premier bistro, L'Express. But for times when you'd rather chat with friends than analyse the meal, drink wine to your heart's content, and wear a pair of khakis instead of your best

Calvins, this restaurant serves up a near-perfect recipe of good food, pleasant surroundings, and congenial service.

LE PARIS BEURRE
1226 Avenue Van Horne (near Bloomfield)
Telephone: (514) 271-7502
Open: Lunch, 11:30 A.M.-3:30 P.M., Monday to Friday;
dinner, 5:30 P.M.-10:30 P.M., daily
Wheelchair access: Yes
Reservations: Recommended
Cards: Major cards
Price range: Starters, $3.75-$9.95; main courses, $15.95-$22.95; desserts, $4.50-$5.50

★★★1/2	$ $ $	REVIEWED 03/00

LE PASSE-PARTOUT

SNAPSHOT · Here is a top French restaurant where the accent is more on the food than on the setting. One goes to Le Passe-Partout for a gourmet experience par excellence. Chef and owner James MacGuire showcases the best local ingredients as well as his stellar technique. The understated atmosphere is welcoming and tranquil. One unique feature is a bakery attached to the restaurant that offers some of the best bread in the city.

THE BIG PICTURE · You can't miss the gourmets at Le Passe-Partout, that unobtrusive bakery/restaurant on an unglamorous corner of Boulevard Décarie. Glassy-eyed, they lovingly admire their plates before lifting the cutlery. They savour every morsel with their eyes half shut. They sip their wine slowly, speaking in muted tones, comparing notes with their equally obsessed companions. They're here to experience the work of chef James MacGuire.

MacGuire's world is one of flavour and texture, showcasing the best local ingredients. French cooking is a fusion of technique and terroir, and few understand this concept better than MacGuire. His style is pure market cuisine, handwritten on a menu that changes daily. Don't expect flashy plate presentations. Unlike many of the city's renowned chefs, a sense of the past clings to MacGuire's cuisine. Look no further than two recent amuse-bouches—cheese puffs (gougères) and ham-filled brioche —classic favourites reborn.

Following in the French tradition, everything at Le Passe-Partout is homemade, save the wine (though I wouldn't be at all surprised one day to see a bottle of Château MacGuire Baron-Lafrenière on the wine list). No other chef offers as personal a dining experience. Everyone serves bread, but few make their own. And nobody makes bread as beautifully as James MacGuire.

The cold appetizers, which are also available at the bakery next door, are mainstays of the menu. The plate of homemade charcuterie is a transformation of country-style meats into four-star-restaurant fare. The mousse de foie de volaille is dense, lush, and masterfully seasoned. MacGuire's duck terrine is chunky and flavourful, while his rillettes de Tours are fine-textured, rich, and melting—the hallmark of well-made rillettes. The house-smoked salmon, served in transparently thin, silky slices with a small cucumber, dill, and yogourt salad, is fresh tasting, lightly smoked and salted—simply divine.

A favourite hot appetizer—and one that goes beyond classic to modern nouvelle cuisine—is the delicate scallop flan served with tender mussels, sautéed spinach, and a pool of intense saffron cream sauce. Another is the hot foie gras, which is given novel treatment here, inlaid in a gâteau of pheasant mousse, wrapped in cabbage, and served with a stew of tiny wild mushrooms. I'd also recommend the squash soup. Swirled with heavy cream and perfectly salted, it's the ideal soup with which to enjoy a crusty slice of pain rustique.

When available, don't miss the duck magret with orange sauce and caramelized pineapple—a dish attributed to MacGuire's culinary mentor, the great French chef Charles Barrier. The rosé slices of duck are crisp-skinned and succulent, the golden pineapple pieces are lightly browned and bursting with sweetness, the orange sauce, dotted with zest, has a lovely tang, and the accompanying potato pancakes are light and crispy around the edges. Wow.

Equally delightful is the striped bass. The generous portion of steamed fish is meaty, meltingly tender, and moist, but it's the sunny Provençal accompaniments — tapenade and tian — that steal the show. The olive, anchovy, and caper tapenade is strong and salty — the most robust condiment around. The tian is intricately assembled into a perfect round of thin, layered slices of zucchini and tomato atop a mound of sautéed onion.

Desserts from MacGuire's kitchen are all charm. A Valrhona chocolate mousse is rich and delicious, if somewhat dry in texture. He pairs it with a luscious Grand Marnier crème anglaise and — an original touch — a thick slice of feathery homemade brioche. For something a bit lighter, try the crisp ladyfingers (biscuits cuillère) sandwiched together with lemon cream and served with strawberries, raspberries, and red fruit coulis. An apple and prune tart made with MacGuire's renowned puff pastry shatters at the touch of a fork and won't be fast forgotten.

IN THE KITCHEN • Chef and owner James MacGuire.

DECOR, DRESS, AMBIENCE • Entering the dining room through the bakery, you get the feeling you're at a secret neighbourhood club — a gourmet speakeasy. The dining room is not much of an attraction. It's small (about 40 places), peach in colour, and rectangular. All the warmth is generated by the charming, professional wait staff under the watchful eye of Suzanne Baron-Lafrenière, the mâitre d' and MacGuire's partner. Diners dress up, but not necessarily in their best. Noise levels are civilized.

WINE LIST • There's a small selection of French, Italian, and Californian bottles, most of which are affordable. Much thought and care has obviously been put into the selection. Enjoy a robust red wine, such as the Domaine de l'Hortus Pic St. Loup for $35 (or $7.50 a glass).

DON'T MISS • The charcuterie, the scallops, the duck, the striped bass, the cheese course, the chocolate mousse, and the homemade ice creams.

WORDS TO THE WISE • Although a meal at Le Passe-Partout is a true gourmet experience, it's not for everyone. Service can be slow on busy nights, and there are only two main-course offerings. Moreover, the restaurant is only open three nights a week, and only two days for lunch. Expect to hang up your own coat. But if you're one of those dedicated (or curious) food lovers in search of the best, you're in for something special. Not only will you walk away from a meal at Le Passe-Partout with a renewed love of French cuisine, but you'll also take home a complimentary loaf of MacGuire's famous bread.

LE PASSE-PARTOUT
3857 Boulevard Décarie (near Notre Dame de Grâce)
Telephone: (514) 487-7750
Hours: Lunch, noon-2 P.M., Tuesday and Friday; dinner, 6:30 P.M.-9:30 P.M., Thursday to Saturday
Wheelchair access: No
Reservations: Recommended
Cards: All major cards
Price range: Starters, $7.50-$11.75; main courses, $28.50; desserts, $7.50

★★★ $ $ $ REVIEWED 05/01

LE PIEMONTAIS

SNAPSHOT • Situated off the beaten track on an unglamorous strip of René Lévesque, east of St. Denis, this well-loved Italian restaurant, popular with celebrating families and the Radio Canada crowd, has been quietly garnering a loyal following since 1977. The cuisine is solid Italian Canadian fare and the wine list is both extensive and affordable. What has the crowds coming back for more is the crackling atmosphere and the professional, courteous service.

THE BIG PICTURE • Though we arrive at Le Piemontais on a busy Saturday night without a reservation, we are welcomed by the maître d' like regulars. Within seconds of being seated at the last available table, crisp fried chicken wings (offered gratis) arrive and drink orders are taken. The waiters do their utmost to please while always maintaining that professional distance. As do their counterparts in so many of Montreal's fine Italian restaurants, these black-vested gentlemen do everything right: dishes arrive like clockwork, cutlery is replaced without hesitation, knowledgeable wine recommendations are made, and grated cheese and pepper are offered before your fork hits the pasta (the waiters also somehow manage to look Italian, dropping the occasional "Grazie" and "Prego," even though most are French Canadian).

The hearty minestrone filled with beans, pasta, and chunky vegetables is as good as it gets. The beef carpaccio is okay—the garden variety. The antipasto plate with canned tuna, artichoke heart, marinated peppers, sliced salami, sardines, oyster mushrooms, and prosciutto and melon, all set around a hard-boiled egg, is good if hardly revolutionary. The Caesar salad is limp, obviously dressed too far in advance.

Main courses fare better. Classic pasta dishes—like penne arrabbiata, spaghetti Bolognese, and lasagna—are offered in both starter and main-course portions. Spaghetti carbonara, that wonderful mix of pasta, fried pancetta, Parmesan, heavy cream, and egg yolks, is a bit dreary, as the pasta is slightly overcooked and the sauce is more creamy than eggy. Baked pastas may be the best choice. Both the spinach-and-Ricotta-stuffed manicotti and the veal-filled cannelloni sauced with béchamel and a tangy tomato sauce are light and flavourful.

Meat dishes are also first-rate. A chicken paillard served with a butter-and-wine-based tarragon sauce is melt-in-the-mouth tender, and the accompanying vegetables—broccoli, cauliflower, roast potatoes—could have been prepared by a loving Italian grandmother. Equally tender and tasty is the saltimbocca Romana. This veal paillard is topped with sliced, sautéed prosciutto and mushrooms, a sprinkling of sage, and it's served with a side of buttered linguini filled with sun-dried tomatoes. Nothing flashy here, just Italian comfort food at its best.

Desserts are authentic, delicious, and, most importantly, made on the premises. A cocoa-dusted frozen tartufo, a dessert rarely made in-house, is scrumptious. Calorie-angst fades in the face of the multilayered cassata and the creamy spumone with raspberry coulis. Those up for the classic Italian egg-based zabaglione will not be disappointed, as the Piemontais version is frothy, delicate, laced with lusty Marsala, and warm—obviously made to order. When made like this, zabaglione is divine—a simple dessert to put all those tuile-laden concoctions to shame.

IN THE KITCHEN • Chefs Claudio DiStefano and Carmelo Maltese.

DECOR, DRESS, AMBIENCE • Le Piemontais is set in an intimate, low-ceilinged room seemingly decorated by a wealthy matron with a penchant for framed prints and the colour beige. The crowd, made up of couples, happy families, and the lunch-and-after-hours crowd from nearby Radio Canada, is animated. Noise levels are high (but pleasantly so), and the tables are close enough to facilitate everyone's favourite pastime: eavesdropping.

WINE LIST • The wine list is another drawing card. The variety and price range are customer-friendly, and there's a fine choice of half bottles and wines available by the glass.

DON'T MISS • The baked pastas, the meats, and the homemade desserts—especially the zabaglione.

WORDS TO THE WISE • Establishments like Le Piemontais succeed in reinforcing the original meaning of the word "restaurant," which is derived from the French word "restaurer," meaning to restore or rejuvenate. My stellar meals here had me rethinking my restaurant priorities. Sometimes it's not solely about the food. Sometimes it's about eating well while in the hands of people whose religion is your pleasure.

LE PIEMONTAIS
1145 Rue de Bullion (near René Lévesque)
Telephone: (514) 861-8122
Open: 11 A.M.-midnight, Monday to Friday; 5 P.M.-midnight,
Saturday
Wheelchair access: No
Reservations: Essential
Cards: Major cards
Price range: Starters, $4.75-$18.50; main courses, $15.75-$47.50;
desserts, $5.75-$8.50

★★1/2	$ $ $	REVIEWED 09/01

LE PUY DU FOU

SNAPSHOT • Dining in a small neighbourhood restaurant like
Le Puy du Fou now and then helps you to put all those trendy
places and fancy hotel dining rooms into perspective. Though the
food is modern French, owner Lionel Gautreau claims his restaurant has no one style and that the menu is based on what he and
chef Nadeige Séguin like to eat. Prices are a bit steep for a bring-
your-own-wine establishment, but rest assured that the quality of
the ingredients is right up there.

THE BIG PICTURE • There was a time when costly china, crystal
goblets, and tuxedoed waiters went hand-in-hand with high-
quality fare. Unfortunately, there are no such guarantees on
today's fine-dining scene; you can walk away from unpretentious
bistros with lasting impressions and leave grand restaurants disappointed.

My hunch is that the majority of restaurant-goers continue to
be seduced by the environment as opposed to the food. To test
this theory, I invited three of my usual dining companions (let's
call them DCs) to Le Puy du Fou, a 40-seat, bring-your-own-wine
bistro situated on a residential strip of Avenue Christophe
Colomb. Anticipating a high-end soirée, the DCs arrive elegantly

dressed, ties and all. Questions arise regarding the restaurant's whereabouts as we weave through the narrow streets of the Plateau. Eyebrows rise as I pull up to the front of this nondescript restaurant and we enter carrying two bottles of wine.

I'm immediately taken with the place. We are greeted like regulars and shown to a corner table set with sparkling stainless steel cutlery and gleaming stemware on an immaculate tablecloth. Though I'm happy to be here, I sense that the DCs, loosening their ties, are underwhelmed.

A simple soup or salad is offered gratis at the outset of the meal. This is preceded by croutons spread with black or green olive tapenade and followed by a choice of about six starters, six mains, a cheese course, and dessert.

After a long wait, the soups and salads arrive. The vegetable soup is decidedly lacklustre, but the green salad, made of frisée lettuce, a few cubes of tomato, and a feisty vinaigrette, is excellent. The other starters, though simple, are right on the money. A goat's cheese salad offers a creamy quenelle of chèvre (and a fine chèvre at that) enhanced with herbs, and arugula dressed with a trickle of thick balsamic vinegar. Homemade pâté de campagne has a meaty/moist texture; its flavour is both rich and complex, a balanced blend of chicken livers and pork. A smoked salmon charlotte consists of a sheet of smoked salmon swirled around a fresh cheese, pink grapefruit, and chive filling, topped with baby watercress (tiny enough to be deemed "microcress"). The fish soup is thick, garlicky, and filled with flakes of snapper and pickerel. Alongside are the usual accoutrements: saffron-enhanced rouille, grated cheese, croutons, and a clove of garlic.

Once the crowd thins out, service picks up and main courses arrive in due time. The quail is fried and served cut into quarters that are crisp on the outside and succulent within. The pieces are set around a mound of thick beet risotto, which at first bite tastes sweet but after a few more bites becomes interesting. The doré (pickerel), cooked in paper (en papillote) with lemon rounds and sliced artichoke heart, is moist, fresh, and delicate.

In sharp contrast to the fish is the meaty duck magret with star anise. Though the edges are a bit tough, the centre slices are tender and ideally cooked (crisp skin, no fat, pink interior).

Lamb shank prepared confit-style (slow-cooked in fat like a duck leg) is not for the faint of palate. It's a rich, flavourful hunk of meat, which falls from the bone at the slightest touch of the fork—a dish serious lamb lovers are sure to remember.

The cheese course includes six varieties, many of them local. For dessert, your best bet is the crème brûlée with griottines. Not only is the cream perfectly cooked and caramelized, but the pungent, Kirsch-soaked cherries add a welcome burst of acidity to every velvety mouthful.

IN THE KITCHEN • Chef and co-owner Nadeige Séguin.

DECOR, DRESS, AMBIENCE • The decor is simple—sponge-painted walls, a large framed mirror, a small bistro bar, urns of dried flowers, and other French country bric-a-brac. The ambience is electric; the customers seem happy, conversing loudly about current events in both official languages.

WINE LIST • Le Puy du Fou is a bring-your-own-wine restaurant.

DON'T MISS • The goat's cheese salad, the quail, the duck magret, the braised lamb shank, the cheese course, and the crème brûlée with griottines.

WORDS TO THE WISE • On the whole, the food, though not flashy, is on a par with that of many of Montreal's higher profile restaurants, where the draw is the flashy decor or a star chef. The restaurant business is notoriously tough and unforgiving. Remove the pretense, reduce the number of seats, focus on the food, take a hands-on approach, and, in my books, you have a winner. As one such establishment, Le Puy du Fou is worth applauding.

LE PUY DU FOU
4354 Avenue Christophe Colomb (corner Marie Anne)
Telephone: (514) 596-2205
Open: 5:30 P.M.-10:30 P.M., Tuesday to Saturday
Wheelchair access: No
Reservations: Essential
Cards: Major cards (and Interac)
Price range: Starters, $7-$9; main courses, $20-$26;
desserts, $5-$6

★★1/2	$ $ $	REVIEWED 10/00

LES CHENÊTS

SNAPSHOT · An evening at Les Chenêts remind us of the days
when haute cuisine was ruled by rotund French chefs wielding
large quantities of butter, cream, and filet mignon, and sommeliers seducing us with rare wines and potent digestifs. For three
decades now, this legendary restaurant has been offering Montrealers classic French dishes like coq au vin, frog's legs, and Dover
sole in a civilized, haute bourgeois setting. Though the gargan-
tuan wine list is one of the finest in North America, many of the
impressive wines and rare Cognacs may be too pricey for most
customers.

THE BIG PICTURE · Whenever my faith in the world of haute
cuisine is quashed by a meal of watermelon risotto, tuna with
brown sugar sauce, and cloudberry crème brûlée, I reach with
desperation for the bible of haute cuisine, the *Larousse Gastro-
nomique*. I find great comfort in flipping through this 1,200-
page tome, soaking up the historical references, the recipes, and
thousands of pictures. From sauce Albufera to vol-au-vent pastry
shells, the Laurousse is *the* reference for traditionalists, who tend
to look down on today's emerging "world cuisine." Les Chenêts
is the ideal restaurant for such epicurians. The ultraclassical menu

is right out of second-year cooking class. The list of selections—escargots bourguignonnes, soupe à l'onion, filets de boeuf Rossini—seems endless, without a whiff of anything ethnic or "nouvelle."

At a recent meal, the first round of starters includes rabbit terrine, cream of watercress soup, and truffled foie gras. The rabbit terrine is the clear winner. This thick slice of pâté, served with a spoonful of chopped aspic, is perfectly seasoned and clearly tastes of rabbit (so many terrines taste only of meat). Though soups are usually a reliable choice in French restaurants, this cream of watercress is a dud. Not only does it lack the fresh, peppery taste of watercress, but also its temperature is no more than lukewarm. Also disappointing is the foie gras. Although the presentation is lovely (the slice of liver arrives on an eye-popping checkerboard-patterned aspic base that must have taken the chef hours to create), the foie gras is grey, cold, and lacking in flavour. The four accompanying toast points are plain white bread, not buttery brioche—the ideal match for foie gras.

The second round of appetizers fare somewhat better. A seafood feuilleté consists of a generous portion of scallops, shrimp, and lobster covered in a cream sauce that's sinfully rich and delicious. Equally decadent, and also topped with a feather-light square of puff pastry, is a bowl of escargots Chablisienne—large, plump snails swimming in a creamy sauce enhanced with mushrooms and white Burgundy wine. On the lighter side is a hearts of palm salad dressed with a mustard vinaigrette so perfectly balanced that one wishes Les Chenêts would sell it commercially.

Main courses include beef Wellington, duck with Cointreau, and a halibut and salmon duo. The filet of beef is toothsome, but instead of being a pastry-wrapped parcel, it's a far less glamorous slice in a ring of soggy pastry with a smear of mushroom duxelles and a button of foie gras in its centre—hardly as luxurious as one would have expected.

I wouldn't hesitate to recommend the duck with Cointreau. The texture of the breast meat is melting, and the flavour, well enhanced with a generous shot of orange liqueur, is superb.

The fish duo, dubbed "Le Délice de Chambord," makes one yearn for somethig modern. The two delicate filets, blanketed in thick, buttery sauces (hollandaise and beurre blanc), are a far cry from today's simple grilled fish with lemon. The accompanying broccoli purée also holds little appeal.

It would be a shame to end a French meal without dessert, especially one of the excellent ones offered here. The Grand Marnier parfait is heavenly. The crêpes Suzette are served with a caramel sauce that is both liqueur-laced and assertively orange. My only complaint is that they aren't prepared tableside, eliminating half the fun.

Service at this establishment is friendly, well paced, and professional.

IN THE KITCHEN • Chef and owner Michel Gillet.

DECOR, DRESS, AMBIENCE • Hundreds of different-sized copper pots adorn the walls of the narrow, two-level dining room. The room is very quiet, with many customers hardly speaking above a whisper. Though times have changed, this remains the kind of restaurant reserved for special occasions, a place worthy of a jacket and tie and expensive jewellry.

WINE LIST • There are a staggering 48,000 bottles on this list, which sits, like an original leather-bound copy of the unabridged *Oxford English Dictionary*, on a wooden bookstand in a corner. The heavy, plasticized pages contain handwritten listings of Burgundies, Bordeaux, Sauternes, Reislings, Champagnes, and the most extensive collection of Cognacs in the world (certified in 1999 by *The Guinness Book of World Records*). Choosing a wine from such a heady list is a challenging and intimidating task. But you'll soon discover that most of the wines are out of range price-wise or listed as part of the restaurant's "collection" (i.e., not for sale). With a few words of advice from the maître d', you'll be fine, though you might end up with a run-of-the-mill selection found on many wine lists around town.

DON'T MISS • The rabbit terrine, the seafood feuilleté, the duck with Cointreau, and the crêpes Suzette.

WORDS TO THE WISE · This restaurant wouldn't be my first recommendation for ambitious gourmets. But for those who still revel in the past or are searching for a taste of days gone by, Les Chenêts provides a civilized, high-class dining experience with plenty of old-fashioned savoir faire.

LES CHENÊTS
2075 Rue Bishop (near de Maisonneuve)
Telephone: (514) 844-1842
Open: Lunch, 11:30 A.M.-3 P.M., Tuesday to Friday; dinner, 5:30 P.M.-11 P.M., daily
Wheelchair access: No
Reservations: Recommended
Cards: All major cards
Price range: Starters, $5.50-$12.50; main courses, $23-$39; desserts, $4.25-$7; four-course table d'hôte menu, $35

★★	$ $ $	REVIEWED 11/99

LES CONTINENTS

SNAPSHOT · If you've already dined at Les Continents, it may have been for one of the table d'hôte specials featuring international menus prepared by guest chefs. If not, you may be disappointed. Like many modern establishments experimenting with fusion flavours and towering plate presentations, Les Continents is attempting to create "world food à la Montréal"—an attempt that falls flat, as the underlying style is classic. Your best bet may be the lunchtime table d'hôte, even if service can be slow.

THE BIG PICTURE · "I had no idea this restaurant was here," says my friend, a resident of Old Montreal, only a stone's throw away. Where are we? At Les Continents, the Hôtel Inter-Continental's upscale restaurant, tucked away in a far corner of the lobby.

In keeping with the name of the restaurant, the menu features favourites of many continents—from Italian penne primavera and French châteaubriand to Indian tandoori chicken and Japanese sushi. The around-the-world-in-80-plates concept is fine, but it seems incongruous when the catchphrase "We promote local products" is printed on the menu.

Everything—from the luxuriously heavy silver-plated cutlery to the perfectly rolled, room temperature butter balls—looks promising. The handsome maître d' arrives to serve the wine. He flashes a charming smile as he slowly eases the cork out of the bottle. Every gesture is studied. Alas, the wine is room temperature—an inexcusable faux pas (room temperature white wine is nothing short of awful). With eyebrows arched, the maître d' immediately submerges the bottle into a bucket of ice, claiming the bottle has come straight from the refrigerator.

Though the service is taken at a slow pace, the appetizers—sea scallops with endives, pink peppercorns, and Pernod, and a green vegetable soup—are heavenly. The combination of sweet, succulent scallops, slightly bitter braised endive, subtle licorice cream sauce, and fruity sharp peppercorns is utterly delicious. The green vegetable potage, unfortunately served warm, has a nice flavour that might have been even better if not for the pronounced taste of fennel.

A plate of duck carpaccio with tabouleh and shredded Pecorino cheese is dominated by a large, pyramid-shaped mound of tabouleh circled by a fan of thinly sliced carpaccio and a small pile of fancy lettuces. Although the portion of duck is small and the lettuce is undressed, the tabouleh is tasty.

The main-course plates of sliced filet of ostrich with a Tatin of endives caramelized in Grand Marnier, and Asian-style orange roughy coated with basil tapenade and crispy vegetables are disappointing. Ostrich may sound tempting, but few have mastered its preparation. Though cooked to the requested medium-rare, the thinly sliced filet is chewy and dry, and the meat lacks intensity of flavour. The accompanying brown sauce made with citrus fruit zest is quite good but insufficiently assertive to enliven the meat. The endive Tatin turns out to be no more than a tiny triangle of sweet endive set atop a soggy piece of puff pastry.

The roughy is colourful and beautifully presented in a bamboo steamer. It's accompanied by white sushi-style rice packed into tight rolls and sprinkled with black sesame seeds. Though properly cooked, the fish is bland and dreary (to be fair, this dish is listed as "heart smart," so perhaps that explains the blandness).

Desserts include a better than average crème brûlée that's rich and creamy, with a perfectly crisp golden caramel topping. The fruit tart, made with buttery pastry and topped with fresh berries, is also delicious, even if a little coulis on the plate would have spun it to a higher level.

IN THE KITCHEN • Executive chef Christian Lévesque.

DECOR, DRESS, AMBIENCE • Les Continents is one of the most elegant dining rooms in the city: a sophisticated setting framed in caramel-coloured wood and decorated in muted tones of beige, with wide-slatted venetian blinds shading floor-to-ceiling windows. Hung from the middle of a vaulted ceiling is a stunning chandelier covered with hundreds of wrought-iron leaves, providing the type of soft light wrinkled movie stars adore.

WINE LIST • Though the list is well varied, prices tend to be steep.

DON'T MISS • The sea scallops, the duck carpaccio, and the desserts.

WORDS TO THE WISE • There's no question that the room is beautiful and a that a meal here can be quite satisfying. Service, however, can be a problem, especially when waiters serving high-priced bottles forget that it's their job to pour your wine during the meal. Be on the lookout for one of the establishment's international festivals, when you can try one of the less expensive table d'hôtes dedicated to a single foreign cooking style.

LES CONTINENTS
360 Rue St. Antoine West (in the Hôtel Inter-Continental)
Telephone: (514) 987-9900
Open: 6:30 A.M.-11:30 P.M., daily
Wheelchair access: Yes
Reservations: Recommended
Cards: All major cards
Price range: Starters, $4.75-$13.95; main courses, $16.25-$29.50;
desserts, $5.25-$6.50

★★★	$$$$	REVIEWED 04/01

LES HALLES

SNAPSHOT · Celebrating its thirty-second anniversary in 2002, Les Halles, Jacques and Ita Landurie's beautiful restaurant, still offers Montrealers a true taste of old-fashioned French gastronomy. With its Parisian-market decor, lavish food, formal service, and French wine list impressive enough to dazzle connoisseurs, Les Halles continues to provide a very grown-up—very French—night of fine dining for well-heeled locals and tourists.

THE BIG PICTURE · Les Halles was the first restaurant to make my taste buds quiver. The occasion was my eighteenth birthday, and the only gift I requested was dinner at this, Montreal's best restaurant. I sat with friends and family at a large table near the front window, soaking up the opulence and decadence of it all. I listened, enraptured, as our very French, tuxedoed waiter recited the daily specials, including force-fed this, caviar that, and sauces with French names they never taught us in high school.

Then, taking a glance at the menu, I spotted a shrimp bisque priced at a startling $18. I turned to my father and apologized for choosing such an expensive restaurant, offering to exit immediately, before anyone had ordered. "That's all right, kid," he answered, unknowingly opening the door for many expensive dinners to come. We proceeded to indulge in a multicourse meal worthy of Escoffier himself. I slurped up that pricey bisque, rolled my tongue around a cream-sauced veal dish, sampled a few pungent cheeses, and stuffed myself silly on several of the magnificent desserts presented at the table. It was a flawless feast, and I still can recall every detail. But years would pass before I'd return for seconds.

Les Halles is a very grown-up restaurant. It's frequented primarily by well-heeled businesspeople who obviously enjoy being fawned over by the stellar wait staff. The menu, though classic French, is less cream-and-butter-laden than in the past—call it "Escoffier lite." It's also long, with many daily specials and an additional table d'hôte. Long menus can indicate a lack of focus, but at Les Halles the kitchen is as focused as they come, thanks to seasoned executive chef Dominique Crevoisier.

The cream of carrot soup has a fresh carrot flavour and is enhanced ever so slightly with the peppery zing of fresh ginger. Also pleasantly gingery is a half lobster served in its shell, topped with grated coconut, and enlivened with a Sauternes sauce. Here is lobster at its best—correctly cooked and adventurously flavoured; sweet, yet piquant and exotic.

One cannot dine at Les Halles without giving in to the temptation of foie gras. One fine choice is the Brome Lake duck breast with hot foie gras. The duck liver is exquisite, perfectly pan-seared, with the desirable pudding-like interior. The thick slices of duck breast are also excellent: crisp-skinned, barely fatty, and cooked just past medium-rare. The entire dish is beautifully arranged, with the meat and vegetables fanned out around the plate as opposed to stacked in the centre. My only complaint is the lack of a sweet element in the composition, always a pleasurable contrasting accent to the earthy flavours of duck and foie gras.

The salmon, from the "Sea & Stream" section of the menu, arrives flash-broiled and sliced into small filets. The pink flesh is fresh, light, and delicate. Only the accompaniments disappoint. The ratatouille is strong and salty, and the green vegetable flan has no discernible green vegetable flavour.

From the section entitled "Animals from the Farm" comes veal with basil and mustard sauce. The three large medallions are melt-in-the-mouth tender, and the assertive basil and mustard cream sauce is absolutely divine.

Desserts are a treat at Les Halles—old-style pâtisserie Française at its best. Of the cakes and tarts presented at the table (including a sumptuous St. Honoré, a rectangular Paris-Brest, and a glistening, pear-topped cheesecake), one of the best is a crisp almond tart topped with glazed fresh raspberries. Another is "Le Bavarois," a two-tiered chocolate and pistachio Bavarian cake that, unlike so many other moussey concoctions, actually tastes like chocolate and pistachio.

Service at Les Halles is terrific. The waiters are veterans who know the menu inside out. The quibble would be the occasional long waits (up to 45 minutes) between courses.

IN THE KITCHEN · Chef Dominique Crevoisier.

DECOR, DRESS, AMBIENCE · At Les Halles, the Landuries have captured the Belle Époque glow of Parisian restaurants such as Maxim's and Le Grand Véfour. It must have something to do with the way the silverware and the off-white linen reflect the glow of the table lamps. The faux Paris market setting, with its trompe-l'oeil panels and striped red-and-white awning, is straight out of *An American in Paris* (one expects Gene Kelly and Leslie Caron to come dancing around the corner). The diners may be formally attired here, but compared to the stuffy atmosphere of the past, today's ambience is welcoming—more bistro de luxe than high temple of gastronomy. Dust off your best outfit or business suit for dinner at Les Halles.

WINE LIST · Next to the smartly chosen, affordable wine lists of many newer restaurants, costly Burgundy-and-Bordeaux-laden lists such as that of Les Halles now seem old-fashioned. Nonetheless, it is impressive, and those willing to splurge will have plenty of choice. There are also affordable bottles for diners on a budget, even if they're fewer in number and hardly inspired.

DON'T MISS · The foie gras dishes, the lobster with coconut and Sauternes, the grilled salmon, and the veal with mustard and basil; desserts are an absolute must.

WORDS TO THE WISE · I wouldn't call an evening at Les Halles exciting. Very good? Yes. Classic French? Undoubtedly. Highbrow? Absolutely. For modern gourmets, though, the spine-tingling moments here may be in the past. Yet for those out for an occasion or a lavish gourmet experience, Les Halles is the place to be.

LES HALLES
1450 Rue Crescent (near Ste. Catherine)
Telephone: (514) 844-2328
Open: 6 P.M.-11 P.M., Monday to Saturday
Wheelchair access: No
Reservations: Recommended
Cards: Major cards
Price range: Starters, $5.50-$36; main courses, $19.95-$37.50; desserts, 6.95-$10

★★★	$ $ $	REVIEWED 05/00

LES REMPARTS

SNAPSHOT · You may have walked past the Auberge du Vieux Port in Old Montreal without an inkling of what was going on downstairs in its restaurant, Les Remparts, which is unlike so many of the old city's fusty French restaurants. Here you'll discover the contemporary cuisine of young Quebec chef Janick Bouchard, a cuisine that features prime local ingredients assembled with plenty of creativity. Service is solicitous, and the atmosphere is warm and romantic. The lunchtime table d'hôte offers great value.

THE BIG PICTURE · I'm at Les Remparts on a tip from a friend who tells me this basement restaurant is "my kind of place." He couldn't be more wrong. The combination of Old Montreal and a hotel restaurant—high prices, passé French cuisine, no parking—is hardly my cup of tea. And it appears I'm not alone, for on a recent Saturday night, only a handful of tables are occupied.

But hold on here. One look at the menu and my eyebrows rise: braised deer shanks, semismoked salmon with sweet potato gratin, and wild mushroom risotto. I'm intrigued. This is definitely not your typical Old Montreal fare.

I can't imagine a more interesting contrast to this Old World setting than the contemporary/classic cuisine of 27-year-old Janick Bouchard. This talented young chef, whose experience includes two years at Citrus under Normand Laprise and three years at Le Passe-Partout under James MacGuire (whom he still refers to as his guru), has been at Les Remparts for the past two years. A style based on five years with the innovator Laprise and the classicist MacGuire is bound to be intriguing.

Take, for example, Bouchard's version of mousse de foie de volaille. The large quenelle of chicken liver mousse is as perfectly seasoned and luscious as the well-loved Passe-Partout signature dish. But Bouchard takes it a step further by adding a stewed pear, mango, cranberry, and onion compote—a welcome boost of tang and sweetness.

Another starter pairs rich duck confit with goat's cheese and wraps them together in a crisp wonton purse. Even the smallest bites are bursting with flavour and well enhanced by the surrounding vegetable jus. Equally delicious are the homemade ravioli, which are filled with tender sweetbreads and set atop a mound of sautéed spinach. In lesser hands, this dish would surely be bland. But bold flavours are another of Bouchard's strengths, and these five silver-dollar-shaped pasta pillows are beautifully enlivened with a veal jus infused with sage.

Main courses are just as impressive. Tenderloin of boar is cooked rosé and served in thin slices fanned out over potato disks, the whole garnished with sautéed shiitake and morel mushrooms. Though this farm-raised boar hardly reaches the gamy heights of wild boar (not commercially available in Quebec), the meat is given a leg up by a confit of shallots and a potent wild mushroom sauce.

Not to be missed is the semismoked and grilled salmon. The lightly charred filet is served with a mound of puréed sweet potatoes topped with crisp sweet potato chips. Spear the fish with a fork and it separates into juicy chunks, which you can then coat with the accompanying coriander butter sauce. With such vivid colours, contrasting textures, and pure flavours, this certainly ranks as one of the most inspired salmon dishes around.

Two other main courses aren't quite there. A filet of beef is tender and perfectly pink, but both the meat and the marrow-herb topping lack flavour. Another dish, orange-stuffed guinea fowl with celery root and chestnut purée, also comes up short. The cooking is impressive in that the roasted breast is moist and the braised legs are tender, yet guinea hen, orange, and celery root turn out to be a pretty dull threesome.

Don't neglect the cheese selection, which, though small, offers high-quality French and Quebec cheeses, correctly served at room temperature.

Desserts are taken seriously at Les Remparts. Bouchard's version of the ever-popular molten Valrhona chocolate cake is served with chocolate ice cream and a swirling disk of hard caramel. A vanilla crème brûlée is sensuously silky, and its bruléed topping has a taste reminiscent of a campfire-toasted marshmallow. My favourite is the banana tart with coconut ice cream. A puff pastry base (as weightless and flaky as a supermodel) is topped with a few slices of soft, ripe banana and served with a scoop of terrific coconut ice cream.

Service is first-class. Informed, discreet, and thoroughly professional, the wait staff at both lunch and dinner is on a par with the city's best.

IN THE KITCHEN • Chef Janick Bouchard.

DECOR, DRESS, AMBIENCE • The decor is in the old-city style: French and pleasantly posh. Enclosed by a low ceiling and chunky, fortlike stone walls, sit well-spaced tables draped in thick white linen. Surrounding the tables are elegant burgundy chairs, high-backed banquettes, and antique mahogany furniture. Though somewhat dark (it is a basement), the overriding effect is more cozy than claustrophobic, and the low lights, soothing guitar music, and shaded candles add a undeniable air of romance to the room.

WINE LIST · The wine list is short and pricey, with many of the selections at close to three times their retail price (at least the bottles are decanted and masterfully served). Wines by the the glass may be the way to go; a full-bodied red Minervois, for example, is available for a mere $6.50.

DON'T MISS · The sweetbread ravioli, the chicken liver mousse, the boar, the grilled semismoked salmon, the cheese course, and the desserts.

WORDS TO THE WISE · Although prices here can be high, bear in mind that all the ingredients are top-notch. Those on tighter budgets should go for lunch, where the all-inclusive $15-to-$18 table d'hôte offers great value. A good time to try Les Remparts is during the international fireworks festival in July, when you can savour multicourse gastronomic dinners on the roof of the auberge with a clear view of the dazzling display.

LES REMPARTS
97 Rue de la Commune East (near St. Gabriel, in the Auberge du Vieux Port)
Telephone: (514) 876-0081
Open: Lunch, 11:30 A.M.-2 P.M.; dinner, 6 P.M.-10 P.M., daily
Wheelchair access: Yes
Reservations: Recommended
Cards: All major cards
Price range: Starters, $7.75-$19.95; main courses, $27.95-$34.95; desserts, $8-$9.50; lunch table d'hôte menu, $15-$18

| ★★★1/2 | $ $ $ | REVIEWED 06/01 |

LE ST. AUGUSTIN

SNAPSHOT • This quaint country restaurant, about half an hour north of Montreal, is a front for some of Quebec's best market cuisine. Le St. Augustin is an unpretentious 50-seat establishment where chef and owner Jean-Paul Giroux proves that with choice ingredients less is more. His food is sensational: vibrant, colourful, and assembled with style. Not only is this one of finest gourmet experiences in, or out of, the city, it's also one of the most affordable. There's an interesting and well-priced wine list too.

THE BIG PICTURE • Purslane is a herb that, more often than not, grows in gardens and fields as a weed. I first tasted it at L'Eau à la Bouche, and later at Toqué!, two Quebec restaurants renowned for their inventive use of local produce. With its young shoots and dark-green leaves, purslane has become quite fashionable in culinary circles, used either in spring salads or as garnish.

I spotted the first purslane sprout of the season propped against an amuse-bouche of cauliflower tabouleh and thin slices of saucisson de Morteau, not at a Relais & Chateau hotel or some downtown hot spot, but at Le St. Augustin.

I'm preparing to toss the purslane under my teeth when I notice, between the wedge-shaped leaves, salt. Not just any salt, but the best: sel de Guérande. That seasoned sprout speaks volumes about Le St. Augustin's chef and owner, Jean-Paul Giroux. Any man who takes the time to season a smidgen of garnish has got to be from France. His choice of salt points to Brittany. The use of purslane—and the other top-quality ingredients featured on his menu, such as Boileau venison, Alberta beef, Maine scallops, Quebec cheeses, and organically grown greens and vegetables— tells me that since arriving in Quebec five years ago, he's kept his eyes open and his ear to the ground.

Like so many of the young generation of French-trained chefs, Giroux has a technique that is solid and a touch that's light. Meats are pan-seared, vegetables are cooked al dente, greens are lightly dressed, and desserts are far from cloying. His heaviest sauce is a beurre blanc. And what a dreamy beurre blanc: lemony, chock-full of chives, swirled around a stack of petit-gris snails and julienned leeks and capped with a thin round of Parmesan.

The other starters are equally ethereal. A generous mound of freshly picked mesclun is ever-so-lightly dressed with carthame oil. Tender, crisp-skinned breast of quail is served with sautéed chanterelles and a trembling poached quail's egg trapped in a thick triangle of toast. A tomato bayaldi—peeled and seeded tomato gratinéed with creamed goat's cheese and a side of baby arugula—is a triumph. It's a masterful combination of three simple ingredients exploited to the fullest. The contrasting flavours, textures, and colours play off each other brilliantly.

Though time between courses tends to drag a bit (Giroux works with a kitchen staff of only three), rest assured that the waits are justified. All main courses are superb.

Roast venison sprinkled with more of that wonderful sea salt and served with pan juices, sweet roasted shallots, and wild mushrooms—oyster, shiitake, chanterelle—has the desired melting texture and lamb-meets-beef flavour. Filet of Alberta beef with a Cabernet sauce is equally toothsome, ranking up there with the most tender cuts of meat ever. Its accompaniments include baby vegetables and the fluffiest, most buttery dollop of mashed potatoes imaginable.

A breast of guinea hen is cooked to perfection—the alabaster flesh is delicate and moist; the skin is crisp and golden. Alongside the hen is a disk of Parmesan-enhanced polenta and pencil-thin white and green asparagus. Best of all may be the scallops. For a mere $19 (half the price of a similar dish downtown) come six spanking-fresh, marshmallow-sized scallops, ideally seared on the outside and silken within. They're set in a circle around baby vegetables and cooked spinach, and the whole is set in a pool of cream and Aperi d'Or-enhanced fumet. Wow.

As if further proof of this kitchen's excellence is needed, enter the desserts. They're all superb: toasted brioche with sautéed Cortland apples and maple ice cream; sautéed bananas and pears sandwiched between sugar cookies and topped with an intense caramel ice cream; and an almond milk crème brûlée, the only variation that outshines the classic.

IN THE KITCHEN · Chef and owner Jean-Paul Giroux.

DECOR, DRESS, AMBIENCE · The two-room restaurant is decorated in a no-frills country style. Dress is casual, and the ambience is quiet — perfect for conversation over a romantic dinner. But diners seated in the front of the restaurant may find the passing traffic distracting.

WINE LIST · The wine list is one of the best selected and affordable around. The excellent Cuvé Prestige Château Lamartine from Cahors costs a mere $40. With prices like these, nondesignated drivers should consider ordering an additional bottle, half bottle, or glass (for only $6.50) to go with the cheese course.

DON'T MISS · The salad, the snails, the scallops, the venison, the filet mignon, and the delicious desserts. And the cheese course is a must.

WORDS TO THE WISE · If you're the kind of diner whose priorities include serious art on the walls, silver flatware, crystal wine glasses, tuxedoed waiters, and harp music cascading in the background, Le St. Augustin is not for you. Here, the luxury is on the plate, not in the setting. And though the service is friendly and professional, you may want to brush up on your conversation skills so you can use them to fill the long waits between courses. Le St. Augustin is a gourmet's lair, where, in chef Giroux's hands, you're in for a unique and memorable experience.

LE ST. AUGUSTIN
15196 Rue de St. Augustin, St. Augustin de Mirabel
Telephone: (450) 475-8290
Open: 5 P.M.-10 P.M., Wednesday to Sunday
Wheelchair access: Yes
Reservations: Recommended
Cards: Major cards
Price range: Starters, $4.50-$8.50; main courses, $17-$24;
desserts, $5.50-$7; three-course table d'hôte menu, $27-$30, and
five-course table d'hôte menu, $37-$46.50

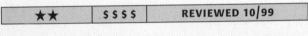

★★ $ $ $ $ REVIEWED 10/99

LES TROIS TILLEULS

SNAPSHOT · Since it opened in the mid-seventies, the restaurant of Canada's first Relais & Château hotel, the Hostellerie Les Trois Tilleuls, has been considered one of Quebec's finer examples of culinary sophistication. The good news is that not much has changed. The food is still classic French, the decor is still institutional country, and the best views of the nearby Rivière Richelieu are still to be had at lunchtime. But be warned: prices are steep.

THE BIG PICTURE · Like other surviving French restaurants of its era—La Sapinière, Les Halles, Les Chenêts—Les Trois Tilleuls is not about cutting-edge cuisine. Ask any waitress here, and she'll candidly tell you that they've tried to serve more modern fare, but the established clientele—comprised mostly of gourmet Montrealers and tourists—balks, demanding a return to the classics. End of story.

This is a good restaurant, save for one problem: consistency. The quail liver parfait, for example, offers a thick slice cut from a terrine that's overly large and far too rich to finish. A better choice of starter is the Richelieu Valley potage. The simple vegetable cream soup is right on—perfectly seasoned, and with a depth of flavour that could only have come from an intense homemade chicken stock.

Another delicious starter is the sweetbreads "façon Trois Tilleuls." A whole shelled lobster claw tops a round pile of sweetbreads layered with sautéed spinach and flecked with perfectly cooked lobster meat. This luxurious, colourful dish comes garnished with a single nasturtium blossom and is served with two matching sauces, lobster and veal.

Main courses reveal more ups and downs. A supreme of guinea hen with maple vinegar and red fruit is an up. Served fanned out next to a pile of warm strawberries and blueberries, the white meat is perfectly cooked, resulting in a melt-in-your-mouth texture. Better yet, the flavour is well matched with the tangy maple sauce.

Expertly prepared by the waitresses tableside, the five-pepper entrecôte features a deliciously creamy Cognac-enhanced pepper sauce. The problem is the taste-to-value ratio: one can easily find the same quality steak in many Montreal restaurants for about half the price.

The salmon and flounder duo comes with a strong butter sauce made from a local beer known as Gargouille. It's a dish worth trying, provided the fish is properly cooked. At times, it can be dry and overcooked, and the butter-beer sauce can be heavy and cloying.

The most satisfying course at Les Trois Tilleuls is dessert. The "Plaisir du Chef" consists of a light custard cream sandwiched between thin sugar wafers, a generous scattering of local wild blackberries, and an ambrosial scoop of strawberry sorbet.

The hot apple tart with vanilla ice cream features a crisp round of pastry covered in a circle of paper-thin apple slices. The homemade ice cream is served in a brandy-snap cookie basket garnished with sliced strawberries. If you're in the mood for chocolate, try the "Assiette Gourmande." The pairing of creamy white chocolate mousse, dark chocolate sorbet, and a chocolate fondant cake with a warm runny centre is sensational.

IN THE KITCHEN • Chef Jean-François Methot.

DECOR, DRESS, AMBIENCE · This restaurant features high-backed maple chairs set around large, linen-covered dining tables. The beamed ceilings and wood-panelled walls hung with Canadian landscapes make for an authentic country feeling. The surrounding terrace has groupings of Adirondack deck chairs arranged for optimum views of the Richelieu. In short, it's everything you'd expect a Quebec country inn to be.

WINE LIST · The wine list at Les Trois Tilleuls is lengthy and varied, with a marked emphasis on prestigious French wines. Prices are fair, and there's a nice little selection of half bottles. A bit surprising for a restaurant of this calibre is the fact that there's no sommelier on hand to answer questions and provide guidance.

DON'T MISS · The sweetbread and lobster starter, the guinea hen, and the fabulous desserts.

WORDS TO THE WISE · Les Trois Tilleuls is situated to take full advantage of its superb location on the banks of the scenic Rivière Richelieu. This is a "destination" restaurant, the kind of place you plan your Sunday drive in the country around. At lunch, prices are more reasonable, and one can see more of the surrounding countryside. The desserts, in particular, make the half-hour drive from Montreal worthwhile.

LES TROIS TILLEULS
290 Rue Richelieu, St. Marc sur Richelieu
Telephone: (514) 856-7787
Open: Lunch, 11:30 A.M.-2:30 P.M.; dinner, 5:30 P.M.-10:00 P.M., daily
Wheelchair access: Yes
Reservations: Recommended
Cards: All major cards
Price range: Starters, $6.50-$17.50; main courses, $32.50-$39.50; desserts, $8.50-$9.75; four-course lunch table d'hôte menu, $18.75

| ★ ★ | $ $ $ | REVIEWED 08/99 |

LE SURCOUF

SNAPSHOT • For the past 23 years, the Bonnot family has been serving traditional French cuisine in this elegant dining room in the heart of Ste. Anne de Bellevue. Muted lighting, dark wood-work, and nineteenth-century paintings help create the perfect backdrop for the classic cuisine and formal service. House specialties include lobster bisque, rack of lamb, Dover sole, and profiteroles. The predominantly French wine list is well selected and reasonably priced.

THE BIG PICTURE • Le Surcouf resides in an Edwardian house set a short distance back from Rue Ste. Anne in the heart of the village of Ste. Anne de Bellevue. Although the place looks like it has seen better days, appearances can be deceiving. This West Island restaurant has plenty to offer.

We're shown to a table by a friendly young woman, Dominique Bonnot, the daughter of owner Michel Bonnot. Bonnot père is a Frenchman, originally from Marseilles, and he has been running Le Surcouf for 23 years.

The menu is textbook French and as traditional as the setting. Of the starters, standouts include a perfectly dressed endive salad, a cold and refreshing cucumber-yogourt soup, and a Cognac-enhanced lobster bisque. Both soups, however, are in dire need of salt (perhaps this restaurant prefers to leave the salting to the customers).

An aspic of leek, goat's cheese, and tomato is an interesting idea, even if an aspic casing may not be the best way to exploit these ingredients; aspic jelly must be served very cold to maintain its structure, whereas the cheese and vegetables lose much of their flavour when chilled below room temperature.

A shared rack of lamb, presented in its entirety on a platter surrounded by a bouquetière of vegetables, turns out to be quite an event. The waiter takes the platter over to the sideboard, where he carves the two racks into portions and divvies up the vegetable bouquets. The small New Zealand lamb chops are perfectly cooked and flavoured with a rosemary crust. The vegetables are well seasoned and delicious. Unfortunately, neither sauce nor pan juices are served with this dish, making it seem incomplete somehow.

The Dover sole is presented in the same manner, then boned and plated at the sideboard. The three thin filets are topped with brown butter and served with many of the same vegetables as the lamb. The fish is firm and delicate, just a bit flaky, and it has a fresh flavour.

Next to the large portion of lamb, the veal medallions with morel sauce seems small. The two sautéed veal medallions are smothered in a thick, cream-based morel sauce and served with the same medley of vegetables.

Desserts are traditional. The profiteroles, the best of the lot, are smothered in a dark, shiny bittersweet chocolate sauce. The crème caramel, cheesecake, and chocolate mousse are all pretty ordinary and, surprisingly, garnished with fennel leaves (no mint?).

Service is friendly and polished, giving one the impression of being a guest at a friend's dinner party.

IN THE KITCHEN • Chef and partner Serge Magnier.

DECOR, DRESS, AMBIENCE • One can't help but be charmed by the surroundings when entering the front hallway. The dining room is framed in dark woodwork with burgundy wallpaper and nineteenth-century paintings. The space is split into three sections: a bright front porch with a view of Lac St. Louis, a front parlour with a fireplace, and a small room (the original dining room) close to the kitchen.

WINE LIST • The wine list is short and French, with wines fairly priced at no more than twice their retail value.

DON'T MISS • The soups, the rack of lamb, the Dover sole, and the profiteroles.

WORDS TO THE WISE · Given that the appeal of classic French restaurants may be on the wane, it's nice to see a hardworking family like the Bonnots at the helm of a fine French restaurant, keeping the old flag proudly aloft. This West Island location is a good half-hour drive from the city centre, but that can be a good thing when an out-of-town excursion is planned.

LE SURCOUF
51 Rue Ste. Anne, Ste. Anne de Bellevue
Telephone: (514) 457-6699
Open: Lunch, 11:30 A.M.-1:30 P.M., Tuesday to Friday;
dinner, 5:30 P.M.-10 P.M., Tuesday to Saturday
Wheelchair access: Yes
Reservations: Recommended
Cards: All major cards
Price range: Starters, $4.95-$10.25; main courses, $18.95-$29;
desserts, $4.95-$8; three-course table d'hôte menu, $23-$31

★★1/2	$	REVIEWED 12/99

LE TAJ

SNAPSHOT · Le Taj's lunchtime buffet is popular with students, university professors, and adventurous businesspeople addicted to the comforting spiciness of Indian food. At dinner, the place comes to life as one of the city's most exotic dining destinations. The assorted classic curries and tandoor-baked flat breads and meats awaken the senses, every bite offering something new. Prices, thankfully, are less jarring than a mouthful of curried carrots. The traditional Indian decor is matched by friendly and solicitous service.

THE BIG PICTURE · Le Taj's menu is divided into standard sections: soups, salads, appetizers, main courses, vegetable dishes, and desserts. Or you can choose a thali—a traditional silver or stainless steel tray that includes little bowls filled with vegetables, raita, dahl, pakoras, and a main-course curry of your choice.

The classic mulligatawny soup, made here with a lentil broth, is hearty, though it lacks the spicing that would justify the name ("mulligatawny" means "pepper water" in Tamil). Alongside are deep-fried papadams studded with cumin seeds, which are perfect for dipping into the fresh coriander chutney—a condiment so fiery with green chilies that it will make your eyes tear.

A selection of tandoor-baked flat breads, the staple of northern Indian restaurants, is outstanding. Buttery, multilayered parathas cut into wedges have a chewy, flaky texture. A large, teardrop-shaped naan is puffy and has a delicious flavour, similar to a grilled pancake or popover. From a platter of assorted appetizers comes seekh kabab, a tandoor-roasted cylinder of minced lamb, redolent of cinnamon and cloves. Another spicy appetizer, onion pakoras, have a gentle onion flavour, the chickpea-flour batter forming a light, crispy crust. The deep-fried potato patties called aloo tikke, and the potato-and-pea-filled samosas, are surprisingly ordinary, even when dipped into the assorted condiments: pickled carrots, yogourt and mint sauce, and that searing coriander chutney.

Service at Le Taj is friendly, professional, and, most importantly, well informed. If you request that your food be spicy, the waiter will place a glass filled with little green chilies on the table. He does this because none of the dishes, as prepared, are particularly hot. All are mildly spiced—accessible to all palates. But be warned: the aforementioned chilies are killers. (The common practice of turning down the heat may be detrimental to some of these dishes. Though serving food hot enough to singe nose hairs may be overdoing it, some heat—and certainly a little more complexity of flavour in the spice department—would be welcome.)

The curries, served in small woks called karhais, are all very good. Saag gosht, a lamb stew with chopped spinach, is lightly spiced and the meat is melt-in-your-mouth tender. Another excellent choice is the murgh jal-farezi, a chicken stir-fry served in a rich, buttery sauce enhanced with fresh coriander. Chef Sharif Khan's makkhani prawns is a wonderful dish of cooked shrimp in a generous serving of tomato-based cream sauce with oranges and ground cashews.

From the tandoori selections, the tandoori chicken arrives warm. The meat is dry and hardly as succulent as you'd expect a marinated, barbecued bird to be. The lamb chops, which arrive on a sizzle platter, have a very strong flavour—a good choice if you're one of the rare people who like older, muttony meat (perhaps Le Taj should consider buying younger and fresher lamb of the local variety).

I have a sweet tooth, but not for most Indian desserts. Predictably, I find Le Taj's offerings too sweet. I'm much happier sipping the lovely cardamom-cinnamon-flavoured Indian tea in this comfortable setting, listening to the soothing sitar background music.

IN THE KITCHEN · Chef Sharif Khan.

DECOR, DRESS, AMBIENCE · The decor is elegant, if spare, with intricate Hindu wood and plaster carvings adorning the high terra-cotta-coloured walls. In the back of the room there's a glassed-in open kitchen, where a chef is usually at work rolling naan bread or pulling skewers out of the tandoor, that classic charcoal-fired clay oven. There are signs of age—cracks in the wall plaster and crockery that's starting to look tired. Nonetheless, Le Taj is generally considered to be the most beautiful Indian restaurant in town.

WINE LIST · There's a small selection of reasonably priced red and white wines, but most patrons prefer the on-tap Double Diamond beer.

DON'T MISS · The breads, the saag gosht (lamb stew with spinach), the murgh jal-farezi (stir-fried chicken served in a butter sauce), and the makkhani prawns (shrimp in a tomato-based cream sauce with oranges and ground cashews).

WORDS TO THE WISE · For a brief and pleasurable moment, Le Taj makes you feel like you're in another world—one flavoured by *The Jewel in the Crown*, Merchant and Ivory films, and Ravi

Shankar. If you're not an expert (or of Indian descent), don't hesitate to rely on your waiter for guidance.

LE TAJ
2077 Rue Stanley (near Sherbrooke)
Telephone: (514) 845-9015
Open: Lunch, 11:30 A.M.-2:30 P.M., Sunday to Friday;
dinner, 5 P.M.-10:30 P.M., daily
Wheelchair access: Yes
Reservations: Recommended
Cards: Major cards
Price range: Starters, $3.95-$6.95; main courses, $5.95-$19.95;
desserts, $3.50-$4.50; lunch buffet, $8.95; four-course table
d'hôte menu, $22.95

★★★	$ $	REVIEWED 01/00

L'EXPRESS

SNAPSHOT • L'Express has been a Montreal landmark since 1979, and it's still the place to be. The secret of its success? The atmosphere. But people wouldn't keep coming back if the food were a disappointment. The kitchen is reliable and consistent, a feat for chef Joel Chapoulie and his staff, who serve reasonably priced bistro fare to up to 400 customers a day. The wine list offers some of the best deals in town. And the service is excellent.

THE BIG PICTURE • North American bistros strive to look old and authentic, transporting the tiled floors, the Ricard water bottles, and the tobacco-stained ceilings of Paris's Boulevard St. Germain to downtown Manhattan, Toronto, or Los Angeles. But somehow these simulated bistros just don't cut it. Something always seems out of place. First, everyone speaks English; and second, the food is all wrong—either too fancy or too foreign. Bistro fare is the original French comfort food. Anything more, and you've missed the point.

In my personal bistro fantasy, the decor is far from film-set perfect. The room has a comfortable, timeworn noblesse, and beauty meets function in all the details: the zinc bar, the black-and-white checkered floor, the papered tables, jars of cornichons on every one. Guess what? I'm not even in Paris. I'm right here in Montreal, and, of course, I'm at L'Express.

The long, crowded room is crackling with Left Bank excitement. When dining with a group, it's best to sit centre stage, between the smokers in the sunny-yellow glass-ceilinged room at the back and the nonsmokers along the glossy-brown mirrored walls up front. For a tête-à-tête, patrons willingly turn their backs to the crowd for a more intimate evening at the bar.

Sip a Perrier and pore over the red-rimmed plastic menus handwritten in the chicest of scripts. There's pot-au-feu, os à la moelle, and confit de canard—no surprises here. Tiny white papers tucked into the corner list daily specials. How refreshing to see a relatively inexpensive menu with no main course over $20.

You might want to start your meal at L'Express with potage à l'oseille or soupe au poisson. Both soups arrive piping hot in deep, lion-head-handled French porcelain bowls. The potage is creamy, perfectly seasoned, and has that distinct, slightly bitter taste of sorrel. The velvety-orange fish soup, made primarily with monkfish, is also delicious, and the accompanying rouille is garlicky and spicy. Only the cheese croutons, which are cold and taste as though they've been gratinéed hours ago, disappoint (everything from the crouton family at L'Express has an undeniable taste of yesterday; it's one of the few missteps of this kitchen).

A heaping portion of delicious celery root salad is dressed with a light version of the classic French rémoulade sauce, made with a mustardy mayonnaise, chopped capers, and parsley.

The starters I love most are the salads made with duck. The salade de confit de canard, served on a bed of mesclun leaves, is rich and moist. Another salad made of baby lettuces—oak leaf, beet green, and arugula—is tossed with a port vinaigrette and served with a fan of tender sliced duck breast dressed with a separate vinaigrette flavoured with orange and mustard.

During the chilly winter months, don't miss that old bistro standby, pot-au-feu. This version is as authentic as can be—

poached chicken, short ribs, and marrow bone served in a flavourful clear broth with root vegetables and a hunk of braised cabbage. The accompaniment is the correct one: a ramekin of French sel de Guérande.

Another fine main course is the roasted quail. Served on a bed of perfectly cooked wild rice with green peas and endive leaves, the succulent birds are served in pieces small enough to eat elegantly with your fingers.

You can tell how good the French fries are by the aroma wafting through the air. L'Express was one of the first places to serve French fries with mayonnaise in Montreal, and maybe that's why this combination has become so popular, especially when eaten with a flavourful, chewy bavette slathered with a melting slab of shallot butter—the ultimate steak-frites!

Desserts could not be more classical. There are homemade favourites, including a good crème caramel, a towering floating island, and somewhat ordinary lemon and chocolate tarts. The pistachio-griottine ice cream cake is probably the best dessert on the menu. If you're too full for dessert, try the 50¢ square of Valrhona chocolate, or, if you're a dipper, have the biscotti with the excellent espresso allongé.

Service at L'Express is excellent. The waiters are uniformly charming—apron-clad Yves Montands, one and all.

IN THE KITCHEN · Chef Joel Chapoulie.

DECOR, DRESS, AMBIENCE · It's all here: the zinc bar, the black-and-white checkered floor, the well-worn walls, and the small, wooden, paper-covered tables. The scene is straight out of the chicest Parisian arrondissement. Wear your best black.

WINE LIST · The extensive wine list offers many interesting, fairly priced bottles (priced between $20 and $200), and the waiters are known to make excellent suggestions.

DON'T MISS · The soups, the duck salads, the quail, the bavette, the French fries, and the pistachio-griottine ice cream cake.

WORDS TO THE WISE · Don't even think about showing up at L'Express without a reservation. This is the most popular bistro in town. Also, as the restaurant's tables are close together, this may not be the best place to discuss the contents of your safety deposit box. But do yourself a favour and dine at L'Express at least once, if for no other reason than to capture the essence of the city itself.

L'EXPRESS
3927 Rue St. Denis (near Duluth)
Telephone: (514) 845-5333
Open: 8 A.M.-2 A.M., Monday to Friday, 10 A.M.-2 A.M., Saturday, and 10 A.M.-1 A.M., Sunday
Wheelchair access: Yes
Reservations: Essential
Cards: Major cards
Price range: Starters, $3.95-$76 (caviar); main courses, $10.95-$20; desserts, $6

★★★	$ $ $	REVIEWED 07/99

L'HABITANT

SNAPSHOT · Set in an eighteenth-century stone house on the quiet banks of the Rivière des Prairies in Pierrefonds, L'Habitant has been a popular gourmet destination for the past 32 years. Owner Pierre Chastel has created a cozy atmosphere where guests are treated to classical French food, flavourful enough to make you forget all that confusing fusion cuisine. With its wonderful food and French Canadian decor, this West Island restaurant is an ideal spot to bring out-of-town guests.

THE BIG PICTURE · Food as entertainment—what a concept. And, quite often, what a mistake. Many of today's star chefs try to impress with newfangled concepts and avant-garde presentations, using exotic ingredients and foreign cooking styles as stars of the show. It's all about flash instead of that most important ingredi-ent: flavour.

I rediscovered flavour recently, and it wasn't in a branché down-town eatery but at L'Habitant, a long-established restaurant set in a 230-year-old stone house across from the Rivière des Prairies in Pierrefonds. Owner Pierre Chastel, originally from Toulouse, has been in business for over three decades, proudly serving his cus-tomers "à la Française." It is Mr. Chastel himself who takes reser-vations, greets customers at the door, pours wine, and often serves meals.

The menu features, among other French classics, frog's legs Provençal, entrecôte Bordelaise, Dover sole, and escargots. The first course is dominated by soups. One whiff of the rich aroma emanating from the consommé au Xérès, and you'll know you're on to something good. Here's a textbook consommé: dark in colour, not a trace of fat, crystal clear, and perfectly salted. It's hard to imagine so much flavour suspended in a single cup of hot liquid.

The pea soup, the country cousin of the noble consommé, is equally delicious. This hearty Quebec favourite, with its pulpy split peas mixed with ham, is thick and textured on the palate.

Main courses include pepper steak, coq au vin, and trout meu-nière. Mr. Chastel himself flambés the steak and warms the pep-per sauce over a copper chafing dish. The sirloin is tender and rosé but lacks the desired seared crust. The meat is also overly em-bedded on both sides with a thick layer of cracked peppercorns.

The coq au vin is simple and elegant. The three meaty pieces of chicken, covered in a delicious red wine sauce, are served with the traditional garnish of sautéed mushrooms, pearl onions, and crisp lardons (thick bacon). The trout from St. Alexis des Monts is prepared in the classic meunière style: seasoned, floured, and sautéed in butter. The pink flesh is moist and delicate, with just a touch of flakiness.

All four main courses are served with broccoli, carrot slices, and potatoes. This often ho-hum combination is anything but. The carrots are potent and sweet, the broccoli is perfectly cooked, and the potatoes (oh, the potatoes!), sliced thin and cooked with a bit of onion and chicken stock, are sublime. Any chef who can rejuvenate these common vegetables and bring them to such heights of perfection is a master.

Desserts, on the whole, are disappointing. To be fair, the crème caramel, with its especially delicious caramel sauce, is quite good. The coffee, which is served in a large pot that holds at least three cups per person, is excellent.

IN THE KITCHEN • Chef Edouard Bischoff.

DECOR, DRESS, AMBIENCE • The decor is pure French Canadian, with antiques everywhere. One piece, a beautiful armoire with glass doors, is as old as the house itself. A small stone fireplace framed with snowshoes, iron pots, and a hunting rifle gives the room an authentic "coureurs de bois" feel, which must be especially alluring in winter, with wood burning in the fireplace and frost covering the windows.

WINE LIST • Each page of the wine list is a collage of vineyard scenes and wine labels, with tiny price tags at the bottom. The wines are all French and reasonably priced. There are also two handwritten pages of expensive Grand Cru wines, obviously aimed at the occasional connoisseur.

DON'T MISS • The soups, the coq au vin, the trout meunière, and, in November, the cassoulet.

WORDS TO THE WISE • Pierrefonds is a West Island community, but it is not as far from the city centre as you might think (depending on traffic, 20 to 40 minutes). L'Habitant is obviously a labour of love for owner Pierre Chastel. You'll feel at home here —from the minute you step into the charming dining room until your last sip of coffee.

L'HABITANT
5010 Boulevard Lalande, Pierrefonds
Telephone: (514) 684-4398
Open: Lunch, noon-2 P.M., Tuesday to Friday; dinner, 5 P.M.-
11 P.M., Tuesday to Sunday
Wheelchair access: Yes
Reservations: Recommended
Cards: Major cards
Price range: Starters, $4.50-$8.50;
main courses, $26-$30; desserts, $4.50-$8

| ★★★ | $ $ | REVIEWED 03/01 |

L'ORCHIDÉE DE CHINE

SNAPSHOT • Those up for Szechwan and Hong Kong-style Chinese food formally served in chic surroundings couldn't do much better than L'Orchidée de Chine. Plate presentations are enticing, ingredients are of the highest quality, and—unlike so many restaurants that drown dishes in the same sweet soy-based sauce—l'Orchidée de Chine features a unique combination of flavours with each of its offerings. Owner George Lau's sophisticated formula appears to be a winner, as his restaurant is packed with upscale families on weekends and discerning business types at lunch. Reservations are essential.

THE BIG PICTURE • L'Orchidée de Chine offers menu items that appear, at first glance, no different than those of the competition. But those familiar with the yin-and-yang world of sweet and sour and hot and cold will note the added level of finesse in this cooking.

Now beginning his sixteenth year in business, owner George Lau has created a restaurant whose success is based on bypassing strict authenticity and favouring Chinese food that's lower in fat and in heat than traditional fare. This updated Hong Kong-style cuisine has proven popular with a great many Montrealers. In keeping with this thinking, Lau places cutlery on the table to avoid "embarrassing the customers" (chopstick aficionados can obtain a pair upon request).

Quality shines through in even the simplest selections. The wonton soup, filled with scrambled egg and tender wontons, all suspended in a robust chicken broth, is one of the best around. The crab and asparagus soup is chock-full of white asparagus and crab meat. And the four-treasures soup, again made with a bold broth, derives its quartet of flavours from bits of shrimp, chicken, shiitake mushroom, and scallop.

One of the best starters is the five-flavoured spareribs. The meat is succulent, crisp, and just spicy enough to awaken the palate for the dishes to come. The pork dumplings with peanut and sesame are, however, a disappointment. The dumplings are all noodle, little filling, and the sauce, a combination of two strong flavours, should be more assertive. Equally lacking char-acter-wise are the spring rolls, which are hot and crisp but offer little more than a faint taste of ginger.

Diners wishing to sample a variety of main-course dishes can request half portions (the ever-popular all-you-can-eat or buffet menu isn't an option here), but on busy nights there might be a wait; it would be preferable to order a few full-size portions as well.

The sautéed shrimp with chili and cayenne pepper are fresh and firm, the chili and pepper adding a spicy kick that doesn't overpower the shrimp's subtle flavour. The sesame-seed-sprinkled breaded beef fingers snap, crackle, and pop with every bite. Also outstanding is the beef with fine Chinese basil. Featuring tender strips of beef, bell peppers, and onions accented with fried basil leaves, this stir-fried preparation is coated in a thin Thai-style sauce devoid of the usual cornstarch.

Of the chicken dishes, I'd recommend the chicken with honey-orange sauce: a flattened, crumb-coated chicken breast sliced into bite-size pieces and served with a honey-orange sauce that's as sweet as candy. The chicken with Szechwan pepper and crispy spinach is another winner. The stir-fried meat is soft and spicy, and the bright-green spinach leaves are deep-fried to a crisp. There's no avoiding that Szechwan favourite, General Tao's chicken. Again, the sauce is light and without the usual cloying sweetness, even if it lacks the heat of dried chili pepper.

Other main-course dishes include a delicious lamb and scallion stir-fry, and an exceedingly delicate Cantonese-style steamed sea bass. Presented in a bamboo steamer and topped with thinly sliced scallion, the pristine morsels of fish are served with light soy sauce infused with ginger. It's an elegant dish, all softness and subtlety, displaying the beauty of fresh ingredients, minimally transformed.

Another of the many high notes is the steamed rice. Less sticky and tastier than most, it's ideal for soaking up the many fine sauces.

Those up for dessert might enjoy the ice cream topped with a ginger maple syrup, the fruit sorbets, or the simple plate of almond and fortune cookies.

Service is professional, if a bit distant. On busy nights, it can feel rushed. Nonetheless, one can't help but admire the waiters' portioning skills as they quickly parcel out equal servings of each dish as it arrives at the table.

IN THE KITCHEN • Chef and co-owner Paul Kiu.

DECOR, DRESS, AMBIENCE • L'Orchidée de Chine stands out for its sophistication, taking a well-loved ethnic cuisine into the realm of fine dining. With four multilevel dining rooms conveying an aura of comfort and elegance quite superior to the city's simpler Chinese restaurants, it sets a high standard that's hard to beat. Noise levels are tolerable, despite the bustling atmosphere and the efficient waiters whizzing to and fro. This is a restaurant that merits one of your better outfits.

WINE LIST • There are two kind of sake, Chinese beer and other imported and local beers, and an international selection of about 30 wines (red and white), which are fairly priced between $23 and $52. There's also a separate list of more expensive wines priced between $60 and $120.

DON'T MISS · The steamed bass, the lamb and scallion stir-fry, the chicken with orange and honey, and the beef with fine Chinese basil.

WORDS TO THE WISE · Almost everyone enjoys Chinese food and has his or her favourite place. This establishment stands out for the finesse with which the standard dishes are prepared and presented. Everything is up a notch or two here. The posh surroundings are different from anything most of us have experienced while enjoying this type of ethnic cuisine. Be mindful, however, that prices (though still reasonable by fine-dining standards) follow suit.

L'ORCHIDÉE DE CHINE

2017 Rue Peel (near de Maisonneuve)
Telephone: (514) 287-1878
Open: Lunch, noon-2:30 P.M., Monday to Friday;
dinner, 5:30 P.M.-10:30 P.M., Monday to Friday,
and 5:30 P.M.-11:30 P.M., Saturday
Wheelchair access: No
Reservations: Essential
Cards: Major cards
Price range: Soups and starters, $3.50-$8; main courses, $13.50-$18.80; desserts, $3-$4.50

| ★★ | $ $ $ | REVIEWED 06/00 |

MAESTRO S.V.P.

SNAPSHOT · There's a good-time atmosphere at Maestro S.V.P. Though oysters are this establishment's raison d'être, there's also delicious calamari—grilled or fried—and other fine seafood selections. The emphasis on dressy plate presentations and strange flavour combinations can sometimes get the better of this kitchen, but the friendly service and laid-back ambience make this one of the Main's most popular casual restaurants.

THE BIG PICTURE • Just as oysters latch on to the ocean's rock-lined shores, so too has Ilene Polansky latched on to oysters as the main draw of her restaurant, Maestro S.V.P. Sure, oysters are available in many Montreal restaurants, but how many can boast an oyster bar where a selection of over 15 varieties is available year-round? Here, oysters are served in many different ways, the most unsual being the oyster shooter. Billed as a refreshing treat, this drink consists of jalapeño vodka, cocktail sauce, and fresh horseradish. Suspended in the centre of this fiery concoction is a raw oyster. Take my advice: unless you live for oysters or crave drinks formulated to put hair on your chest, order a martini.

Far more appealing are the fresh raw oysters, which are served on the half shell with lemon, Tobasco, or red wine vinegar. Eating oysters is a bit of an indulgence. Prices can mount quickly, especially if you order individual specimens at $4.25 a pop. Still, it's a wonderful way to begin a meal.

Oyster offerings change frequently. A recent tasting included a Kumamoto from Washington, an Aspy Bay from Nova Scotia, a Malpeque from Prince Edward Island, a Yaquina Bay from Oregon, a Belon from France, and a Martha's Vineyard from Massachusetts. To my taste, the Kumamoto has the gentlest flavour, while the Malpeque is more metallic. The Aspy Bay and the Yaquina Bay are briny and redolent of cantaloupe, respectively. The nutty-tasting Belon, with just a squirt of lemon, makes a fine match for a glass of chilled Muscadet wine.

After these fresh and salty mouthfuls, a serving of four hot oysters Rockefeller falls flat. This version combines oysters on the half shell with spinach and pesto, the whole covered in a gratinéed blanket of Swiss cheese. The spinach works, the cheese doesn't (it's greasy and overpowering), and you can hardly taste the pesto. I'm not sold on the Louisiana crab cake either. The cake is insufficiently crispy, and it's thicker than usual. It's also under-seasoned and served with a red pepper coulis that adds sweetness and little else.

A far better choice for a hot appetizer is the calamari. At Maestro S.V.P. you can have it two ways: deep-fried or grilled. Both are outstanding. The grilled calamari are tender, spicy, and matched with grilled peppers and a summery red pepper, black bean, and corn salsa. The accompanying red pepper coulis works in this dish, as it provides a mellow contrast to the spicy seafood.

The fried calamari is even better. With a sauce made with sour cream, gin, and cayenne, the crispy rings have a sweet flavour, a tender texture, and a light coating that's not at all greasy.

The highlight of the main-course offerings is a fish and seafood pot-au-feu. A small heating element is brought to the table and a large, shallow bowl, piled high with seafood, is placed on top. The mussels are heavenly: plump, juicy, and beautifully enhanced by an aromatic pastis and saffron broth that's heavy on the pastis and light on the saffron. The salmon is also ideal, as it's juicy on the inside and just lightly crusted on the outside. But the high praise ends here. The remaining seafood — jumbo shrimp, clams, a single scallop — is unevenly cooked. Some bites are tender, others are tough and chewy. The broth, though, saves the dish. Gutsily salted and filled with a julienne of carrots, onions, and peppers, it's delicious enough to stand on its own.

Another dish marred by overcooked seafood is the squid ink pasta with tomato sauce, Kalamata olives, and grilled shrimp. The shrimp have little of the smoky flavour we expect of grilled food. The rest of the dish is quite good, though the black pasta is tasteless and appears to be there for looks only.

The "Thai-style" chicken satay is served with rice, stir-fried vegetables, and deep-fried rice noodles. Sounds good, but after a few bites enthusiasm wanes. Though the accompanying peanut sauce provides a sweet complement to the chicken, the meat itself is on the dry side and only lightly grilled. The rest of the dish tastes not of lemon grass and ginger, but also of coconut milk.

Equally marred by flavour conflicts is the bigeye tuna with a dark rum and sugar sauce. Set atop a thick stalk of sugarcane, the tuna tournedos is warm, grey in the middle (instead of deep crimson), and coated in a sweet, syrupy sauce. The accompaniments include unseasoned blue potatoes, carrots, and a rum sauce better suited to an ice cream sundae than seafood.

Desserts are also ambitiously dressed up; the fresh fruit, tuiles, and elaborate coulis designs are worth the price of admission alone. But take away all the decorations and you aren't left with much. The best choice is a sorbet plate that offers three full-flavoured sorbets: mango, coconut, and wild berry.

Service at Maestro S.V.P. is friendly, casual, and competent.

IN THE KITCHEN • Chef Yves Therrien.

DECOR, DRESS, AMBIENCE • Situated on the grungy yet oh-so-fashionable strip of Boulevard St. Laurent between Prince Arthur and des Pins, this seafood bistro boasts a decor that may best be described as Maine meets the Main. The room is painted in deep tones of sea blue, burgundy, and burnt sienna. Half shells of favourite oysters are nailed to one wall, each identified for curious onlookers. Modern touches include trendy high-backed chairs and blue halogen lights; bistro touches include mirrors, a small bar, and a large blackboard listing the day's selection of imported oysters. Musical instruments lining the top of the walls provide the only visual clue to the restaurant's unusual name.

WINE LIST • The international wine list is fairly priced and features about 30 oyster-friendly white wines priced between $28 and $175, and about as many reds priced between $30 and $500.

DON'T MISS • The calamari (fried or grilled), the fresh oysters (of course), and the sorbets.

WORDS TO THE WISE • Good food needs little or no embellishment to shine. At Maestro S.V.P., less is more. Unless you're up for exotic flavour combinations, stick to the house specialty—the humble yet luxurious oyster.

MAESTRO S.V.P.
3615 Boulevard St. Laurent (near Prince Arthur)
Telephone: (514) 842-6447
Open: 11 A.M.-11 P.M., Monday to Friday, and 4 P.M.-11 P.M.,
Saturday and Sunday
Wheelchair access: Yes
Reservations: Recommended
Cards: All major cards
Price range: Starters, $6-$16 (oysters, $40 a dozen);
main courses, $14-$39; desserts, $7.50-$8.50

★★★	$ $ $	REVIEWED 02/01

MIKADO

SNAPSHOT • This stylish and wildly popular Outremont restaurant offers inventive Japanese fare, superb tempura, and beautiful sushi. Chef Mikio Owaki's goal is to modernize traditional Japanese fare, allotting it the same level of glamour we've awarded to sushi. He appears to be well on his way. This Avenue Laurier walk-up, now 11 years strong, is booked solid night after night.

THE BIG PICTURE • Seated at Mikado's sushi bar, I observe my fellow diners: beautiful women, young couples, and an especially stylish, leather-clad, fortysomething couple regaling the sushi chef with anecdotes about their recent foray into the New York sushi scene. In front of me, a young chef prepares intricate maki rolls, every ingredient—nori, sushi rice, raw fish, tempura flakes—within reach. On the far right are dozens of wooden trays of all shapes and sizes containing sashimi, nigiri sushi, and slices of colourful, spicy crisp and soft maki. Mikado also appears to do a brisk takeout business, as illustrated by the dozens of sushi-laden Styrofoam trays being whisked off the counter.

The atmosphere has a impressive, bustling appeal, but it certainly isn't unique. Unable to match the heights of piscine freshness or variety of either Japan or New York, Montreal's top sushi restaurants have compensated with creativity. Maki rolls—un-commonly heavy on the salad fixings and light on the raw fish—reign. But the drawback of sushi being given a starring role is that many of the city's Japanese establishments have neglected the traditional dishes. Not Mikado.

There are 35 non-sushi/sashimi-related selections on the menu, including traditional offerings like teriyaki and innovative ones like tuna tempura (a dish also served at that most cutting edge of restaurants, Toqué!). The overall look of much of Mikado's food is more in the French/Japanese fusion vein than strictly Japanese.

The à la carte menu begins with the inevitable miso soup, which is hot and refreshing. The pork and cabbage dumplings—gyoza—are also piping hot, not a bit clammy, and generously salted, highlighting the filling's meaty flavour. The spring rolls, haru maki, arrive upright and sliced at an angle, like fat spears. Filled with chicken, shrimp, and vegetables, the golden rolls lack only seasonings. The classic shrimp and vegetable tempura doesn't disappoint either. The batter is thin, crisp, and ever-so-slightly greasy. The vegetables are toothsome; the jumbo shrimp, utterly delicious.

The tuna tempura is superb. Wrapped in nori and deep-fried, sliced, and fanned onto a bright-yellow plate, the red-fleshed big-eye tuna is paired with a sweet, thick Mikado sauce strewn with sesame seeds.

The main-course selection of sushi and sashimi includes scallops, red tuna, and octopus: all are superfresh and perfectly cut (the scallops literally melt in the mouth like butter). The nigiri sushi selections—salmon, shrimp, whitefish, mackerel, and more tuna—are also excellent. The rice is especially pleasant, as it's lightly packed, not cloying, and just slightly sweetened and vinegared. The maki-roll assortment includes everything from the standard tuna and spicy tuna to the exotic Kamikaze (made crunchy with the addition of tempura flakes), Mikado (crab, salmon skin, and caviar), and Tempura (filled with deep-fried shrimp and cucumber).

Chicken katsu and the Mikado plate are fine choices for those not up for the raw-fish experience. The chicken is pounded into a flat paillard, coated with Japanese bread crumbs, and deep-fried, resulting in the lightest and crispiest piece of chicken imaginable. Though the chicken is terrific, the soy-based katsu dipping sauce is sweet—and not much else. The Mikado plate, a combination of marinated grilled meats and stir-fried vegetables with teriyaki sauce, also comes up short. The steak is very good—medium-rare and tender—but the skewered chicken is dry and tasteless.

There are only a few desserts at Mikado, but they're a cut above. A selection of sorbets (litchi, cassis, mango, and strawberry) and ice creams (green tea and vanilla) is presented on a dish shaped like an artist's palette. Those in dire need of a chocolate fix will enjoy the round two-chocolate mousse cake decorated with fresh fruit and a vanilla crème anglaise.

Despite the crowds and small space, service at Mikado is smooth. The only long waits are for the elaborate sushi platters.

IN THE KITCHEN • Chef Mikio Owaki.

DECOR, DRESS, AMBIENCE • Mikado is usually very crowded, and there's often a line at the door. Noise levels are high, but tolerable. The room is simply decorated in a modern style. The customers range from groups of trendy Outremont thirtysomethings to sushi aficionados eating solo at the bar.

WINE LIST • There are three varieties of sake priced between $24 and $52, and about 40 bottles of red and 40 bottles of white wine (French and Californian) priced between $28 and $300.

DON'T MISS • The chicken katsu, the Mikado plate, the tuna tempura, the pork dumplings (gyoza), and the sushi and sashimi.

WORDS TO THE WISE • This is a cuisine that fits all seasons: reenergizing in winter; pared-down, healthy, and chic in summer. At Mikado you can expect many pleasant surprises and feel confident in trying some of the more exotic offerings you might shy away from at other sushi emporiums. The sheer volume of patrons passing through this establishment also tells you that the fish is always fresh.

MIKADO
368 Avenue Laurier West (near du Parc)
Telephone: (514) 279-4809
Open: Lunch, 11:30 A.M.-2:30 P.M., Monday to Friday;
dinner, 5:30 P.M.-10 P.M., Sunday and Monday,
and 5:30 P.M.-11 P.M., Tuesday to Saturday
Wheelchair access: No
Reservations: Essential
Cards: Major cards
Price range: Starters, $2.50-$9.50; main courses, $12-$24;
desserts $6-$7.30

| ★★★ | $ $ $ $ | REVIEWED 11/99 |

MILOS

SNAPSHOT • Milos is one of Montreal's most fashionable restaurants. This is the place where visiting celebrities, socialites, and business leaders come to drop serious mazuma on Greek food at its best: simple salads, fried vegetables with tzatziki, and grilled fish and seafood laced with lemon, oregano, and fruity olive oil. Owner Costas Spiliadis insists on the best ingredients, and his stylish Mediterranean decor sets the mood for a relaxed night of indulgence.

THE BIG PICTURE • For my first meal at Milos I was seated next to a long, rectangular lobster tank. I have nothing against lobsters, but a hundred doomed creatures killing time in a tank next to my dinner plate is not my idea of ambience. I politely asked to move and we were shown to another table near a large open kitchen. After five minutes of waiters bumping into the back of my chair and being distracted by other diners hovering around the fish display selecting specimens, I asked to move again. This time we found ourselves close to a smaller open kitchen near a vine-covered loggia nestled between large ceramic olive-oil urns.

Within minutes, a waiter arrived to pour some of the house olive oil (available commercially as My Sister's Own) into a deep saucer topped with snippings of fresh Greek oregano. A basket of grilled bread was provided for dipping. And then nothing. No menus, no drinks, and no service. It wasn't until 30 minutes later that my dining companions and I were offered drinks. After 15 more minutes, spent watching the young chef in front of me making salads, I grabbed the first waiter I could find and pleaded for menus. We were in the restaurant for a full hour before our orders were taken.

Obviously, service can be a problem at Milos when the crowds descend. They're here, of course, for good reason: the food is some of the best of its kind. Ordering can be another problem. Starters are straightforward; the only difficulty is choosing, as they all sound so good. Main-course fish dishes, however, can get complicated. Depending on the size of the fish on a given day, only a few selections are available for one person. Many are for two people or more.

An outstanding starter, not to be missed, is the deep-fried calamari (squid)—light, crisp, and tender. Also memorable is the Milos special: a stack of deep-fried, paper-thin zucchini and eggplant disks topped with fried Kasseri cheese and served with a perfectly balanced tzatziki that's flavourful yet not too heavy on the garlic. Milos is famous for its shrimp, and rightly so. The starter of five grilled shrimp are not only smoky and delicious but also firm—the hallmark of superfresh shellfish. The ever-popular Greek salad is composed of the freshest cucumbers, green peppers, tomatoes, and onions, along with triangles of salty, firm Feta cheese, intensely flavoured Kalamata olives (imported from Greece by the restaurant), and hot pepperichio peppers.

One of the star main-course offerings is the loup de mer. This perfectly cooked white-fleshed fish is soft, moist, and flaky (apparently, at the acclaimed New York City branch of Milos, Estiatorio Milos, loup de mer is so popular they have trouble keeping it in stock). Also perfectly cooked is another white-fleshed Mediterranean fish, called sargos. Though firmer, fishier, and not quite as refined as the loup de mer, it's a succulent specimen— outstanding in every way.

The brochette of swordfish is a disappointment. Although the marinated, grilled swordfish cubes are flavourful and tender (they fall apart at the slightest touch of the fork), they lack that meaty consistency one expects of swordfish. Moreover, the accompanying vegetables—steamed broccoli, carrots, and cauliflower—are underseasoned and undercooked, and the brochetterie-style French fries are soggy.

There aren't many desserts at Milos, but all offerings are authentic and delicious. The goat's milk yogourt (from Ontario) is creamy and contrasts well with a topping of spiced, marinated quince and a spoonful of honey. Crisp homemade baklava, served with soft dates, litchi fruit, and slices of Israeli pitahaya (also known as dragon fruit), is a dessert full of subtle Mediterranean flavours. It happily rejuvenates taste buds grown tired of chocolate.

IN THE KITCHEN • Chef and owner Costas Spiliadis.

DECOR, DRESS, AMBIENCE • Dress at Milos is casual chic, the ambience is relaxed and festive. The decor is modern Mediterranean, with open kitchens, displays of vegetables and seafood on ice, large paintings, and oversized urns filled with branches and dried flowers. It's all rather fabulous—even the washrooms.

WINE LIST • The wine list includes Greek, French, Californian, and Italian wines priced between $34 and up, up, up . . . Try the best-selling Greek white wine Domaine Hatzimichalis, ideal for fish and priced at a reasonable $47.

DON'T MISS • The Greek salad, the grilled octopus, the Milos special (fried vegetables with tzatziki), the grilled loup de mer, the sargos, and the goat's milk yogourt.

WORDS TO THE WISE • The copious side dishes at Milos are extra. If you're smart, you'll skip them entirely. Also be careful when ordering fish or lobster by weight, as you might end up with a few unwelcome surprises come bill time. Remember too that fish entrées are served without accompaniments.

MILOS

5357 Avenue du Parc (near St. Viateur)

Telephone: (514) 272-3522

Open: Lunch, noon-3 P.M., Monday to Friday;

dinner, 5:30 P.M.-midnight, Monday to Sunday

Wheelchair access: Yes

Reservations: Essential

Cards: All major cards

Price range: Starters, $7.50-$15; main-course fish is sold whole for $22.95-$32 a pound, and veal and lamb chops are $28; desserts, $6.50 to $7.50

★★1/2	$ $ $	REVIEWED 12/99

MOISHE'S STEAK HOUSE

SNAPSHOT · You might get the feeling that everyone at Moishe's is related, and many probably are. This Boulevard St. Laurent landmark comes about as close to a Jewish social club as you'll find in Montreal. Yet this is no sectarian enclave. The big and welcoming steak house has broad appeal, and you'll see people of many different ethnic backgrounds enjoying the mouthwatering steaks, top-notch wines, and kosher pickles. Even with a reservation, expect to wait for a table on a busy night.

THE BIG PICTURE · When I call for an eight o'clock reservation at Moishe's Steak House, I'm told by the young man who answers the phone that 8:30 is the best he can do, but I should be there at eight to ensure a table by 8:45. What? "Take it or leave it," he says. "That's the way it is here on busy nights."

So even with a reservation you're expected to wait until called, which can take up to 30 minutes. Annoying it is; unbearable it isn't. The reason? The mouthwatering aroma of charred meat, and the crowded anteroom, which turns out to be a great place to observe one of the best schmooze fests in town.

Once you are seated, two bowls—one of kosher pickles and the other of homemade coleslaw—are placed on the table. These are high-quality pickles—so crisp and refreshing that you could easily wolf down four before dinner, along with a few slices of the kimmel or black bread that the restaurant buys from Boulangerie St. Laurent, across the street.

Moishe's isn't a delicatessen, but it's famous for a few deli-type specialties. The chopped liver is often regarded as the best in town, and it is very good. The shrimp cocktail is a letdown, however, as it contains no more than five bland shrimp, a dollop of cocktail sauce, and a lettuce leaf. The Caesar salad—small, limp, and coated with salty, low-quality cheese—is also lacking.

Apparently, Moishe's beef is imported from Colorado. Portions are more than generous. Many of the steaks are large enough for two (the grilled Arctic char could easily feed three). But the rib steak is so flavourful and juicy that you won't want to share; if it weren't for the upscale onlookers, you'd probably be tempted to pick up the bone and have a good gnaw.

The New York cut sirloin doesn't fare too well. Though toothsome, it's a leaner cut than the rib steak and could use a bold sauce to liven it up (forget the pepper sauce, which is peppery in name only).

Sauce, schmauce—the Arctic char is wonderful. Served as a filet close to seven inches long, it is perfectly cooked, delicate, and rich. Considering that this is a steak house, it's nice to see that the nonsteak items are given the attention they deserve.

Main courses are served with excellent French fries or a Monte Carlo potato: a twice-baked potato filled with delicious chive-studded mashed potatoes and a sprinkling of paprika. The potato latkes, which taste like a cross between onion rings and hash browns, are served piping hot, crisp, and soft on the inside.

All vegetable side dishes are extra and big enough to share. They may not be worth the added cost, however. The grilled oyster mushrooms are overly charred. The spinach is watery and unseasoned, and it's served with the tough stalks intact—about as exciting as a cheese sandwich.

For such a powerhouse restaurant, desserts are surprisingly mediocre. The marble cheesecake is the dullest I've ever eaten. Another dessert—called "Chocolate! Chocolate!"—is boring! boring!—more homemade-style than restaurant quality.

The wait staff at Moishe's is efficient and friendly and certainly ranks among the best in Montreal.

IN THE KITCHEN • Chef Fotis Sagris.

DECOR, DRESS, AMBIENCE • The dining room is deep and rectangular, with masculine wood panelling, wine racks, and modern paintings. The closely placed tables are filled with animated types, all of whom appear to be talking at the same time. Don't be surprised to run into your lawyer or accountant—this is where they hang out.

WINE LIST • If you read *Wine Spectator*, you know that many steak houses have been featured in the magazine for their wine lists. With an impressive collection of over 175 wines, Moishe's is among this elite. Take note: impressive wine lists usually have equally impressive prices.

DON'T MISS The rib steak, the Arctic char, the pickles, the coleslaw, the Monte Carlo potatoes, and the potato latkes.

WORDS TO THE WISE • One goes to a steak house for a serious hunk of meat—not foie gras or kumquat crème brûlée. Skip the entrées and desserts and splurge on a good bottle of wine. What you see is what you get, and what you get at Moishe's is delicious steak house fare.

MOISHE'S STEAK HOUSE
3961 Boulevard St. Laurent (near Duluth)
Telephone: (514) 845-1696
Open: 5:30 P.M.-11 P.M., Monday to Friday;
5 P.M.-11 P.M., Saturday and Sunday
Wheelchair access: No
Reservations: Essential
Cards: All major cards
Price range: Starters, $5.75-$12.15;
main courses, $23.75-$37.50; desserts, $2.75-$6.50

★★	$ $ $ $	REVIEWED 07/01

NEWTOWN

SNAPSHOT · Since throwing open its doors in June 2001, Jacques Villeneuve's glamorous resto/bar has been going full tilt. Its Rue Crescent location is ideal, as this is the epicentre of Grand Prix mania every summer. Though the predictable menu doesn't quite live up to the racy setting, the high-octane crowd doesn't seem concerned. Reservations are a must.

THE BIG PICTURE · Jacques Villeneuve claims that his restaurant is "a great place to have a quiet coffee—my new pied à terre in Montreal." A quiet coffee? On the first floor of Newtown, you'll see an imposing square bar usually buzzing with big-haired blondes, macho guys, and rakish baby boomers. Revellers spill out onto the outdoor terrace. It's a high-octane crowd—très sexy —the ultimate meet market. The scene is a bit more subdued one flight up, in the restaurant—but just a bit. The room is noisy, the lights are low, and the ambience is electric. Villeneuve has good taste; this place is beautiful.

One look at the menu shows that Newtown aims to compete with the big boys. Prices are high, and the selection includes luxury items such as foie gras (hot and cold), caviar, Dover sole, and filet mignon. What strikes one immediately is the simplicity of the menu descriptions coupled with the lack of a distinct culinary style. It looks like a list of someone's favourite meals, possibly those of Villeneuve himself; I can imagine him describing, to an appropriately obsequious chef, an espresso-crusted rack of lamb he once tasted in Milan during the Italian Grand Prix.

Simple can be good, and the terrine de foie gras shows us why. Two rounds of velvety foie gras are perfectly seasoned and have a sweet liver flavour devoid of bitterness. A sprinkling of fleur de sel adds sparkle to every bite. A crab and spinach tart baked in a phyllo shell is also tasty. The crab flavour is pronounced, and the filling is hot and melting—the perfect foil for the crisp phyllo base. But the presentation leaves you cold; the squeeze-bottle tic-tac-toe grid of balsamic reduction and yellow pepper sauces is just so passé.

Unfortunately, simple can also be dreary, especially if the ingredients aren't first-class. A plate of artichoke hearts topped with Parmesan shavings and dressed with Tuscan olive oil is a case in point, as the artichokes are watery and practically tasteless and the oil is no more fruity or peppery than the supermarket variety. The Parmesan, a controlled substance, provides the only strong flavour.

Main courses fare better. The grilled fish and vegetable entrée consists of a salmon pavé, a few scallops, and a single jumbo shrimp served on a bed of grilled yellow squash, zucchini, peppers, and eggplant. The fish and seafood are ideally moist and succulent, the salmon winning out flavour-wise. The veggies are also nice. But grilled food—especially a whole plateful—is an easy score.

Halibut Niçoise better displays this kitchen's talents. The generous pavé, pan-seared to perfection, is very nice; the alabaster flesh breaks into juicy chunks as opposed to dry flakes. Halibut is an austere fish with a subtle flavour that shines with gutsy accompaniments. The Niçoise-style vegetables—melting yellow and red peppers, black olives, potato, and onion—provide just that.

Carnivores with a taste for luxury will no doubt opt for the foie-gras-topped Newtown filet. Though flavourful, the filet mignon is small and on the tough side, as is the foie gras topping. Served alongside is a dish of scalloped potatoes that appears to have been thrown together at the last minute. If you're going to name a dish after your restaurant, give it a little lovin' care — right now, it's a $39 disappointment.

Desserts are nice, but, again, nothing makes it to the checkered flag. The best of the lot turns out to be crêpes folded around Grand Marnier pastry cream, reminding us what miracles this sublime orange liqueur can work on the palate.

The waiters are friendly and competent, though they are more plate carriers than seasoned pros. Considering that this establishment boasts a staff of 160, it's surprising to see water glasses sitting empty all night long.

DECOR, DRESS, AMBIENCE · The decor is modern: the square room is done in tones of white, black, and grey, with polished wood floors and undulating, textured walls. The space is divided in half by a wide, glassed-in wine refrigerator, and there's a marble mirror-backed bar by the entrance. It's all quite chichi and upscale, which is perfectly in keeping with the stylish crowd.

WINE LIST · The wine list at Newtown is filled with French and Californian bottles priced for profit, though not egregiously so.

DON'T MISS · The terrine de foie gras, the grilled fish and vegetables, the halibut Niçoise, and the Grand Marnier crêpes.

WORDS TO THE WISE · Clearly, there's plenty of potential here, but if Mr. Villeneuve and partners want to make a mark on the city's fine-dining scene, they'll have to work on the menu and plate presentations, which right now are a bit unsure for such an elegant pit stop.

NEWTOWN
1476 Rue Crescent (corner de Maisonneuve)
Telephone: (514) 284-6555
Open: Lunch, 11:30 P.M.-2:15 P.M., Monday to Friday;
dinner, 5:30 P.M.-10:30 P.M., Monday to Wednesday and Sunday,
5:30 P.M.-11 P.M., Thursday and Friday,
and 5:30 P.M.-11:30 P.M., Saturday
Wheelchair access: No
Reservations: Essential
Cards: Major cards
Price range: Starters, $11-$78 (caviar); main courses, $16-$39;
desserts, $9

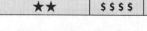

★★ $ $ $ $ REVIEWED 05/00

NUANCES

SNAPSHOT · With its impressive wines, fancy French food, elaborate setting, and impeccable service, Nuances may be the ideal restaurant for high rollers. But with inconsistencies in the menu, it's a risky proposition for those seeking the ultimate gourmet experience. Not to be missed, however, are the frequent special events featuring international guest chefs, when the kitchen seems more focused.

THE BIG PICTURE · As most gambling devotees are aware, Nuances is one of the city's most acclaimed restaurants. It's situated on the third floor of the Casino de Montréal. There's neither direct access from outside nor a discreet elevator to swoosh you up in style. No, the only way to get to the restaurant is to make your way past slot machines, blackjack tables, and hordes of chip-toting, wide-eyed gaming enthusiasts. Roulette before dinner? Why not. Getting accustomed to being separated from large sums of cash sets the right tone for the evening.

An excellent reason to dine here is that you will be waited upon hand and foot by one of the most gracious and knowledgeable wait staffs in town. Few restaurants try as hard to please. But making menu choices can feel like placing bets on the table. The lobster salad is priced at $22, the roasted scallops are $39.75, and the pigeon is $44. This is where the real gambling begins.

The first dish to arrive is the amuse-bouche: a delicious nugget of poached red snapper smothered in lobster sauce, presented in a small ramekin on a slab of green granite. Flanking the ramekin, and towering over the dish, is a gilded letter N. This objet d'art, a not-so-subtle reference to the restaurant's name, is — like the setting — impressively garish.

Though the decor may not be to my taste, two lobster starters certainly are. The first, a "not so classic lobster à l'américaine," pairs warm chunks of meat from the tail with olive oil, lobster bisque, cilantro, confit of shallots, and crushed tomatoes. Served in a large triangular glass dish with a whole, shelled, au naturel lobster claw on the side, this irresistible starter gets the meal off to a flying start. The second starter is a cold salad consisting of a lobster and roasted tomato timbale, with another whole claw on the side. The sweet and tender meat is well matched with the melting tomato, and the colourful mix is lightly accented by an olive oil and balsamic vinegar dressing.

Other starters aren't as successful. A caviar-topped gâteau (referred to as a "tian") is made with alternating layers of home-smoked salmon, buckwheat pancakes, and a Mascarpone and chive lemon cream. It's served with a small salad of mixed greens covered with an overly acidic dressing. Granted, the individual ingredients in the tian are rich and good-tasting, but such a generous portion, weighed down by the thick crêpes, is heavy going at the outset of the meal.

Also disappointing is the foie gras mille-feuille: a two-inch-high round of foie gras laced with thin slices of maple-wine-poached prunes. The flavourless liver cake, as firm as cold butter, appears to have come straight from the refrigerator. The little accent — a blah quenelle of warm diced apple and sweet prunes — adds a boost of sweetness and little else.

Main-course choices include scallops, duck, pigeon, and beef. Plump and decoratively branded with crisscross grill marks, the five medium-rare roasted scallops are served in a pool of delicate Chardonnay butter sauce. A confit of sliced shallots tops a mound of puréed potatoes, the whole again topped with a teaspoon of Atibitibi caviar.

The orange-and-spice-marinated duck magret falls flat. No sooner does the plate arrive than the waiter notes that the meat is undercooked and suggests taking it back to the kitchen. Cooking problems aside, the accompanying poached orange halves are inedible. The bittersweet spicy-orange sauce is quite intriguing, however, and the other accompaniment, a few caramelized endive halves, are really quite delicious.

And what about the pigeon? The roasted dark meat is rich and moist, and the skin is crisp and succulent. It's served with gratinéed mashed potatoes and a stew of pigeon meat, giblets (livers and hearts), and chanterelles. The sauce, made with veal and chicken stock blended with cream and foie gras, is pure heaven.

The intense red wine sauce served with a coeur de filet mignon turns this well-known dish into a triumph. The thick beef filet is cooked to perfection and is served with two whimsical fan-shaped tuiles of dried prosciutto as well as a few red-wine-braised shallots. Once again, the main vegetable accompaniment is mashed potatoes—this time flecked with black truffles (even though all the potatoes are excellent, one would think a restaurant of this calibre could come up with more inventive vegetables).

Portions at Nuances are large, which makes dessert seem unnecessary. Standouts include a hot caramelized banana served with whisky-raisin ice cream and a shard of coconut caramel. The house ices—mango and raspberry sorbets, crème-fraîche-basil ice cream, and maple-pecan ice cream—are all very good. The heavily soaked baba au rhum is served with a passion fruit sabayon over sliced bananas and pineapple. Just before you dig in, it's re-topped with a cloying exotic fruit punch—a fun dessert better sampled at midday than at the end of such a copious meal.

IN THE KITCHEN · Executive chef Jean-Pierre Curtat.

DECOR, DRESS, AMBIENCE · Nuances is formal; jackets are required. The space, surprisingly small for a grand casino restaurant, with has high ceilings, intimate booths, and a twinkling cityscape view (obscured by useless curtains). The heady mix of futuristic light fixtures, dreary flowered upholstery, mosaic trim, and Doric columns—all done up in old rose, brown, and burgundy—comes off as kitschy as opposed to glitzy.

WINE LIST · Nuances features a wine list of medium length filled with a fine selection fairly priced international bottles.

DON'T MISS · The lobster starters, the pigeon, the filet mignon, and the sorbets.

WORDS TO THE WISE · A meal at Nuances can easily cost you $100 per person with wine and tip. A lot of money? Not for big gamblers. But for those in search of a surefire gourmet experience, not necessarily a good bet.

NUANCES
1 Avenue du Casino, Île Notre Dame
(in the Casino de Montréal)
Telephone: (514) 392-2746
Open: 5:30 P.M.-11 P.M., Sunday to Thursday, and 5:30 P.M.-11:30 P.M., Friday and Saturday
Wheelchair access: Yes
Reservations: Recommended
Cards: All major cards
Price range: Starters, $7.75-$22; main courses, $29.95-$44; desserts, $9.50-$12

★ ★	$ $ $	REVIEWED 06/01

OPUS II

SNAPSHOT • Opus II has been going through an identity crisis since opening in 1997. Many chefs have made their way through this hotel restaurant, which has now returned to a contemporary French menu best suited to its eye-catching modern decor. The fairly priced wine list is another draw. Service, especially in the evening, can be uneven.

THE BIG PICTURE • Opus II is a restaurant that's hard to pin down. There have been many highs and lows. The last menu was Mediterranean. Or was it French? There were some blissful meals to be had here during that all-too-brief period in 1998 when the late Nicolas Jongleux ruled the kitchen and maître d' and sommelier Don-Jean Léandri coordinated the service.

Opus II's chefdom then passed to another Frenchman, Thierry Baron, whose reign was also short-lived and who today can be found manning the stoves at Chorus. After Baron came executive chef Abdessattar Zitouni, who, for a brief period, brought in a Mediterranean influence.

The restaurant now shows the battle scars of past regimes. The seating has diminished in favour of an increased bar area, and the young woman who greets patrons at the door, though charming, does not command the room like the former maître d's. The background music is also disheartening. In a room this elegant one expects Mozart, not Madonna.

The menu is refreshingly short for a hotel restaurant: ten starters, four fish dishes, four meats, six desserts. Thankfully, it also lacks clichéd hotel favourites like châteaubriand and tournedos à la something or other. The cuisine is now modern French and features grilled fish, meats, and seafood boosted with herbs and spices and surrounded by wild mushrooms, delicate greens, the occasional slice of fruit, and some jazzy vegetables.

The sautéed foie gras is an all-out winner. The generous portion of liver is fried just so — crusty on the outside, velvety within.

It's sprinkled with equally rich and buttery macadamia nuts, and paired with a brunoise of licorice-poached pears; the whole is topped with a mound of paper-thin yellow potato chips that provide the ideal contrasting texture. It's a clever spin on this popular dish, using ingredients more akin to sweet than savoury to complement the inherent earthiness of the liver and potatoes.

Also delicious are the Spanish red peppers stuffed with crab meat, beet greens, and a drizzling of lobster oil. Despite the strong flavours of each ingredient, none overwhelms; each retains its personality without fighting for first place.

Not all sailing is smooth. Case in point is the vegetable salad with Îles de la Madeleine lobster. The lobster flesh, pulled with difficulty from a half tail and claw, is cold and mushy, obviously prepared much earlier in the day. This starter is also poorly presented, for without lobster-cracking implements one can't get to all the claw meat.

A main-course tuna mi-cuit is perfectly half-cooked and spanking fresh. My only quibble is with the ratatouille-like fondu of vegetables and bok-choy-garlic confit, which, though delicious, offer strong flavours that would be better suited to game or red meat. The poor tuna can hardly compete.

Also outshone by its accompaniments is the red snapper. The fish, overcooked to a degree, is pushed aside in favour of the risotto, a creamy mound of leek-spiked pearls as comforting as mom's rice pudding.

The best of the mains is the chicken seared in coarse sea salt. Though the white and dark meats are moist and flavourful, they're salty enough to turn heart patients away. But this classic has character, and the wild mushroom Tatin and gently flavoured red wine and licorice jus provide fine accompaniment.

Desserts at Opus II rise above predictable hotel fare, especially the chocolate desserts, which are made with the world's best: Valrhona. Chocolate soup (yes, please!), served with a large truffle is good fun: crack its coating and coffee ice cream oozes out. The ubiquitous chocolate moelleux cake has the requisite molten centre and intense chocolate flavour. A red fruit tart with strawberry sorbet is a favourite, especially in berry season.

Service can be problem in that it tends to start out strong and then peter out.

DECOR, DRESS, AMBIENCE • Fronting one of the city's highest-rent corners (Peel and Sherbrooke), Opus II's dining room is open and elegant. There are cushy beige banquettes and blond-wood tables draped in thick linen. One off note in this sleek setting is the pop music playing in the background. Nonetheless, this is a fancy restaurant where one's best garb is de rigueur.

WINE LIST • The wine list is short but well chosen and fairly priced—a rarity in hotel dining rooms.

DON'T MISS • The hot foie gras, the crab-stuffed red peppers, the chicken seared in coarse salt, and the chocolate desserts.

WORDS TO THE WISE • Although this kitchen is taking some interesting risks with its menu, there's still work to be done to bring the service up to the level expected of a first-class establishment. You might want to keep this restaurant on the back burner —a possible choice for a night out when you just don't feel like driving a long way or hassling with crowds or parking. It's also a good lunchtime destination.

OPUS II
1050 Rue Sherbrooke West (corner Peel, in the Hôtel Omni)
Telephone: (514) 985-6252
Open: 6 A.M.-1 A.M., daily
Wheelchair access: Yes
Reservations: Recommended
Cards: Major cards
Price range: Starters, $6.25-$22.50; main courses, $23-$32.50; desserts, $6.50

| ★★1/2 | $ $ $ | REVIEWED 07/01 |

PRIMADONNA

SNAPSHOT · For close to ten years, Primadonna has been the place where fashionistas flock for sushi, pasta, and a bustling see-and-be-seen atmosphere. Although classified as an Italian restaurant, this Boulevard St. Laurent hot spot stays in tune with recent food trends by featuring many North American-style plate presentations and flavour combinations. On the downside, noise levels can be trying, and service, provided by some fine-looking young waiters, tends to lag.

THE BIG PICTURE · When Primadonna opened in 1993, many passersby froze in their tracks. The decor was so modern, so original, so glamorous. The brilliant idea of offering two separate menus—Italian and sushi—was also revolutionary at a time when many local chefs were experimenting to varying degrees of success with Franco-Asian fusion cuisine.

Not much has changed over the years. The crowd is just as fashionable, if a bit older. The comely baby boomers still flock to this establishment to show off their tanned, toned, and expensively garbed bods.

To avoid international conflict on the palate, you might want to order sushi before your meal. The nigiri sushi—salmon, red snapper, halibut, and tuna—is fresh, and the rice is subtly seasoned and ideally cooked. The few maki rolls—tuna and cucumber—are also quite nice. À la carte Kamikaze rolls are a disappointment, however, as they're a bit dreary and poorly cut.

The starters are impressive and would be an asset to any of the city's nouvelle cuisine establishments. Four plump scallops, served on a bed of guacamole, are ultrafresh, tender, and have a melting texture and grilled flavour that pairs perfectly with the creamy cubes of avocado. The wild mushroom mille-feuille offers a chunky, herb-enhanced mushroom duxelle layered between thin slices of toasted pumpernickel. Another starter presents a goat's-cheese-stuffed beefsteak tomato set atop a flying-saucer-shaped cracker placed on a bed of chopped arugula. With its peppery greens, tangy cheese, crisp cracker, and melting tomato, this appetizer offers a beautiful array of bright flavours and opposing textures.

Primadonna has a reputation for outstanding pastas—for good reason. Available in all shapes and sizes, the pastas are home-made and appropriately matched to original sauces. Chitarra di pasta fresca con aragosta combines guitar-string-sized pasta strands with a generous helping of lobster morsels and shiitake mush-rooms in a cream-based, ever-so-slightly spiced tomato sauce. The lobster is especially tender, and a few arugula leaves help to cut down on the inherent richness and heaviness of the dish.

The fettuccini with lamb ragù is also outstanding. The lamb flavour is subtle and the pasta is luscious, every fat noodle coated with the thick sauce.

From the meat selections, a veal medallion served with Tuscan beans and asparagus doesn't quite cut it. Though its flavour is ex-cellent, the meat is tough. Turn your attention instead to the veg-etables (mixed with veal juices and few drops of truffle oil), and you'll taste fat white beans that dissolve on the tongue and as-paragus spears that have true asparagus flavour.

Desserts include an intense chocolate cake with a dry texture that requires a larger helping of vanilla ice cream than your waist-line can afford. The tiramisu has a nice flavour but its filling has been gelatinized (tiramisu à la française?). Those up for something luscious are better served by the crème brûlée, which couldn't be more perfect.

DECOR, DRESS, AMBIENCE • Primadonna's much-copied decor features pale-wood furniture, curved yellow walls, a sea-blue bar, and gold eggcup-shaped pillars. Lights are low, seating is crowded, and whoever sets the volume of the background music obviously doesn't believe in intimate conversation. Of course, this is the Main, not some sleepy hotel dining room, and the trendy atmosphere is Primadonna's principal claim to fame.

WINE LIST • There are many fine wines on the list, but don't count on your waiter to recommend anything out of the ordinary for less than $60.

DON'T MISS • The sushi, the scallops, the pastas (especially the lamb ragù), and the crème brûlée.

WORDS TO THE WISE • Appealing to both trend seekers and gourmets isn't an easy row to hoe. But judging by the glamorous crowds that still congregate here, it would seem that Primadonna's formula is still on the money. Be warned: unless you're into this kind of scene, you may feel uncomfortable.

PRIMADONNA
3479 Boulevard St. Laurent (near Sherbrooke)
Telephone: (514) 282-6644
Open: Lunch, noon-3 P.M., Monday to Friday; dinner, 6 P.M.-
1 A.M., Monday to Sunday
Wheelchair access: No
Reservations: Essential
Cards: Major cards
Price range: Starters, $10-$19; main courses, $20-$33;
desserts, $7.50

★★★	$ $ $	REVIEWED 10/99

QUELLI DELLA NOTTE

SNAPSHOT • Set in the heart of Little Italy, this exciting restaurant, frequented by a young, slick crowd, offers fabulous decor and delicious, authentic Italian cuisine. Though service can unravel on busy nights, and you might pay dearly for a good bottle of wine, chances are you'll walk away from Quelli Della Notte thoroughly satisfied.

THE BIG PICTURE • Just when Italian food in Montreal was starting to look predictable, along came Quelli Della Notte. Set amid the cafés and Italian grocery stores on the northern stretch of Boulevard St. Laurent, this flashy Italian restaurant stands out like a Versace-clad supermodel in a room full of Girl Guides. No wax-covered Chanti bottles here. This place pulls out all the stylistic stops.

The Italian/English or Italian/French menu lists soups, risotti, antipasti, primi piatti (pastas), secondi piatti (main courses), and grilled dishes. It also states that sushi "complements our cuisine" and there are two pages of sushi and sashimi selections as well.

The ravioli ai funghi porcini offers a generous portion of homemade veal-stuffed ravioli covered with sautéed porcini mushrooms and lightly sauced with a potent mushroom veal stock. Each of these fragrant, rich, and woodsy little pillows is cooked to the ideal al dente.

Another homemade Italian favourite, gnocchi verde, is as delectable as the ravioli. Like pasta, gnocchi must be cooked al dente, and so these are, offering just a touch of resistance on the first bite before melting on the second. The accompanying three-cheese sauce, made with Provolone, Fontina, and dry Ricotta, is the ideal foil for the small potato dumplings, providing a lovely marriage of texture and flavour accented by a few slices of nutty artichoke.

Equally swoon-worthy is the sliced warm salmon topped with green peppercorns. The thin slices of fish are just barely cooked, thus maintaining their delicate saltwater flavour.

A main-course serving of veal medallions is wonderful. The medallions are perfectly pink inside, tender, and juicy. Though the meat itself is incredibly flavourful, the topping of first-rate prosciutto di Parma and thick slices of salty Parmigiano-Reggiano takes this dish from delicious to sublime. The veal is served with nothing more elaborate than tender boiled new potatoes and sautéed rapini.

Here's a kitchen that obviously excels in meat and fish cookery. Is any local restaurant serving swordfish as skilfully prepared as Quelli Della Notte? This grilled seafood steak easily surpasses its beef counterpart. The fish is firm and succulent without being heavy or filling. It, also, is served with simple accompaniments: sautéed baby bok choy, potatoes, and red peppers.

But there is such a thing as too much simplicity, even in a cuisine as pure as Italian. One of the menu's only low points is the fettuccine served with buffalo Mozzarella and fresh tomatoes. A mound of undressed fettucine is topped with cherry tomato halves and Mozzarella speckled with basil. Although it is genuine buffalo Mozzarella, most of it is in the bottom of the plate. Also, the cherry tomatoes are underripe, a shame given that Jean Talon Market is only few blocks away.

Desserts are not in phase with the rest of the cuisine. The frozen nougat is good, but awfully sweet, and the Zuccotto cake is mediocre at best.

Service is a problem at Quelli Della Notte. So many waiters serve each table that you won't know who to turn to come bill time. Yet, to be fair, they seem to work nonstop; so either the system is faulty or the restaurant is understaffed.

IN THE KITCHEN · Chefs Peter Triassi and Pasquale Vari.

DECOR, DRESS, AMBIENCE · The low-lit dining room is dotted with chic burgundy chairs and well-spaced tables, and it's adorned with large pleated swatches of floor-to-ceiling fabric. The attractive, vivacious crowd, though comprised of diners of all ages, includes more than its fair share of Italian stallions and their equally glamorous girlfriends.

WINE LIST · There are a dozen wines priced between $30 and $50, and many more at higher prices. No half bottles are listed, but if you drink half a bottle of wine in the $30-to-$50 price range, you'll be charged half price. Red and white wines by the glass are available for $7 or $8.

DON'T MISS · The salmon with green peppercorns, the veal ravioli, the gnocchi with three-cheese sauce, the veal medallions, and the grilled sworfish.

WORDS TO THE WISE · In spite of certain weaknesses, Quelli Della Notte has something original to offer. The food, at times, shows flashes of true brilliance while trying to maintain an authentic flavour. If there's one restaurant in Montreal that can be called "sexy," this is it.

QUELLI DELLA NOTTE
6834 Boulevard St. Laurent (near Dante)
Telephone: (514) 271-3929
Open: Lunch, noon-3 P.M., Monday to Friday;
dinner, 5 P.M.-11 P.M., daily
Wheelchair access: No
Reservations: Recommended
Cards: Major cards
Price range: Starters, $8.75 -$10.75; main courses, $13.75-$29.75;
desserts, $7-$8; table d'hôte menu, $24-$36

★★1/2	$ $ $ $	REVIEWED 08/00

QUEUE DE CHEVAL

SNAPSHOT • Queue de Cheval is one of the most extraordinary restaurants in Montreal. With its pharaonic decor, its orgiastic attitude towards food, and its upmarket American tourists bursting with cash, it's a steak lover's Disneyland. Large-stomached, cell-phone-toting businessmen rule. This downtown den of indulgence is a haven for carnivores who like their steaks marbled, aged, and grilled to glistening perfection. There's excellent seafood as well. The wine list is appropriately steak-friendly and—no surprise—pricey.

THE BIG PICTURE • Queue de Cheval is a restaurant that aims to please. The staff works so hard that you'll wonder whether management has set up a surveillance camera in every corner. You're sure to notice the details: the logo of a running horse emblazoned on the plates and glasses, the refrigerated cases at the door displaying sides of aged Kansas and Colorado beef, the fresh fish on ice, and the tank of obscenely large lobsters. Fancy lamps and elegantly framed cards that list steak seasonings embellish every table. Men are provided with chunky-handled steak knives; women's knives are thin and sleek. No expense has been spared.

"Expense" is a key word here. Be prepared for high numbers when cruising through the menu. According to the waiters, Queue de Cheval serves "nothing but the best." Well rehearsed, they explain the desirable characteristics of aged meat. Exhibit one: a raw Delmonico steak sealed under a tight layer of cellophane. The waiter points to the impressive marbling of meat and fat and then smacks the steak through the plastic. With the same purpose in mind (to show the lack of oozing blood in aged red meat), he picks up a raw rib steak — exhibit two — by the bone and flings it down onto another plate. It's a harmless bit of show-and-tell, but hardly helpful in guiding one through the selection of à la carte steaks, which range from $28 for a ten-ounce petit filet mignon to $40 for a 28-ounce porterhouse (described on the menu as the "Cadillac").

Ordering fish is equally trying. By 8 P.M. many selections are sold out. When enquiring about cost, you'll be given the market price. (Beware: market price is per pound, not per serving. One of the less expensive fish, Mediterranean snapper, goes for $24.99 a pound, or $37.49 a serving.)

Starters include two steak house favourites: Caesar salad and shrimp cocktail. The Caesar is very good — coated with a delicious cheesy dressing — but it's made with an abundance of the limp outer leaves of the romaine as opposed to the more desirable crunchy hearts. The shrimp cocktail consists of three U8 shrimp (large specimens that weigh in at eight crustaceans per pound), a lettuce leaf, and some spicy cocktail sauce. The shrimp are meaty and well enhanced by the sauce, but this old-fashioned starter seems dated next to today's more innovative offerings.

Far more appealing is the tuna tartare. Although pricey at $18, this tower of diced fresh tuna, topped with mashed avocado and salmon roe and surrounded by a ring of sliced cucumber, provides a pleasant taste sensation at the outset of a steak-and-potatoes dinner.

Of the steaks, the Delmonico is too fatty, a fact that becomes obvious when one looks down at the large pile of fat that's left on the plate after the meat is eaten. Also disappointing is the blackened T-bone. It's also fatty, and it lacks the charred exterior or spicy coating of blackened meats.

With steaks like this, you could easily write off Queue de Cheval as just another over-priced tourist trap. But you'd have missed something. Talk to your waiter, and describe the steak of your dreams (mine's charred on the outside, medium-rare on the inside, with a meaty mineral flavour and as little fat as possible—the kind of steaks cowboys in Wyoming devour 'neath the starry skies). Chances are he'll consult Louïs, the man in charge of aging and butchering the steaks, who has been here since day one. They'll find you something good, like 20-ounce ribeye (called "Lou's Cut"), which lends itself well to a smothering of garlic and steak spices. If you like it charred yet still pink and juicy inside, ask that it be grilled Pittsburgh style. You won't be disappointed.

If it's fish you're after, try one of the daily specials, like the snapper. The two large filets are grilled to perfection, every bite is delicate and melting, and the taste—a gentle mix of sweetness and saltwater—is a triumph. Another winner is the Chilean sea bass. This à la carte offering is served with fresh herbs and a wrapping of prosciutto.

Side dishes include superb garlic mashed potatoes, terrific jumbo onion rings, and potent sautéed spinach with garlic. The most outrageous side order is the "Garbage Baker": a five-inch stuffed baked potato covered with melted Cheddar and bacon bits. Despite its unglamorous name, this gigantic spud is a winner and certainly could be a meal in itself.

If you're not embarrassed to order dessert after all this, there's a "Death by Chocolate" cake, which the waiters describe as "layers of fudge, cake, fudge, cake, fudge, cake." There's also a white chocolate cheesecake that's white, creamy, and not much else.

IN THE KITCHEN • Chef Stéphane Dumas.

DECOR, DRESS, AMBIENCE • Framed in dark wood, with chandeliers, lush paintings, and studded leather banquettes, the setting is as macho as the clientele. The space is cavernous. Two large floors are divided by a curved staircase; young waiters carrying heavy trays bound up and down it. The main floor is dominated by an open kitchen, the focal point being an enormous grill topped by a copper exhaust hood, similar in size and shape to an inverted out-of-ground swimming pool. As far as the eye can see, waiters bustle, decanting wine, serving huge steaks, and dishing up freshly tossed salads.

WINE LIST • The wine list is pricey. Not only are many bottles offered at triple their retail cost, but there are few selections for less than $50. Especially frustrating is the small choice of half bottles priced between $39 and $85, and the few mediocre selections by the glass at close to ten dollars each.

DON'T MISS • The garlic mashed potatoes, the "Garbage Baker," the jumbo onion rings, the Chilean sea bass, the red snapper, and the 20-ounce ribeye ("Lou's Cut," smothered in garlic and steak spices, grilled Pittsburgh style).

WORDS TO THE WISE • At Queue de Cheval, the ingredients are stellar and the cooking style is simple. But if you're not mindful of the details (what to order and how it should be prepared) you can go terribly wrong here and pay dearly for it. The good news is that when the steak and fish are good, they're really good. And when it's that good, the he-man-size price tag hurts a bit less.

QUEUE DE CHEVAL

1221 Boulevard René Lévesque (near Drummond)
Telephone: (514) 390-0090
Open: Lunch, 11:30 A.M.-2:30 P.M., Monday to Friday;
dinner 5:30 P.M.-10:30 P.M., Sunday to Wednesday,
and 5:30 P.M.-11:30 P.M., Thursday to Saturday
Wheelchair access: Yes
Reservations: Essential
Cards: All major cards
Price range: Starters, $8-$19; main courses, $28-$41 (market-priced items as well); desserts, $11-$13

★★1/2	$ $ $	REVIEWED 12/00

RESTAURANT BONAPARTE

SNAPSHOT · With its pared-down classic French cuisine, impeccable service, and romantic auberge setting, this Old Montreal restaurant, situated on a cobblestone side street next to the Centaur Theatre, has become a popular destination for theatre-goers and tourists alike. The six-course tasting menu offers great value. The wine list is well chosen and affordable.

THE BIG PICTURE · Plenty has happened at Restaurant Bonaparte in the past decade. It added a third dining room six years ago when it expanded into the space formerly occupied by the pastry shop next door. Three years later, management made the shrewd move of renovating the rooms upstairs and opening one of the old city's most upscale small hotels, the Auberge Bonaparte.

The restaurant is still wildly popular with the pretheatre crowd — who come to catch an early dinner before performances at the Centaur, Notre Dame Basilica, or Place des Arts — or couples and tourists out for a evening in a romantic Old Montreal setting.

Bonaparte's menu offers a wide choice of bourgeois French fare, either à la carte, as a three-course table d'hôte, or a six-course tasting menu that includes a lobster bisque, mushroom ravioli, a goat's cheese salad, a seafood plate, a choice of duck or veal, and dessert.

The lobster bisque, flavoured with ginger, arrives steaming. Though its scent is heavenly, the lobster taste is understated and benefits from a dash of salt. The thin-skinned mushroom ravioli are filled with a flavourful duxelle and enhanced with a thin cream sauce perfumed with sage. The goat's cheese in the salad arrives wrapped in phyllo and is set atop mesclun greens and tomatoes. The seafood tasting plate offers a small salmon filet, two tender shrimp, and sliced, seared scallops paired with a vanilla cream sauce. The salmon, served with a dribble of citrus butter, is perfectly grilled: crusty on the outside, translucent on the inside.

The next course is the highlight of the menu de dégustation. The magret de canard (duck breast) flavoured with maple syrup and berries is superb: the meat is pink, the consistency is melting, the fat is minimal, and the taste is deeply satisfying. The medallions of veal filet are equally tender, and the accompanying morel sauce provides a serious wild mushroom kick without overshadowing the meat.

Desserts include small squares of lemon cheesecake and two layered chocolate mousse cakes, one enhanced with coffee, the other with praline. A crème brûlée displays the ideal combination of creaminess and crunchiness. Take note: hot soufflés, a rare treat on today's restaurant menus, are available at Bonaparte if ordered 30 minutes in advance.

Although the tasting menu is an all-out winner, some à la carte selections turn up disappoinments. The main fault appears to be that many of the dishes are undersalted. The potage St. Germain, France's version of pea soup, is as blah as a bowl of oatmeal. A phyllo purse filled with sautéed snails and oyster mushrooms is also pretty dreary. If all this faintly flavoured food has you doubting your taste buds, opt for the game terrine, which is chunky, garlicky, and well seasoned.

Some main courses also fail to measure up. The confit de canard lacks depth of flavour. The Dover sole meunière arrives filleted atop a mound of rice pilaf and vegetables. It's good, if a bit dull, lacking the delicacy, the buttery flavour, and the glamour of many Dover soles boned at the table in the classic French restaurant tradition. The wild boar, by contrast, has a terrific flavour and is well matched with a hearty red-wine bordelaise sauce.

For polish and professionalism, Bonaparte gets top marks. Plates arrive like clockwork, with rarely more than a five-minute wait between courses.

IN THE KITCHEN · Chef Gérard Fort.

DECOR, DRESS, AMBIENCE · The elegant L'Impératrice room, with its tall benjamina trees, ornate ceilings, working fireplace, and flickering table lamps, makes for a relaxed and romantic setting. Among the most coveted spots are the tables in the low-lit alcoves in the front of the restaurant, overlooking Rue St. François Xavier.

WINE LIST · The wine list is made up of predominantly French bottles, all more than reasonably priced, with many half bottles and a few wines available by the glass (for as low as five dollars).

DON'T MISS · The six-course tasting menu, the terrine, the wild boar, and the desserts.

WORDS TO THE WISE · This is a smooth operation, ideal for couples, family groups, and the theatre- and concert-going crowd, which has obviously already found a home here. The faults of the kitchen are offset by the pleasures of dining at a leisurely pace and in pleasantly elegant surroundings, as well as by the wait staff, who are neither too formal nor overly solicitous.

RESTAURANT BONAPARTE
443 Rue St. François Xavier (near Notre Dame)
Telephone: (514) 844-4368
Open: Lunch, noon-2:30 P.M., Monday to Friday;
dinner 5:30 P.M.-10:30 P.M., daily
Wheelchair access: No
Reservations: Essential
Cards: Major cards
Price range: Starters, $4.50-$18.50; main courses, $19.50-$30.50;
desserts, $3.50-$7.50, six-course tasting menu, $52.50

| ★★1/2 | $ $ $ | REVIEWED 08/01 |

RESTAURANT LE MCHAFFY

SNAPSHOT · Looking for a place in the Eastern Townships to enjoy a romantic dinner or an après-ski gourmet meal? Cowansville's McHaffy's might just be the place. This converted-house restaurant run by chef and owner Pierre Johnston offers sophisticated Quebec cuisine in a quaint country setting. Service is excellent.

THE BIG PICTURE · Cowansville does not share Knowlton's social scene or Bromont's fast-emerging French Canadian country cachet. It's more of a quiet town, with small businesses and clapboard houses set right on the main street, Rue Principale. But what it does have is one the best chef-owned restaurants in L'Estrie (the Eastern Townships): Restaurant Le McHaffy, known affectionately to locals as McHaffy's.

Chef and owner Pierre Johnston, who is a highly regarded caterer as well, offers a menu filled with local ingredients prepared in the modern Quebec style. All the dishes—from classic seared squab with lentils to edgy tuna sashimi with tuna tartare—sound enticing.

Another of McHaffy's lures is its format and pricing. The five-course menu (amuse-bouche, starter, soup or salad, main course, dessert and coffee) makes for a generous, well-paced meal for less than $40 per person—a steal at a time when main-course prices at many of Montreal's better restaurants exceed the $30 mark.

What a pleasure it is to sit in McHaffy's country setting and be served a cosmopolitan-style starter, like the shrimp martini. Johnston offers six tiger shrimp enticingly perched on the thin edge of a martini glass filled with gazpacho and topped with saffron cream. The shrimp have a smoky grilled flavour and meaty texture that contrasts well with the refreshing cold soup.

Also scoring high flavour-wise is the warm paillé goat's cheese layered with oven-roasted tomatoes, sautéed spinach, and red peppers. These fanned-out concoctions are real taste tinglers, especially when rolled around in the accompanying smoked jalapeño jus and roasted garlic. Those up for something a little less intense at the outset of the meal should opt for the seared squab. All-too-rare on restaurant menus, this luxurious bird is served here in two pieces — a plump breast and leg — with a mound of lentils studded with mushrooms, a baked fig, leek confit, and summer truffles. Unlike so many insipid farm-raised birds, this one is especially notable for its rich, gamy flavour.

The next course — a choice of leek soup or baby organic greens — is also successful. The soup is perfect: neither too thick nor too thin, as well as ideally seasoned and redolent of leeks. The salad is fine, though the addition of chewy, unreconstituted sun-dried tomatoes is a off note. Also off the mark is the trou normand (a midmeal palate-cleansing sorbet). Though the combination — mango, lemon, and tequila — is inspired, the crusty texture of the sorbet leads one to believe it's been languishing in the freezer since the chef's last trip to Mexico.

Main courses rise to the level of the starters. The pan-seared Angus filet mignon is tender and delicious, as are the potato and parsnip purée, and the sautéed rapini. The rack of lamb is another winner: the chops are rosé and the lamb flavour is pleasantly subtle. Also much appreciated are the mashed white lingot beans underneath, and the melting braised endive.

The pan-seared pork tenderloin doesn't quite cut it. The flavour is very good (on the menu, Johnston credits local pork producer F. Ménard), but the meat is just this side of overcooked and dry. No complaints about the accompaniments, however — especially since the sliced portobella mushrooms and potatoes are seasoned with fresh thyme and doused with a satisfying brown pork sauce.

The cheese selection is small, and none of the ones offered are local. As for desserts, your best bet is one of the Valrhona chocolate mousse cakes. Service is superb: as professional as that of a four-star restaurant and as friendly as that of a corner bistro.

IN THE KITCHEN • Chef and owner Pierre Johnston.

DECOR, DRESS, AMBIENCE • The restaurant is divided into several small, cozy rooms decorated with flowered wallpaper, potpourri, and country furniture. Given the location, the atmosphere is subdued and ideal for an intimate tête-à-tête. If you're into hand holding with your significant other, this is the place to do it.

WINE LIST • The wine list, which could serve as an example to many a restaurateur, ranges from the lovely white Spanish house wine offered by the glass to serious Bordeaux and Burgundies.

DON'T MISS • The shrimp martini, the goat's cheese starter, the filet mignon, the squab, and the rack of lamb.

WORDS TO THE WISE • McHaffy's combination of a rustic setting and a sophisticated, modern menu is intriguing. Granted, some of the food is less than stellar. Nonetheless, it's a wonderful spot for a gourmet meal amid the resplendent autumn colours, or for a romantic dinner during the ski season. Bear in mind that this restaurant is about an hour's drive from Montreal.

RESTAURANT LE McHAFFY
351 Rue Principale, Cowansville
Phone: (450) 266-7700
Open: Lunch, 11:30 A.M.-2 P.M., Tuesday to Friday;
dinner, 5:30 P.M.-11 P.M., Tuesday to Saturday
Wheelchair access: Yes
Reservations: Recommended
Cards: Major cards (and Interac)
Price range: Starters, $10.50-$15; main courses, $21.50-$25;
desserts, $7.25-$8.25; five-course prix fixe menu, $35.75-$39.75

| ★★1/2 | $ $ $ $ | REVIEWED 12/01 |

RESTAURANT TENTATION

SNAPSHOT • Restaurant Tentation is an ambitious newcomer on the Montreal scene. The menu lists a dazzling array of dishes that includes oysters, caviar, lobster, foie gras, pigeon (flown in from France), fancy fish, and a $15 chocolate dessert. There's an amuse-bouche at the outset of the meal and mignardises with coffee. Wine orders are taken by a sommelière, and during dinner the chef makes an appearance at every table to inquire whether diners are enjoying their food.

THE BIG PICTURE • Located on a quiet strip of Boulevard St. Laurent in Little Italy, Restaurant Tentation is a luxurious 40-seat establishment that has taken over the modest locale formerly occupied by Luca Bianca. One senses a commitment to excellence even before the food arrives. Three varieties of superb homemade bread—sea salt, rye, and pumpkin seed—are offered along with a spoonful of tuna tartare (light on the tuna and heavy on the raw onions).

Oyster season is taken seriously here. The first page of the menu lists 30 different preparations, ranging from raw oysters with sherry vinegar and shallots to an oyster spring roll with wasabi. At a recent meal, opting for something simple yet inventive, I chose the oysters with julienned, lime-perfumed cucumber and chlorophyll jelly. The combination was a bit of a letdown, as the cucumber flavour outshone all the others. The oysters, served out of their shell, were practically tasteless, lacking the sea-salt bite one relishes in an oyster (a different variety might have held its own next to the cucumber). And as for the lime and chlorophyll, if they weren't noted on the menu, you'd never know they were there.

The plates at this restaurant are assembled with flair. The most impressive starter is a small stack of braised rabbit and Yukon Gold potato slices layered atop one another on a small square plate and christened the "parmentier de lapereau." The rabbit meat is especially good: meltingly tender, full flavoured, and ideally enhanced with a subtle thyme jus.

Other starters don't fare as well. The lobster strudel is made with overcooked phyllo dough that tastes bitter, and the filling contains but a scant few morsels of lobster and bits of chewy chanterelle mushroom. A single, plate-sized ravioli (called a "voile") is equally lacking. Though the menu promises a white truffle, shrimp, and leek filling, there are no more than two small sliced shrimp and a spoonful of leeks; the truffles appear to be there in essence only, and on top of it all, the voile wrapper is gummy. Fortunately, the Chardonnay reduction served alongside is delicious, a real French sauce made with wine, butter, and stock reduced to a velvety liquid packed with rich flavours (sauces appear to be one of the chef's strengths).

Main courses again display this kitchen's talent for plate presentations. A large filet of St. Pierre (John Dory) is topped with two small slices of foie gras and accompanied by a red-wine-enhanced demi-glace, baby pattypan squash, and yellow carrots. The St. Pierre—a common item on French menus, yet scarce in Montreal's top restaurants—is a real treat. Perfectly cooked and moist, this lovely, white-fleshed fish has a consistency between monkfish and sole and a rich and delicate taste sophisticated enough to upstage the foie gras.

A plate of deer loin isn't as successful. The meat is cooked well past the ideal rosé—a shame, since it is tender and has a deep, gamy flavour. I like the choice of side dishes, however, especially the toothsome mound of kamut grains and a scattering of intensely flavoured dried blueberries.

The roasted wild turkey with a chestnut purée and cranberry sauce also comes up short. Though the meat is very good, it doesn't taste all that different from your average domestic turkey, especially when paired with a strong flavour like cranberry. Moreover, for $28, I expect something a bit more exciting.

In the dessert department, pastry chef François Lacasse has

composed a short but interesting menu that displays his strong technique and adventurous palate. A small organic carrot cake is topped with a thick goat's cheese cream and served with a scoop of cinnamon sorbet. His chocolate plate presents chocolate in many delightful guises: two bittersweet chocolate raviolis, a quenelle of thick white chocolate cream, a scoop of milk chocolate ice cream topped with a macaroon, and a few slices of miniature chocolate tart. Every bite offers chocolate at its best, my only complaint being that the $15 portion is less than generous.

IN THE KITCHEN · Chef and owner Giovanni Apollo.

DECOR, DRESS, AMBIENCE · The dining room is long and narrow, with a small bar, fireplace, and open kitchen set between the two dining rooms. Though a noticeable effort has been made to gussy up the place, the layout is the restaurant's weak point: the space is cramped, there are more undesirable tables than choice ones, and the small back dining room feels like Siberia. Management is obviously aware of these limitations and does its best to distract diners by way of frequent tableside visits and artfully assembled dishes.

WINE LIST · Though the wine list contains a fine selection of reasonably priced bottles, I would suggest casting it aside and allowing sommelière Véronique Dalle to make suggestions. Such a diverse menu cries out for wines by the glass, and Dalle's recommendations are invariably winners.

DON'T MISS · The oysters, the braised rabbit, the St. Pierre (John Dory), the venison, and the desserts.

WORDS TO THE WISE · In a town where cafés and bistros appear to be taking over and chefs rarely venture past their kitchen's swinging doors, Restaurant Tentation's attention to detail offers a rare taste of French savoir faire. True, the kitchen's high ambitions have yet to be met—at this writing, the food is a bit fussy and the menu needs more focus—but the welcoming ambience and the enthusiasm of the staff (especially chef Apollo) make up for a lot.

RESTAURANT TENTATION
7076 Boulevard St. Laurent (near Jean Talon)
Telephone: (514) 274-3343
Open: 5:30 P.M.-midnight, Tuesday to Sunday
Wheelchair access: No
Reservations: Recommended
Cards: All major cards
Price range: Starters, $5-$67 (caviar); main courses, $19-$39;
desserts, $8-$15; seven-course tasting menu, $72

★★1/2	$ $ $ $	REVIEWED 01/01

RIB 'N REEF

SNAPSHOT • Behind its dreary, modern façade, Rib 'n Reef is one elegant steak house. Diners can expect juicy char-grilled USDA Prime steaks, Caesar salads, and fluffy baked potatoes at this beloved Montreal landmark. From the reef, there are excellent fresh fish and seafood. Despite the formal decor and service, the ambience is relaxed and family-friendly.

THE BIG PICTURE • Rib 'n Reef celebrated its thirty-eighth anniversary in 2001. This Boulevard Décarie favourite, under the management of Peter Katsoudas and his wife, Chris-Ann Nakis, for the past seven years, was completely renovated in August 1999. The menu still offers standard steak house fare with a marked emphasis on seafood, perhaps more so than at similar establishments.

One could easily forgo starters, as main-course portions are he-man sized (and, in keeping with the Montreal steak house tradition, garlicky dill pickles and fresh coleslaw are offered gratis at the outset of the meal). Of the ones sampled, the crab cakes, served with a delicious grainy-mustard cream sauce, are a definite must. The clam chowder is thick and rich but stingy on the clams and too subtle in flavour to compensate for all the calories. A phyllo shell filled with sautéed Parisian mushrooms and pink pepper-corns is pleasant, but after the first few bites it becomes dull (a few wild mushrooms would liven it up).

The best of the starters is that steak house classic, Caesar salad. Prepared with passion and flair by the waiter tableside, this is a Caesar to put all those preplated versions to shame. The romaine is freshly cut, the croutons are the real deal, the creamy vinai-grette has the right tang and garlic punch, and the bacon bits and grated Parmesan add an edge of decadence — the ideal overture for the serious feeding frenzy to come.

The steak at Rib 'n Reef is advertised as USDA Prime mid-western beef, aged 21 to 30 days and hand cut daily. It lives up to its billing. An 18-ounce half-inch-thick ribeye offers a charred ex-terior, a juicy pink interior, and the intense mineral meat flavour sought after by steak aficionados. It's juicy and full of flavour, but it's neither too fatty nor too sinewy — just delicious. A New York cut sirloin, almost an inch thick, is also first-rate, though certainly less flavourful than bone-in, thinner cuts, like the ribeye.

Rack of lamb is another good choice, for the six New Zealand chops are individually grilled for maximum flavour. Side-dish potato offerings include fat French fries and delicious baked pota-toes — heaven when slathered with sour cream and topped with bacon bits and chives.

From the reef, you'll find the standard favourites — lobster, scampi, and shrimp — along with fresh fish, such as red snapper. The snapper is served in a portion as generous as the meats, and it's perfectly pan-seared, the succulent flesh falling off the skin in moist and tender chunks.

If you're up for dessert at the end of such a copious meal, re-consider. Desserts are heavy, American-style concoctions — one of the few letdowns at Rib 'n Reef.

The wait staff, however, is superb: from the maître d' and coat-check girl to the waiters and busboys, everyone is friendly and thoroughly professional.

IN THE KITCHEN • Chef Odile Messier.

DECOR, DRESS, AMBIENCE • Following the traditional steak house style, the decor has a masculine feel, with wine-coloured panelled walls, deep banquettes, and armchairs upholstered in dark striped fabric. Small shaded lamps at every table, wall sconces, and recessed spotlights provide the kind of low lighting that everyone over 30 appreciates. Waiters wear tuxedos; busboys sport white jackets and bow ties. The casually attired, upscale crowd is comprised of middle-aged couples and families. The atmosphere is subdued and civilized.

WINE LIST • The wine list features many impressive, if costly, bottles. For those less willing to splurge, there are a few good bottles, including a $48 Beringer Merlot, which goes well with the meaty menu selections.

DON'T MISS • The crab cakes, the Caesar salad, the ribeye steak, the lamb chops, and the fresh fish.

WORDS TO THE WISE • It's a pleasure to dine at Rib 'n Reef. In spite of the formal setting, there are no hassles and no pretensions, just good steak house fare and the kind of professional service you'd expect from an establishment with such a track record. If you're an out-of-towner, you may not know that the Boulevard Décarie location, while quite a distance from downtown, is still easily accessible via the Montreal subway system; the de la Savane stop is within walking distance.

RIB 'N REEF
8105 Boulevard Décarie (near de la Savane)
Telephone: (514) 735-1601
Open: 11:30 A.M.-midnight, daily
Wheelchair access: Yes
Reservations: Recommended
Cards: Major cards
Price range: Starters, $6.95-$23.50; main courses, $20.95-$44.50; desserts, $4.75-$12.95

| ★★★1/2 | $ $ $ $ | REVIEWED 01/00 |

RISTORANTE DA VINCI

SNAPSHOT · Montrealers have the Mazzaferro family, owners of Ristorante Da Vinci, to thank for their first taste of anchovies, home-delivered pizza, and espresso coffee. That was back in the 1960s. Today the legacy continues. Though the takeout operation is long gone, the second generation still prides itself on introducing locals and visitors to authentic Italian cuisine at its best. Seamless service is just another facet of this restaurant's commitment to excellence. And the beautiful Victorian townhouse setting creates the most civilized and romantic of moods.

THE BIG PICTURE · Italian fare has undergone a renaissance over the past few years, shunning modernity for a return to authentic regional cooking and high-quality imported ingredients —a concept still slow to be adopted in this city. There are a few Italian restaurants in Montreal making an effort to serve authentic cuisine. Ristorante Da Vinci is one of them.

Although southern in spirit, this restaurant offers a repertoire of popular dishes from the various regions and provinces of Italy, all interpreted with elegance and finesse. The typical carpaccio and Mozzarella starter comes to life at Da Vinci. The key to this carpaccio is the high quality and intense flavour of the thinly sliced, wine-marinated beef tenderloin. Every melting mouthful of meat is enhanced with peppery, olive-oil-dressed arugula and slivers of Parmigiano-Reggiano. Superb.

Carpaccio lovers are also sure to enjoy the rustico di bresaola, another beef, cheese, and arugula combination, which, though similar in appearance, offers the stronger flavours of lean, salty cured beef and pungent Fontina cow's milk cheese. A salad of Mozzarella, tomatoes, and basil is also a cut above, as the cheese —imported buffalo Mozzarella—is so much richer and more flavourful than the standard, tasteless Bocconcini (it's also about five times as costly).

Of the dishes sampled from the pasta and risotti menu, the standout is definitely chef Vincezo Bonfa's hearty potato gnocchi with lamb ragù sauce. The homemade gnocchi are soft yet firm, and the creamy tomato-based sauce has a gentle lamb and rosemary flavour. Pasta medallions served with a lively fresh tomato sauce are also outstanding. The pasta pillows are filled with ground veal, Parmesan, and nutmeg—each as meaty as a tiny tourtière. A generous portion of spaghettini Santa Maria is made with a delicious sauce of scallions, smoked salmon, perfectly cooked shrimp, and diced tomato.

Prices can run high on this menu, and the $32 seafood risotto is a case in point. Though some might prefer the rice be cooked a bit more al dente, others would argue that this version is just right. The taste, however, is not an issue. Laced with saffron, seafood, and only a hint of fishiness, it's simply sublime. And considering the generous portion of seafood—clams, jumbo shrimp, mussels, scallops, and calamari—the price is justified.

A $36 Quebec veal chop is a wallet cruncher as well. The two-inch-thick chop is portioned in-house and marinated for 48 hours in olive oil, rosemary, and thyme. It's then grilled to the lightest rosé, topped with crisp fried onions, and served with a braised potato, sautéed rapini, and roasted carrots.

Though Italians are rarely known for their desserts, Da Vinci has taken care to offer the best of the classics at very reasonable prices. You could finish your meal with a shot of excellent espresso, but you'd be missing out on the silky semifreddo, packed with caramelized hazelnuts and chocolate shards, and served with crème anglaise, chocolate sauce, and strawberries. A dreamy panna cotta—beautifully enhanced with a red berry coulis and a handful of berries—is made with reduced, vanilla-flavoured heavy cream and just enough gelatin to hold together the conical shape. The lemon granita has a fresh-squeezed flavour and an ideal creamy texture. The best dessert at DaVinci might just be the Sicilian specialty, cannoli. This bubbly, crisp dough is so dry you'd never know it emerged from boiling oil. The nutty, spicy flavour and crunchy texture of the cookie offers the ultimate contrast to the sweet and creamy Ricotta filling enhanced with orange and lemon zests.

One can't help but be impressed by the high level of confidence and professionalism in this room. Also appreciated is the attention to little details: the bowl of walnuts served before dessert, finger bowls for seafood eaters, homemade amaretti cookies with coffee, and waiters who are smart enough to turn away before one makes the inexcusable faux pas of asking for grated Parmesan cheese on a seafood pasta or risotto.

IN THE KITCHEN • Chef Vincenzo Bonfa.

DECOR, DRESS, AMBIENCE • The dining room occupies two floors of an elegant Victorian townhouse. The sponge-painted yellow walls are hung with oil paintings depicting Montreal winter scenes. Frosted-glass panels divide the ground floor into cozy sections, and everywhere you look there are wine bottles gleaming in the candlelight. Diners are greeted by Salvatore Mazzaferro, who most nights mans the reservation book, points waiters and customers in the right direction, and clears the occasional plate.

WINE LIST • As they are at many fine Italian restaurants in Montreal, wines here are on the expensive side. Finding a good bottle at a reasonable price can be difficult. Your waiter, however, can provide good advice.

DON'T MISS • The carpaccio, the gnocchi with lamb ragù, the seafood risotto, the veal chop, and the desserts.

WORDS TO THE WISE • Given that everything here—ambience, service, food, and decor—is in sync, you can feel confident in choosing this restaurant for a celebratory meal (lunch or dinner) or for a memorable night out with guests or a group of friends. Chances are you'll have one of the best Italian meals you've had in a while.

RISTORANT DA VINCI
1180 Rue Bishop (near Ste. Catherine)
Telephone: (514) 874-2001
Open: Noon-midnight, Monday to Friday, 5 P.M.-midnight,
Saturday, and by request on Sunday
Wheelchair access: Partial
Reservations: Recommended
Cards: All major cards
Price range: Starters, $5.50-$16.50; main courses, $13.50-$39;
desserts, $4.75-$7.50

★★1/2	$ $ $	REVIEWED 05/00

RISTORANTE LUCCA

SNAPSHOT · With its simple yet elegant decor, authentic cuisine, and friendly wait staff, Lucca is the ideal Italian trattoria. The crowd is sophisticated—from the yuppies at dinner to the locals at lunch. There's no set menu, as the Italian market cuisine, which uses the freshest local ingredients, changes daily. Pastas, grilled meats, and seafood are standouts. The soft polenta alone is worth the search for a parking place.

THE BIG PICTURE · You may have driven past Ristorante Lucca many times without knowing it. Sandwiched between triplexes and other nondescript restaurants on Rue Dante in Montreal's Little Italy, its broad white awning is easy to miss.

Chef and owner Domenic Armeni has slowly transformed this cozy restaurant into a satisfyingly upscale eatery, taking the neighbourhood trattoria to a whole new level. Unlike many of the area's restaurants, which prepare standard Italian Canadian fare (claiming the public demands it), Lucca offers adventurous Italian dishes based on the concept of market cuisine.

As there's no set menu, daily specials are listed on a large blackboard. But there are a few house specialties—like fried calamari—that never leave the board. No surprise, as the generous portion of crisp squid rings and spiders is piping hot, tender, and grease-free. The accompanying tomato-basil sauce with garlic and pepper is tasty, but hardly necessary, for the fish flavour is subtle and a squirt of fresh lemon is more than sufficient.

Warm-weather fare includes fruit and seafood salads, such as grilled shrimp with exotic fruit (mango, star fruit, papaya, passion fruit) and baby lettuce leaves coated with a vanilla dressing. In arugula season, don't miss the arugula salad, which is simply enhanced with shaved Parmesan and a light lemon dressing.

Antipasto misto is another sure bet. This plate contains a neatly arranged assortment of thinly sliced meats, Provolone cheese, and vegetables. Smoked and salted meats include top-quality salami, prosciutto, capicolo, and bresaola. And—unlike so many other antipasto plates, which are loaded with canned vegetables soaked in low-quality olive oil—this selection includes marinated fresh artichoke hearts, red peppers, eggplant, and a mixture of small cut vegetables such as carrots, mushrooms, and olives. It's an antipasto plate that doesn't spoil one's appetite for the main course.

This kitchen certainly knows its way around two well-loved Italian specialties: grilled veal chop and braised osso buco. The veal chop is slightly rosé, meltingly tender, and—thankfully— not of the prehistoric proportions served in many places around town. In a word, it's fabulous. Its accompaniments include grilled red peppers, sautéed spinach, and delicious, perfectly seasoned, soft white polenta. So much better than all those pasty polentas made with water, this recipe includes milk, cream, garlic, and basil, resulting in a polenta with a fluffy texture and an appealing flavour.

The osso buco is equally impressive. The meat is falling-off-the-bone tender and the shank contains a blob of gelatinous marrow—decidedly gruesome, but undeniably delicious. The accompanying wild mushroom risotto made with fresh porcini, shiitake, oyster, and button mushrooms has a rich earthiness, but the consistency leaves something to be desired; like so many restaurant risottos, it's just this side of overcooked.

The rigatoni is correctly al dente. Tossed with spinach, bresaola, and wild mushrooms, each ribbed tube is also coated with a splendid cream-enhanced mushroom sauce. Another excellent pasta dish is the fettuccini with a generous portion of perfectly cooked salmon, scallops, and shrimp, the whole covered in a tomato sauce with spinach.

There are a few disappointments. Made sans beans, peas, or pasta, the minestrone is a sad and sorry affair. The simplest of the pasta entrées, penne with tomato, also fails to satisfy, as the pasta quills are overcooked and the tomato sauce is harsh and lacking in any interesting flavour accents.

Desserts, on the other hand, are not only very good but also made from scratch. The chocolate mousse is a treat, with a super-smooth expensive-chocolate flavour and an original crunchy base made with white chocolate, pine nuts, and crumbled cookies. The cakey, coffee-soaked tiramisu is divine. The panna cotta is absolutely authentic—just barely gelatinized, sprinkled with vanilla beans, and topped with fresh raspberries. It's a simple Italian dessert all too rarely seen in our city's restaurants.

There's plenty to like about Lucca, and not just in the kitchen. Service is excellent—an expert balance between casual friendliness and professionalism, so well epitomized by one spiky-haired busboy, who walks around with a towel on his arm and a permanent smile on his face. Everyone looks happy to be here.

IN THE KITCHEN · Chefs and owners Domenic Armeni and Claudio Fabielo.

DECOR, DRESS, AMBIENCE · The decor is pared down and elegant—completely free of flash, pretension, or (the flip side) checkered tablecloths. The walls are sponge-painted in soothing tones of beige, the plain wooden chairs are comfortable, and there's a lovely fresh-flower arrangement at the bar. The lighting is low at dinner and bright at lunch, when the smell of fried calamari permeates the air. Noise levels can be alarmingly high, since the room is small—there are only 42 seats and a few choice places at the bar.

WINE LIST · Lucca's wine list is short and pricey. Food this good deserves good wine, but there's nothing here for under $50 to match the quality of the food. Ask your waiter for a few suggestions within your price range. Wines by the glass, though generous, are also expensive.

DON'T MISS · The antipasto, the calamari, the grilled veal chop, the osso buco, the panna cotta, and the tiramisu.

WORDS TO THE WISE · Few would dispute that this is one of the coziest trattorias in town. Parking can be a problem. Lucca is near the Jean Talon Market and Little Italy, two destinations popular with shoppers and restaurant-goers. Consider taking a cab or public transportation, or be prepared to make a couple of loops around the block. Also, remember that food this good comes at a fairly hefty price.

RISTORANTE LUCCA
12 Rue Dante (near St. Laurent)
Telephone: (514) 278-6502
Open: Lunch, noon-3 P.M., Monday to Friday; dinner, 6 P.M.-
11 P.M., Tuesday to Saturday
Wheelchair access: No
Reservations: Recommended
Cards: All major cards
Price range: Starters, $10-$12; main courses, $15-$33;
desserts, $6; lunch table d'hôte menu, $12-$22

| ★★1/2 | $ $ | REVIEWED 04/00 |

SHO-DAN

SNAPSHOT · The Montreal love affair with sushi carries on, and those up for fine sashimi, sushi, and funky makis should bypass the sleepy downtown dinner scene for a night at Sho-Dan. The modern, sleek setting is ideal for risk takers willing to try blueberries and pineapple in their maki rolls. The traditional sushi-bar offerings are also delicious—ultrafresh and beautifully presented.

THE BIG PICTURE · When the sushi craze broke in Montreal in the early eighties, many chefs and ambitious home cooks ran out to purchase bamboo mats, powdered wasabi, and Kokuho Rose rice. Suddenly, sushi was on every caterer's canapé platter, maki rolls were available at the corner dépanneur, and sushi bars were popping up faster than Honda dealerships. The smell of nori (seaweed) was everywhere. But once butterfly-shaped maki rolls and fruit and chocolate sushi desserts starting appearing, one would have assumed that the trend seekers would leave this Japanese import behind.

Wrong! Sushi was in the right place at the right time. Exotic, aesthetic, low fat, and guilt-free, no food better embodies the current Zeitgeist of healthy eating and tranquil living. Sushi is today's soul food. Montrealers' fling with sushi has deepened into a committed relationship. Local Japanese restaurants (along with a handful of trendy Italian restaurants) are reaping the benefits— Sho-Dan among them.

The menu lists well-known sushi and sashimi combinations, single à la carte selections, and, for those who shun sushi, a variety of salads as well as several teriyaki and tempura dishes. Sho-Dan also excells in the preparation of adventurous maki rolls, reflecting the North American take on this traditional Japanese favourite.

Three in-house creations include the Twister, the Sushi Pizza, and the Romeo and Juliet. All are knockouts. The Twister is a panfried, oval-shaped maki roll that contains rice and strips of whitefish, carrot, and scallion. Sliced thin and fanned out on a baby-blue plate, it's served with a tangy teriyaki-lemon mayonnaise. Every bite, coated in a crispy tempura-flake crust, offers a contrasting crunchy and smooth texture — it's reminiscent of good fried chicken, and even more fun.

The Sushi Pizza is even better. A chewy baked rice cake is topped with spicy sauce, thin slices of raw tuna, smoked salmon, and small mounds of gleaming orange-and-green (wasabi-enhanced) flying-fish roe. The Romeo and Juliet is as funky a sushi creation as one can imagine. Check out these ingredients: pineapple chunks, blueberries, raspberries, rice, shrimp, and spicy sauce. Everything is layered, wrapped, rolled in nori, deep-fried, thinly sliced, and . . . served with orange segments! It tastes better than it sounds. The subtle fruit flavour is given a boost by a terrific teriyaki sauce made with ginger and sesame seed oil.

From the à la carte sushi menu, don't miss Sho-Dan's version of the Kamikaze maki roll. Made with salmon, avocado, cucumber, and crispy tempura flakes that provide a pleasant "Snap, Krackle & Pop" with every bite, this roll has created legions of addicts, who frequent the restaurant for nothing else but. The Vancouver roll, a uramaki (a reverse roll with the rice on the outside), contains smoked salmon, avocado, cucumber, smelt roe, and ginseng. The remarkable quality here is lightness; there's no hint of the cloying stickiness found in the hard-packed, rice-laden concoctions of lesser establishments.

Traditional sushi-bar offerings are also first-rate. A variety of sashimi includes maguro (red tuna), syake (salmon), and shiromi (whitefish). Of the sushi selections, the basic nigiri includes thin slices of shrimp, salmon, whitefish, and tuna, each draped over a hand-shaped quenelle of vinegar-flavoured rice with a generous swash of wasabi. Both the perfectly seasoned and cooked rice and the ultrafresh fish literally dissolve on the palate, the richness and the soft texture so perfectly capturing the sensual sushi experience.

Nonsushi selections are hit and miss. A spicy octopus salad scores high. Blanched and marinated in a spicy soy sauce, the octopus pieces are fresh and tender. The tempura is surprisingly disappointing. The batter is light, crisp, and grease-free, but the vegetables are stone cold. The jumbo shrimp are also no more than warm. Tepid tempura? No thank you.

The beef teriyaki is an attention grabber, as it's served atop a large mound of bean sprouts and the whole plate arrives at the table sizzling hot. How hot? Too hot, for the steak is overcooked. In addition, the meat is insufficiently flavourful to stand up to the robust, sweet sauce.

For dessert, skip the the red bean ice cream, which isn't all that different from good old vanilla. The ginger ice cream is a better choice, as it's packed with nuggets of peppery candied ginger. The rich and creamy crème brûlée is perfect.

IN THE KITCHEN • Chef Romeo Pham.

DECOR, DRESS, AMBIENCE • The dining room is modern and sleek: high ceilings, angular beige-and-cream-painted walls, tubular spotlights, and contemporary furniture—not especially Japanese, but neither is the jazzy background music.

WINE LIST • There are three kinds of sake available, along with about 30 international wines priced between $28 and $60.

DON'T MISS • The octopus salad, the sushi and sashimi, and the house makis: the Twister, the Sushi Pizza, the Romeo and Juliet, and the Kamikaze.

WORDS TO THE WISE • Count on about $60 per person for dinner at Sho-Dan, which, considering the quality of the ingredients and the creativity of the presentations, is more than reasonable. In a time when it's common to pay top dollar for grilled steak, this exquisite fare can lay claim to being one of the best values around. For a bit of entertainment, find a seat at the sushi bar and watch the chefs do their thing. And don't be too shy to strike up a conversation; they'll be happy to guide you in your choices.

SHO-DAN
2020 Rue Metcalfe (near de Maisonneuve)
Telephone: (514) 987-9987
Open: Lunch, 11 A.M.-2:30 P.M., Monday to Friday;
dinner, 5 P.M.-10:30 P.M., Monday to Saturday
Wheelchair access: Yes
Reservations: Recommended; essential at lunch
Cards: Major cards
Price range: Starters, $2.50-$12; main courses, $10.95-$22;
desserts, $2.95-$5.95

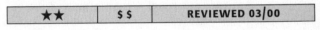

| ★★ | $ $ | REVIEWED 03/00 |

TERRA

SNAPSHOT • Terra is a hotel restaurant like no other. The food is showy, and the glamorous, all-white setting is worthy of Old Hollywood. Though the menu is primarily Mediterranean, there are Italian, French, and fusion dishes as well. If you're not up for a full dinner, Terra would be a good choice for a post- or pretheatre drink, nibble, or dessert.

THE BIG PICTURE • Entering Terra is like stepping onto cloud 9 or into a winter wonderland. Snap out of it and you'll realize you're on Drummond below Ste. Catherine inside the glamorous white-on-white dining room of the newly renovated Hôtel Europa.

Terra's cuisine is described as Mediterranean, which immediately conjures up images of grilled fish, lamb, olive oil, hummus, couscous, and baba ghannoush. But among the 26 starters and 30 main courses on this menu there's a bit of everything — not only Mediterranean, but also nothern Italian, French, fusion, and more.

National styles aside, Terra's cuisine turns out to be trendy — even flashy. Decorative presentations and unpredictable combinations and colours jump off the plate, all the more so since absolutely everything in the surrounding environment is devoid of colour.

Starters looks promising, which is to be expected from a
kitchen where plate presentation rules. A deep-fried rice-paper
basket holds a cascade of baby lettuces topped with nuggets of
sautéed lemon chicken. It's a lovely display, but the chicken has
no discernible taste of lemon, and the salad is doused with an
underseasoned, oily vinaigrette. A scallop fricassée with young
celery leaves fares somewhat better, though the accompanying
salad is as dull as the first. The dish is saved by three fresh scallops
that are plump, lightly seared, and topped with strips of oven-
roasted tomato.

The risotto starters are hit and miss. The first, made with sun-
dried tomatoes, pine nuts, and black olives, combines three strong
ingredients that aren't compatible; there's a battle of flavours
being fought on this plate. Worse may be the soupy, overcooked
rice—an unforgivable faux pas in the world of risotto.

Fortunately, the second risotto is a winner, especially as it's
prepared with pearl barley, a popular new alternative to the classic
starchy Italian rice. The round, al dente grains—deliciously nutty
—are paired with a flavourful stock and a generous portion of
sautéed oyster mushrooms.

Main courses reveal some interesting ideas. As strange as it
sounds, a dish consisting of perch (walleye), candied pineapple,
and spinach works. The pan-seared fish has a subtle flavour that's
pleasantly enhanced by the fruity pineapple and earthy spinach.
It's all rather light and refreshing. Pineapple and perch? Who
would have thought?

Another creative pairing is the red mullet and beets. In this
dish, the mullet filets lean against a mound of puréed yellow beets
surrounded by a pool of red beet juice. Although beautifully presented, the fish is bland and the beet purée and sauce are nothing
more than sweet.

Meats fare better. A towering braised lamb shank is served with
a fabulous, full-flavoured reduced lamb jus dotted with a miniature mirepoix. The meat is meltingly tender—perfectly braised.
The accompanying couscous is spicy and redolent of cinnamon.

The pork tenderloin is also first-rate. Served with roasted garlic potatoes and fanned zucchini, the moist pork filet is cooked slightly rosé, sliced on the diagonal, and served upright alongside the potatoes.

Desserts are decorated with many tuiles and gaufrettes. Underneath the cookies you'll find a warm molten chocolate cake that's rich and delicious. The vanilla crème brûlée has the requisite silky-smooth texture. A cake with layers of chocolate mousse and praline cream is nice, but too rich to finish. Coffee is very good, and tea, a high-quality Earl Grey blend served in lovely little pots, is a real treat.

Service at Terra is friendly, well paced, and professional.

IN THE KITCHEN · Chef Denis Payen.

DECOR, DRESS, AMBIENCE · Swoopy puckered drapes hang from the ceiling, and tiny table lamps illuminate white banquettes lined with quilted fabric. You'll feel like Jean Harlow sinking slowly into an overstuffed white sofa. The overall effect is quite stunning—original and good fun.

WINE LIST · The wine list is a bonus. Not that prices are a deal (some bottles creep close to three times their retail value), but there's a large selection available for under $40.

DON'T MISS · The barley risotto, the perch with pineapple, the pork tenderloin, the braised lamb shank, and the molten chocolate cake.

WORDS TO THE WISE · Terra is feast for the eyes; few restaurants in Montreal can elicit such a "wow" response. The food doesn't quite live up to the glamorous setting (not much could). Nonetheless, for an over-the-top occasion, you might want to give it a go. It's not every day you'll have dinner in a place like this.

TERRA
1240 Rue Drummond (near Ste. Catherine, in the Hôtel
Europa Royal)
Telephone: (514) 866-8910
Open: 7 A.M.-11 P.M., Monday to Friday, 7 A.M.-3 P.M. and
5 P.M.-midnight, Saturday and Sunday
Wheelchair access: Yes
Reservations: Recommended
Cards: Major cards
Price range: Starters, $3.95-$14.95; main courses, $11.95-$39.95;
desserts, $5.95-$8.95

★★1/2	$ $	REVIEWED 05/00

TOKYO SUKIYAKI

SNAPSHOT · Don't be turned off by the obscure setting. Montreal's oldest Japanese restaurant, divided into 15 private tatami
rooms, offers red lanterns, kimono-clad waitresses, and delicious,
authentic Japanese food. The teriyaki and tempura dishes are not
to be missed.

THE BIG PICTURE · "This couldn't be the right place," I say as
we pull up to Tokyo Sukiyaki. "Oh yes it is," says a friend, whose
last visit to this, Montreal's oldest Japanese restaurant (it opened
in 1961), was in the late sixties. From the outside, Tokyo Sukiyaki
appears to be nothing more than an old house that has definitely
seen better days. "I know it doesn't look like much," he says, with
an air of excitement, "but behind those doors are bubbling streams
filled with goldfish, little bridges, and great Japanese food." I don't
believe any of it, and I insist that he check things out before we
park. A good sport, he runs in and emerges a few moments later,
giggling and claiming that the restaurant hasn't changed a bit.
And so we enter—three of us, two adventurous, smiling men and
sceptical me.

We're greeted by an elderly, kimono-clad lady who kindly asks us to remove our shoes. She then hands us plastic slippers — red for me, black for the men — and leads us down a mysterious corridor. Shuffling along, I soak up this curious scene. We are invited to enter our own private dining room, where we sit cross-legged on straw mats at a round, black-lacquered table (there's a convenient well under the table into which one may insert one's legs — a bonus for less agile diners). An air of mystery pervades the secluded little room. Though there are no other diners to be seen, voices make it plain that we are not alone. Peeking through the soji screens, I catch a glimpse of a group of well-dressed twenty-somethings and a family with small children. Obviously, these private rooms are ideal for dining with youngsters (I dare say they're also ideal for couples carrying on discreet affairs).

Our waitress, our sole contact with the outside world, enters with menus listing classical Japanese favourites, including sukiyaki, shabu-shabu, teriyaki, yakitori, and sushi. When I ask about the shabu-shabu — a fondue-style specialty of beef and vegetables cooked in steaming broth — she tells me to have the beef teriyaki instead. I inquire about the cut of meat, but she hasn't a clue. She's equally confused about the composition of the yakitori sauce and the sushi. With a complete air of indifference, she eventually hands us a small card of sushi selections. I've seen gas station attendants with more enthusiasm than this. We order the teriyaki, the yakitori, and the sushi. Each is the main dish of a five-course set menu. Rubbing my hands in my steaming towel (oshibori), I'm still grumbling, predicting a bleak outcome to this meal, when the food arrives.

We start with a cold salad of fine white rice noodles, carrot, and celery. It's lively and fresh — three simple ingredients brightened up with a marinated ginger, sake, vinegar, and sesame oil vinaigrette. In the true Japanese spirit, we noisily slurp up every last noodle.

A clear soup, suimono, is the second dish of a traditional Japanese menu, and Tokyo Sukiyaki's offering includes chicken with chopped green onion and scrambled egg. Served in the traditional lidded bowl, this simple broth is as fragrant as the most complex, ingredient-packed homemade chicken soup.

Next up is a grilled dish: yakimono. My companions are served chicken yakitori, while I'm offered a dish of a half-dozen strips of beef teriyaki. The chicken is textbook Japanese—moist and just tinged pink at the bone. The sweet yakitori marinade, made with soy, sugar, onion, and garlic, provides an exotic lift to the grilled flavour of the meat, especially with the delicious hot chicken juices milling around in there.

My companions devour their chicken in seconds, complaining that two small legs are hardly enough. Little do they know that the beef is even better. The homemade sauce, made with sake, mirin, and soy, is exceptionally tasty and worlds apart from those ready-made sweet and oversalted teriyaki sauces served in many establishments around town. But it's the beef that steals the show: sublimely tender, glazed, crusty, and full flavoured.

Dish after dish proves my initial impressions incorrect. Take the tempura, that ubiquitous Japanese specialty. Tokyo Sukiyaki's version is golden and lacy, with the fried batter wrapped around jumbo shrimp as well as sliced potato, carrot, green pepper, and green beans. Everything is light, piping hot, and not the least bit oily. And, instead of the soy sauce served in most Japanese restaurants, the dipping sauce here is the real deal: light soy with grated daikon and ginger.

Two of our main courses are larger servings of the fantastic yakitori and teriyaki. The accompanying stir-fried vegetables—potato, onion, carrot, scallion—are perfectly seasoned and pleasantly crisp. Our third main course is the sushi platter, which turns out to be the evening's only disappointment. A large, rectangular wooden tray holds four cucumber maki rolls, a flying fish roe maki, and a wide assortment of nigiri sushi. Topped with fresh, high-quality tuna, octopus, salmon, red snapper, whitefish, shrimp, and crab, the rice, though correctly prepared (sticky but not clammy), is underseasoned, providing a dull base for the lovely fish. Compared to the creative sushi concoctions found in Montreal's modern sushi bars, this platter falls short.

We finish up with excellent green tea, which is served with a wedge of ungarnished honeydew melon—an authentic and welcome close to our copious meal. On the way out, we're surprised to see our shoes laid out for us at the door. Little touches like these make the evening memorable. So does the price. Our feast for three, including sake and Japanese beer, came to only $130.

IN THE KITCHEN • Chef Hiro Onda.

DECOR, DRESS, AMBIENCE • The restaurant is divided into 15 closed tatami rooms of various sizes. Dark-red lanterns line the tops of the walls. Little red bridges crisscross a rock-lined stream that meanders through the room towards a small bar. Alas, the goldfish are long gone.

WINE LIST • There is one sake available, at $25, and about five wines priced between $20 and $33.

DON'T MISS • The tempura and the beef and chicken teriyaki.

WORDS TO THE WISE • If ever there was a case for not judging a book by its cover, it's Tokyo Sukiyaki. The unusual decor and top-quality cuisine are completely at odds with the obscure location and the somewhat seedy impression the restaurant conveys from the outside. I recommend that you pull on your best pair of socks and give it a try.

TOKYO SUKIYAKI
7355 Avenue Mountain Sights (near Jean Talon)
Telephone: (514) 737-7245
Open: 5:30 P.M.-11 P.M., Tuesday to Saturday,
and 5:30 P.M.-10:30 P.M., Sunday
Wheelchair access: No
Reservations: Recommended
Cards: Major cards
Price Range: Starters, $4; main courses, $19-$20; desserts, $3.50;
four-course dinner, $27

| ★★★★ | $$$$ | REVIEWED 09/01 |

TOQUÉ!

SNAPSHOT · Take a look at his press clippings, and you'll get the impression that Toqué!'s chef and co-owner, Normand Laprise, can do no wrong. And it's not just about his personality or his endless quest for choice ingredients. The man can really cook, and he knows exactly how to showcase all those exquisite foodstuffs. Toqué! is considered by many to be Montreal's best restaurant. Everything tastes better at Toqué!

THE BIG PICTURE · How do you feel about milkweed pods with your tuna? Or, for that matter, cold cod soup, sea parsley, or sautéed fairy-ring mushrooms? At Toqué!, you never know quite what to expect. You just have to trust Normand Laprise, indefatigable innovator and numero uno chef in these parts. Chances are that whatever he creates will be fabulous.

One of Toqué!'s Christmas menus included the most perfect classical terrine de foie gras imaginable. A risotto that followed would be the pride of the best Italian restaurant. Strewn around the steaming mound of rice were vegetables, each ideally al dente and bursting with flavour. And this was in December, a month when most chefs gripe—with reason—about flavourless produce.

He's also a curious one, this Laprise, travelling far and wide in search of ingredients and cooking techniques to the benefit of Montrealers who need journey no further than Rue St. Denis for a taste of something new. A dinner in October 2000 featured dishes bathed in frothy sauces, no doubt influenced by a pilgrimage to Europe's restaurant of the moment—El Bulli, north of Barcelona. There were also razor clams at that meal, with organic, multicoloured cherry tomatoes lined up inside the long, rectangular shell. Why razor clams? Oh, just another discovery from an ingredient-seeking sojourn to the Îles de la Madeleine.

Lately, Laprise's inspirations have run a bit closer to home. Milkweed pods, glasswort, wild purslane, wild spinach, and wild mesclun are featured on the plates, as are other plants and herbs from François Brouillard, an "artisanal forager" and friend of Laprise's since the early 1990s. The chef's tastes now run to the sauvage, and so strong is this man's influence on our local dining scene that soon many aspiring chefs are sure to be doing the "wild thing."

Though eye-catching ingredients are added or subtracted from the menu each season, the Laprise touch is always present. He's in no hurry to radically change his style; its evolution may be slow, but it isn't forced or contrived. A tartare of tuna with avocado, chives, marinated radish, ginger, and taro chips (also prepared with duck) is a variation of an old Toqué! favourite, salmon tartare, which has been on the menu since the restaurant's opening, a decade ago. Signature dishes, like the gratin of Tournevent goat's cheese with spinach and Yukon Gold potatoes, and a simple salad made with the best greens and herbs of organic farmer Pierre-André Daignault, still hold an honoured place on Toqué!'s menu.

Of the starters, who could resist a taste of chilled cod soup with lobster, wild purslane, and glasswort? The cod flavour is ideally subtle and well enhanced by the sweet lobster meat and succulent greens. The soup's creamy consistency and alabaster colour come from the addition of fresh whole milk. Little garlic croutons provide a pleasant crunch amid the various mouth feels. Though this big bowl of cold soup arrives looking awfully bland — like the underbelly of a whale — its well-matched flavours and varying textures turn out to be the revelation of the evening.

Over the years, there has usually been a quail dish among the appetizers. Laprise's current "ode to the quail" features a roasted Cap St. Ignace quail with green asparagus, sautéed morels, shallots, wild mesclun, and a red wine vinegar reduction. Laprise is famous for his foie gras "à la Toqué!" — meaning, prepared following the inspiration of the moment. A recently sampled plate pairs the panfried liver with a white bean purée.

In the past, Toqué!'s starters have often outshone the overly generous main courses. Lately, the main courses have been beyond reproach. Boileau venison done two ways — grilled upper filet and roasted haunch — is tender and flavourful enough to explain why beef is a rarity on Toqué!'s menu. To top it off, it's served with beautiful accompaniments: woodsy sautéed fairy-ring mushrooms, chubby roasted carrot halves, potent wilted baby spinach, and puffy potato gnocchi (at this restaurant, the word "accompaniment" seems demeaning, as each element is an intrinsic part of the whole).

The assembly of pan-seared Îles de la Madeleine sea scallops with glasswort, a quenelle of sweet pea purée, grilled portobello mushroom, and a warm vinaigrette of wild Abitibi blueberries with tarragon is rather Dali-esque—artistic, if a bit creepy. The resilient texture of the scallops might lead you to believe they're overcooked, but a few bites later you'll realize they're just meatier and less watery than most—perhaps the best scallops you've ever tasted.

Also outstanding is the roasted Bas du Fleuve saddle of lamb with cauliflower purée, sautéed Western Canadian girolle mushrooms, coco beans, roasted fingerling potatoes, and baby pak choi from the greenhouse of Mr. Daigneault. The meat is wonderful: pink, moist, delicious, and melt-in-the-mouth tender—utterly amazing. The beans, mushrooms, and pak choi are also superb, as are the potatoes.

Desserts are a bit serious, lacking a spark of whimsy (too masculine?). A mascarpone tart piled high with wild Quebec blueberries and served with ginger ice milk is good, if somewhat bland; it lacks a bit of sweetness to make it all come to life. Chocolate desserts—molten Manjari cake with a red wine reduction and spices, and a caramelized chocolate brioche with creamy Manjari, clove ice milk, and port reduction—are delicious, but the spice/chocolate/wine combination might be better suited to a winter menu.

Under the watchful eye of co-owner Christine Lamarche, service has remained casual as opposed to stuffy—a refreshing approach for such a high-end restaurant. There's nothing stodgy about the place; it's all about the food, and when it comes to describing the food, the waiters score high as well.

IN THE KITCHEN • Chef and co-owner Normand Laprise.

DECOR, DRESS, AMBIENCE • Toqué! is a comfortable restaurant. The decor is eclectic. The long, narrow space is split into four colourful rooms. There's a large bar near the door for predinner cocktails. In summer, the small outdoor terrace is the ideal spot for your after-dinner Illy espresso. Dress up, if you like, but don't expect to see many ties or flouncy dresses around you.

WINE LIST • The wine list is made up of an interesting array of international selections, and it has been increasing in size, quality, and complexity, year after year.

DON'T MISS • The foie gras, the fish tartares, the quail starter, the Quebec lamb entrées, the Boileau venison, and the Îles de la Madeleine scallops.

WORDS TO THE WISE • Despite the fact that Toqué! may appear to receive heaps of attention, this magical restaurant is often taken for granted. Some say they're bored with the place or boast that they've already "done it." If you love fine food and haven't been lately, consider a return visit, for every meal offers something you haven't experienced before. At Toqué!, you're in the hands of a world-class chef who is perfecting his craft, honing a unique style. Laprise has taken his cuisine up a notch of late. What he will come up with next leaves his many fans breathless in anticipation.

TOQUÉ!
3842 Rue St. Denis (near Roy)
Telephone: (514) 499-2084
Open: 5:30 P.M.-10:30 P.M., daily
Wheelchair access: No
Reservations: Essential
Cards: Major cards (and Interac)
Price range: Starters, $8-$21; main courses, $23-$34;
desserts, $10-$11

★★★	$ $ $	REVIEWED 07/01

TREEHOUSE

SNAPSHOT · The man behind the hype surrounding Treehouse, one of the city's most exciting restaurants, is Tri Du, a chef revered for his form-equals-substance inventions. Using traditional Japanese cuisine as a starting point, he relies on the freshest local and imported ingredients to fuel his seemingly endless imagination. To date, he has won over the most discerning fashionistas, who collectively rave about Treehouse, not only for the inventive sushi and sashimi, but also for such daring concoctions as sea urchin tempura, miso-marinated black cod, and oysters that are suitably named "Tri-afeller."

THE BIG PICTURE · I arrive on a Saturday night with three serious—and ravenous—sushi aficionados, none of whom have sampled chef Tri's creations, but all of whom know him by reputation. Riding the elevator to the restaurant's second-floor location, our group is quietly giddy. The excitement is palpable. We step out into the bar area and are welcomed by an Amazonian hostess and some cute waiters, everyone clad head-to-toe in black.

Facing the panoply of appetizers, sushi, sashimi, new-style sashimi, maki, tempura, and house specialties, we turn to our waiter for guidance. He suggests the chef's tasting menu, called "Omakase," paired with cold Black and Gold Gekkeikan sake.

The kitchen tunes up with a starter as ordinary as a seaweed salad that consists of a multicoloured mound of julienned daikon, carrot, seaweed, and cucumber; the dish is laced with a sweet ginger vinaigrette, sprinkled with fried potato, and garnished with a blue pansy. It's the ideal palate cleanser for the serious taste sensations to come.

The main meal starts with a bang. We're offered two plates of sashimi—one of salmon, the other of lightly grilled (new-style sashimi) Hawaiian opa. Both are sensational, but I'd give the opa, with its char-grilled accent, top marks. A perfectly balanced ponzu sauce adds spice to the here-it's-cooked/here-it-isn't paper-thin slices. We devour both plates of fish in seconds, locking chopsticks over every last melting morsel.

Served along with the sashimi are oysters "Tri-afeller." This take on the classic oysters Rockefeller consists of Japanese oysters with spinach, shallots, and béchamel sauce. They're quite nice, but they might have been out of this world had the blanket of béchamel been velvety, as opposed to curdled.

Two more fish courses follow: black cod and Chilean sea bass marinated in miso, and grilled tuna and Californian striped bass tataki. Here the fish is perfectly cooked, easily breaking into succulent chunks grilled just beyond translucency. The cod and bass retain their distinct flavours while the miso marinade enhances without overwhelming. Initially, I prefer the cod, then the bass. In the end, there's no denying it: both are outstanding.

The tataki course is different, for here the sauce commands centre stage. At first it seems a shame to mask such high-quality fish with a thick sauce. After a few bites, however, one becomes accustomed to the spicy and slightly sweet flavour and smooth mouth feel, which enable the tuna and striped bass flavours to shine through. It's an outstanding combination, exploiting fish to its fullest potential. Don't bother inquiring about the composition of the sauce; apparently, it's a well-guarded secret (no doubt residing in the same vault as the recipes for Coke and the Colonel's seven herbs and spices).

After such highs, there are bound to be a few lows. A serving of grilled squid with basil offers an equal number of tender morsels and rubbery ones—a shame, since the basil-squid pairing is lovely. Beef tartare, served atop a bowl of ice, is spicy but otherwise bland. The hand-minced beef is topped with black flying fish roe, which provides a welcome bit of crunch, but little in the way of flavour.

Two riceless sushi maki rolls are also lacking. The makis—Tri's Deluxe, with smoked salmon, cucumber, black caviar, and Alaskan crab; and the Eye of the Dragon, with fresh salmon, squid, flying fish roe, and shiso—are a feat of engineering. The colourful ingredients are encased in tempura and flash-fried, resulting in a light, crispy blanket around a cold roll. Both rolls are on the dry side; the Tris Deluxe roll is salty, and its pronounced smokiness isn't all that pleasant.

An impressive and generous sushi platter includes pristine salmon and tuna sashimi, halibut and red snapper nigiri sushi, and killer combination makis. The white-on-white nigiri sushi looks fantastic, and the ultrafresh fish melts on the tongue. Too bad the rice doesn't live up to its promise, as it's underseasoned and just this side of overcooked. The rainbow maki and spider rainbow maki—the spider being soft-shell crab—are absolutely delicious, an intriguing combination of flavours and textures, and nearly as dry as the tempura maki (though the end bits are cumbersomely large).

In complete contrast to the usual sushi-restaurant desserts, Treehouse offers a welcome surprise: chocolate soufflé. Though not the towering French variety, this soufflé has the ideal pudding-like centre, light texture, and dense chocolate flavour.

Service throughout the meal is attentive and well paced. One wishes, however, that the waiters were better informed about the composition of the dishes and sauces.

IN THE KITCHEN • Chef Tri Du.

DECOR, DRESS, AMBIENCE • The large, square room was obviously conceived as office space, but it's now filled with dark furniture and the requisite winding sushi bar topped with spotlights. Having imagined chef Tri's lair as something more exotic (considering the name, I had visions of a jungle decor, replete with bamboo, toucans, and swinging monkeys), this oh-so-common sushi bar is a bit of a letdown.

WINE LIST • There are eight varieties of sake, priced between $30 and $90. There's also an extensive choice of mainly French and Californian wines, priced between $32 and $550 (Château Mouton-Rothschild).

DON'T MISS · The new-style sashimi, the black cod and Chilean sea bass marinated in miso, the grilled tuna and Californian striped bass tataki, and the sushi.

WORDS TO THE WISE · No doubt about it, Treehouse is an exciting dining destination with an eye to the future. The herd instinct isn't always a reliable indicator of quality, but chef Tri's legions of devotees seem to be on to something good.

TREEHOUSE
4120 Rue Ste. Catherine West (near Greene)
Telephone: (514) 932-7873
Open: 5:30 P.M.-10:30 P.M., Sunday, Tuesday, and Wednesday, and 5:30 P.M.-midnight, Thursday to Saturday
Wheelchair access: Yes
Reservations: Recommended
Cards: Major cards
Price range: Starters, $6-$17.50; main courses, $14-$28; desserts, $8-$11.95; Omakase tasting menus, $65, $85, and $120

★★	$ $	REVIEWED 01/01

ZEN

SNAPSHOT · Zen offers an eye-popping selection of Chinese and Szechwan favourites in one of the city's sleekest contemporary dining rooms. The prix fixe menu includes a wide choice of all-you-can-eat hors d'oeuvres and main-course dishes. The crispy duck is one of the best versions of this classic to be found in Montreal. Those up for spicy dishes, however, may be disappointed.

THE BIG PICTURE · My first taste of Szechwan cuisine was at Zen in the early nineties. A good friend of mine worked upstairs, in the Four Seasons Hotel, and for half price (about ten dollars cach) we would eat our way through the menu about three times a month. Though never a fan of Chinese buffets or dim sum gorge fests, I cherished these meals.

Despite an attempt to alter the restaurant's formula in the mid-nineties, the menu at Zen isn't all that different from the one offered a decade ago. Prices are still reasonable: $27 for an unlimited (all you can eat) choice of hors d'oeuvres and main-course dishes.

Ordering is a no-brainer at Zen; you simply pick whatever sounds appetizing. Mistakes won't set you back a penny. Hot and sour soup has the correct brilliance and syrupy consistency and is indeed very hot. Sweet corn soup with chicken provides another soothing start to a meal. Within minutes of the soup bowls being cleared, dish after dish of appetizers begin to appear. Standouts are moist barbecued satay chicken brochettes with a terrific chunky peanut sauce, and piping hot, crisp chicken spring rolls. Everything else falls somewhat short. The vermicelli-and-vegetable-stuffed chicken wings taste warmed-over. The steamed shrimp dim sum are wrapped in a thick, gummy casing, and the pork Hunan dumplings, which arrive cold and clammy, are served with an insipid peanut sauce.

The crispy, aromatic Szechwan duck makes up for the kitchen's shortcomings. A boned, flattened, and fried piece of duck is presented on a dinner plate before being shredded by the waiter into manageable strips. It's served with a steamer basket filled with thin crêpes, side dishes of sliced scallion and cucumber, and a sweet, thick hoisin sauce. The ritual is to fill a crêpe with the ingredients, top it with sauce, and form it into a roll.

Main dishes can be a letdown. Those marked spicy are uniformly bland. And few, save for the sautéed filet of chicken with black pepper and crispy spinach served on a sizzle platter, arrive hot. Sesame orange beef, which used to be considered one of the best items on this menu, lacks the requisite heat and any orange flavour. Another favourite, the General Tao's chicken, is devoid of heat as well as the sweetness of the Szechwan classic. A dish described on the menu as both spicy and a house specialty, Szechwan chicken, is a dull concoction of warm stir-fried chicken, al dente red and green peppers, and little else. Even the simple dishes, Szechwan green beans and steamed rice, fall short in the spice and temperature department.

One course where a bit of chill is welcome is dessert. Zen's lemon sorbet is sweet, tart, and delicious. A large profiterole filled with cappuccino ice cream is smothered in a heavenly chocolate sauce.

IN THE KITCHEN · Chef Simon Shum.

DECOR, DRESS, AMBIENCE · With its chrome and black-leather furniture, glass-topped bar, wide red pillars, and bold yellow-and-blue walls, Zen is one of the most stunning contemporary dining rooms in the city. But when it comes to ambience, there appears to be no middle ground: it's either bustling when packed, or dreary when half empty.

WINE LIST · There is one kind of sake, 15 red wines, and 20 white wines (French, Californian, and Italian) priced between $30 and $56.

DON'T MISS · The hot and sour soup, the sweet corn soup, the crispy duck, and the desserts.

WORDS TO THE WISE · Although service at Zen is gracious and efficient, there's obviously a problem getting the food to the table while it is still satisfyingly hot—an absolute must for fried and steamed food. In the past, everything appeared to be cooked to order. Today one thing is clear: we need a little more heat coming out of this kitchen in more ways than one. Don't hesitate to request spicier food, if that is your preference.

ZEN
1050 Rue Sherbrooke West (corner Peel, in the Hôtel Omni)
Telephone: (514) 499-0801
Open: Lunch, 11:30 A.M.-2:30 P.M., Monday to Friday;
dinner, 5:30 P.M.-10 P.M., daily
Wheelchair access: Yes
Reservations: Recommended; essential on weekends
Cards: Major cards
Price range: Lunch table d'hôte menu, $13.95-$14.95; brunch,
$19; all-you-can-eat dinner menu, $27

CASUAL DINING

AU BISTRO GOURMET

Serving bistro fare gussied up to the hilt, this is a restaurant that merits its name. Wildly popular with downtown locals and the business crowd, Au Bistro Gourmet offers delicious, reasonably priced food ranging from classic French to upscale nouvelle cuisine. There's a short wine list to match. Take note, however, that their new, fancier satellite operation, Au Bistro Gourmet 2, located on Rue St. Denis, fails (at present) to live up to the quality of the maison mère.

Favourite dishes: Duck confit salad, bavette aux échalotes, rack of lamb, pork chop with chestnuts, salmon with white wine sauce, French apple tart, and crème caramel.

Two locations:
2100 Rue St. Mathieu (near de Maisonneuve)
Telephone: (514) 846-1553
And
4007 Rue St. Denis (corner Duluth)
Telephone: (514) 844-0555
Open: Lunch, noon-2:30 P.M., Monday to Friday;
dinner, 5:30 P.M.-10 P.M., daily
Reservations: Essential
Price range: Table d'hôte menu, $19.95-$26.95;
desserts, $4.50-$6

AU PETIT EXTRA

Lunch at Au Petit Extra is the perfect antidote for a bleak winter afternoon. Dinner is like a big party. Packed to the rafters with jovial regulars, this expansive neighbourhood bistro is remarkably warm and friendly. Waits for tables can be long, so order a glass of wine and hang out at the bar with everyone else. The wine list offers a good selection of affordable bottles; daily specials are listed on the blackboards around the room. Though the location is a little off the beaten track, this is the ideal place for out-of-towners to experience a taste of French Montreal.

Favourite dishes: Terrine, leg of lamb, salmon, duck confit, and bavette.

AU PETIT EXTRA
1690 Rue Ontario East (corner Papineau)
Telephone: (514) 527-5552
Open: Lunch, 11:30 A.M.-2:30 P.M., Monday to Friday;
dinner, 6 P.M.-10 P.M., Monday to Wednesday, 6 P.M.-10:30 P.M.,
Thursday to Saturday, and 5:30 P.M.-9:30 P.M., Sunday
Reservations: Essential
Price range: Starters, $4.25-$15; main courses, $19.75-$23;
desserts, $4-$7

BEAUTY'S

Montrealers have been flocking to Beauty's, an institution if ever there was one, since 1953. Owner Hymie Sckolnick is always there to greet you with a "How are you, dahling?" Beauty's is the place where Root's-clad couples, yuppies, and families converge to eat breakfast all day long—otherwise known as brunching. And nobody does it better than Beauty's. If the decor is strictly *American Graffiti*, the fare is an homage to the city's best feel-good food: the bagel. One word of advice: beware the weekend crunch (they don't take reservations).

Favourite dishes: Beauty's special, comprised of a Montreal bagel, cream cheese, and Nova Scotia smoked salmon (lox); and mishmash omelette, spinach salad, homemade banana bread, and velvety Tofutti.

BEAUTY'S
93 Boulevard Mont Royal West (corner St. Urbain)
Telephone: (514) 849-8883
Open: 7 A.M.-4 P.M., Monday to Friday, 7 A.M.-5 P.M., Saturday, and 8 A.M.-5 P.M., Sunday
Reservations: Not accepted
Price range: Breakfast, $10-$15

CAFÉ INTERNATIONAL

Although its name implies a restaurant with a world-food menu, Café International is strictly Italian, with an à la carte selection of pastas and pizzas and daily specials including market-fresh salads, risotti, and meat and fish dishes. The food is simple and delicious, and the price/quality ratio is excellent. There are also at least a dozen red and white wines offered by the glass. There's nothing fancy about the decor, but there's always plenty of atmosphere at this Little Italy bistro, especially in summertime, when tables spill out onto the sidewalk of Boulevard St. Laurent. At lunch these outdoor seats fill up quickly with local residents and the television crowd from the Quatre Saisons/CFCF building up the street.

Favourite dishes: Pizza, sandwiches, and daily specials, which include two pastas, risotti, and various meat, fish, and veal dishes.

CAFÉ INTERNATIONAL
6714 Boulevard St. Laurent (near St. Zotique)
Telephone: (514) 495-0067
Open: Lunch, 11 A.M.-3 P.M.; dinner, 6 P.M.-10 P.M., daily
Reservations: Recommended
Price range: À la carte menu items, $ 7.95- $16.95;
table d'hôte menu, $7.95-$16.95

CAFÉ MÉLIÈS

Much has changed at this ultramodern restaurant located in Ex-Centris, Montreal's most luxurious independent cinema and multimedia complex, since it opened in June 1999. Chef Lindsay Petit has transformed the simple menu, favouring creative bistro fare made with the finest local ingredients. Open from morning to night, Café Méliès is also a good choice for breakfast, brunch, or a late-afternoon snack. The bar is often filled with moviegoers having a cocktail before viewing the latest foreign film. Ask for a table next to the windows, one of the Main's primo people-watching sites. Or, better yet, take a look at who is eating at the table next to yours, for Café Méliès is known as a popular draw for international celebrities, politicians, and artists. Service is friendly and efficient, and the wine list is full of interesting selections at prices that are more than fair.

Favourite dishes: Brandade de morue, mussels, marinated salmon, bavette, roasted scallops, seafood pot-au-feu, braised lamb shank, and desserts.

CAFÉ MÉLIÈS
3536 Boulevard St. Laurent (near des Pins)
Telephone: (514) 847-9218
Open: 8 A.M.-11 P.M., Monday to Wednesday and Sunday,
8:30 A.M.-midnight, Thursday, Friday, and Saturday
Reservations: Recommended
Price range: Starters, $5-$20; main courses, $17-$29;
desserts, $8-$10

CHEZ CLO

For the past 18 years, fans of Chez Clo have been flocking to this east end eatery not only for eggs, bacon, beans, and cretons, but also for the homey ambience and friendly service. Don't be discouraged by the lineups; the authentic Québecois-style cooking —all at ridiculously low prices—is worth the short wait. The old-fashioned decor, which adds to the fun of this family-run restaurant, makes it the ideal spot for a meal with children. At lunch and dinner, the menu includes Québecois specialties such as tourtière, poutine, ragoût de boulettes, and pouding chômeur. Chez Clo is a great place to pick up a bit of local flavour.

Favourite dishes: Pea soup, assiette Québécoise (ragoût de boulettes, tourtière, pig's feet, salad, vegetables, potatoes), pork roast, breakfast special with cretons, date squares, and homemade pies and layer cakes.

CHEZ CLO
3199 Rue Ontario East (corner Desiré)
Telephone: (514) 522-5348
Open: 6 A.M.- 8 P.M. (10 P.M. in summer), daily
Reservations: Not accepted
Price range: Full meals start at $4

⅃ANGO

Don't expect mariachi bands, birdbath-sized margaritas, or cheese-and-salsa-laden Americanized Mexican dishes at Fandango. Chef and owner Ward Deal and his wife/partner Diane Gagnon have taken Mexican cuisine to new heights at this gem of a bistro, located in the heart of the Plateau Mont Royal. Everything here is skilfully prepared, elegantly presented, and filled with flavours that range from subtle to explosive. Start your meal with a mojito, and cap the night off with a tequila or Mexican coffee. The wine list is short but inexpensive, with some fine Chilean and Californian (and one Mexican) wines to choose from. The decor is simple, the ambience is relaxed, and the service is first-rate.

Favourite dishes: Guacamole, black bean soup, shrimp cocktail, tacos al carbon (with grilled steak or pork), mole with chicken breast, enchiladas verdes, birria (marinated lamb braised in a guajillo and ancho chili broth), coconut crème caramel, and rice pudding.

FANDANGO
3807 Rue St. André (near Roy)
Telephone: (514) 526-7373
Open: 5 P.M.-11 P.M., Tuesday to Saturday
Reservations: Recommended
Price range: Starters, $4-$9; main courses, $14-$20;
desserts, $5-$6; table d'hôte menu, $28

FONDUMENTALE

This is a fun place for diners who enjoy the convivial atmosphere that develops around a pot of hot fondue (it's also the ideal date destination). The restaurant is set on the main floor of a beautiful old house on one of the most crowded strips of branché Rue St. Denis. Fondumentale is especially popular with young people who are new to fondue or aren't necessarily out for a gourmet experience (though foodies are sure to find the many fondue options amusing and impressive). Despite this restaurant's strengths, service can be slow and a bit distant.

Favourite dishes: Wild mushroom fondue, Chinese fondue (broth), bourguignonne fondue (oil) served with plates of game meats or seafood, and chocolate fondue.

FONDUMENTALE
4325 Rue St. Denis (near Marie Anne)
Telephone: (514) 499-1446
Open: 5:30 P.M.-10 P.M., Sunday to Thursday, 5:30 P.M.-11 P.M., Friday and Saturday
Reservations: Essential
Price range: Starters, $4.50-$11.50; main courses, $14-$26; desserts, $4-$8; table d'hôte menu, $24-$38

GANDHI

Gandhi, open since 2001, could be described as Montreal's pretti-est Indian restaurant (though perhaps not its most authentic). Curries here consist of meats—lamb, chicken, beef, and seafood —topped with a choice of sauces in a pick-and-choose style of cooking not usually associated with the slow-simmered prepara-tions of Indian cuisine. Starters such as the vegetable samosas and pakoras are delicious, and the lovely raita (cucumber with yo-gourt and coriander) will soothe an overheated palate. Authentic-ity sticklers may be disappointed, yet owner Mohammad Farouk Ahmed has made Gandhi a popular destination by placing the emphasis on a beautiful, inviting ambience where crisp white tablecloths, sunflower-yellow walls, high ceilings, and floor-to-ceiling windows overlooking Rue St. Paul create an irresistible charm. The wine list comprises over 50 selections, including fine red and white French wines along with a few choice rosés and Champagnes.

Favourite dishes: Aloo (potato) chat and chicken chat, tandoor duck, lamb korahi, butter chicken, chicken tikka jalfrezi, Malaya chicken, sagwala shrimp, vegetable dishes, and phirni (rice pud-ding).

GANDHI
230 Rue St. Paul West (near St. Pierre)
Telephone: (514) 845-5866
Open: Lunch, noon-2:30 P.M., Monday to Friday;
dinner, 5 P.M.-10:30 P.M., daily
Reservations: Recommended
Price range: Starters, $3-$7.50; main courses, $9.50-$20.50;
desserts, $3

ISAKAYA

Since its opening two years ago, Isakaya has quickly established itself as the most authentic Japanese restaurant in town. Though the setting may not be as fancy as those of many of the city's sushi emporiums, the lineup at the door, as well as the impressive number of Japanese patrons, tells the story. Chef and owner Shige Minagawa, a 25-year veteran of the restaurant Katsura, has a reputation among local fishmongers as the man who chooses the best fish and seafood, to which he does justice by serving it (cooked or raw) as simply as Japanese cuisine dictates. Look for daily specials — such as yellowtail neck, toro (choice tuna belly), deep-fried oysters, or lobster sashimi — listed on the chalkboard behind the kitchen. Not the spot for fashionistas seeking a sushi-bar scene, or trendies with a hankering for fruit-filled maki rolls, Isakaya is the place for foodies looking for the real deal.

Favourite dishes: Miso soup, gyoza dumplings, tempura, tuna and pork spring rolls, yakitori brochettes, sushi and sashimi, octopus omelette, grilled scallops, and shrimp with ginger sauce.

ISAKAYA
3469 Avenue du Parc (near Milton)
Telephone: (514) 845-8226
Open: Lunch, 11:30 A.M.-3 P.M., Tuesday to Saturday; dinner, 6 P.M.-10 P.M., Tuesday to Friday, and 6 P.M.-11 P.M., Saturday
Reservations: Essential
Price range: Starters, $1.50-$8.75; main courses, $14-$23; desserts, $2.50

LA PARYSE

Your quest for the perfect burger stops here. Nestled among the nondescript buildings facing the CEGEP de Vieux Montréal, this resto caters largely to the student crowd, which accounts for its bohemian ambience. To sink your teeth into one of their famous hamburgers is to have a culinary epiphany of sorts. Corny as it may sound, the girls at La Paryse put a lot of loving care into making their burgers, restoring a much-maligned classic with a little homemade integrity. The fries are pretty good too.

Favourite dishes: Hamburgers, club sandwiches, La Paryse sandwich (egg, mushroom, and cheese), French fries, and wicked milkshakes.

LA PARYSE
302 Rue Ontario East (corner Sanguinet)
Telephone: (514) 842-2040
Open: 11 A.M.-11 P.M., Monday to Friday, noon-10 P.M.,
Saturday and Sunday
Reservations: Not accepted
Price range: Full meals (burger or sandwich, fries,
and a drink), $10

LA RACLETTE

The popularity of this charming resto proves you don't have to be Swiss or a skier to crave a plate of hot melted cheese for dinner. If you do fancy raclette or fondue, this is the place to indulge. There are various affordable menu options, service is stellar, and the Swiss-modern decor is romantic (even the bathrooms are candlelit). In winter, the room is crowded with groups of revellers feasting on soups, salads, and large platters of raclette beneath cuckoo clocks. In summer, it's bright and airy, with a large terrace in front and wonderful smells of melted cheese and sautéed meats emanating from the gleaming open kitchen. Don't even think of showing up without a reservation.

Favourite dishes: Raclette (starter or main course), salads, fondue, émincé de veau Zurichoise, salmon with Meaux mustard, and poire Belle Hélène.

LA RACLETTE
1059 Rue Guilford (corner Christophe Colomb)
Telephone: (514) 524-8118
Open: 5:30 P.M.-10 P.M., daily
Reservations: Essential
Price range: Starters, $5.95-$7.25; main courses, $15.45-$22; desserts, $4.25-5.50; three-course table d'hôte menu, $15.45-$22.95, and five-course table d'hôte menu, $27-$31

LA SPAGHETTATA

Don't let the name or modern logo fool you. This Outremont landmark, in business since 1978, offers some the best and most reliable Italian food in town. The decor is modern and unpretentious, the service is efficient and professional, and everything is fresh and prepared with care. Spaghettata also boasts one of the most interesting and affordable (primarily Italian) wine lists around, with many fine choices by the glass. This is the ideal spot for lunch when shopping on fashionable Avenue Laurier. Note: there's a children's menu as well.

Favourite dishes: House-smoked salmon, antipasti Spaghettata, Caesar salad, lasagna, carbonara and puttanesca pastas, and homemade desserts.

LA SPAGHETTATA

399 Avenue Laurier West (near Hutchison)
Telephone: (514) 273-9509
Open: 11:30 A.M.-10 P.M., daily
Reservations: Recommended
Price range: Starters, $4-$9;
main courses, $11-$27; desserts, $6; weekly two-course table d'hôte menu, $18-$26, and lunch table d'hôte menu, $8-$14

LE BISTINGO

Here is another small (26-seat) Outremont bistro that features southwestern French food and a well-priced wine list. What makes Le Bistingo stand out is the personal touch of owner Christian Truchot, who greets customers, makes wonderful wine and menu recommendations, and oversees the whole shebang. The food is always fresh, inventive, and delicious. Once you've dined at Le Bistingo a couple of times, Mr. Truchot is sure to remember you. And on those nights when you show up hungry and without a reservation, he'll do his best to squeeze you in somewhere. Chances are you'll fare better in summertime, when the large outdoor terrace doubles the seating capacity.

Favourite dishes: Cervelle de veau (calf's brains), bavette a l'échalote, duck magret and confit, gingerbread with poached pears, tarte Tatin, and prune ice cream with a shot of Armagnac.

LE BISTINGO
1199 Avenue Van Horne (corner Bloomfield)
Telephone: (514) 270-6162
Open: Lunch, noon-2 P.M., Monday to Friday; dinner, 6 P.M.-9:30 P.M., Monday to Wednesday, and 6 P.M.-10 P.M., Thursday to Saturday
Reservations: Recommended
Price range: Starters, $3.95-$6.95; main courses, $10.95-$24.95; desserts, $3.95-$8.95; daily menu, $15.95; tasting menu, $29.95

LE GRAIN DE SEL

This tiny east-end bistro could easily be found on a quiet Paris side street. The narrow room's Old World ambience is enlivened by a small bar and an open kitchen, where toque-wearing chefs busily assemble plates. The menu lists such bistro classics as goat's cheese salad, pheasant terrine, asparagus vinaigrette, and bavette Maître Queux, but once the plates arrive, you're sure to appreciate the kitchen's flair for unusual flavour combinations. Chef and owner Hop Lam Dao incorporates many Asian accents and exotic ingredients into his dishes, along with Quebec products such as raw-milk cheese, beer, and iced cider. Service is efficient, and the wine list offers many affordable, food-friendly selections.

Favourite dishes: Five-spice quails, mussels cooked in beer, salmon pavé with lemon and ginger, and sweetbreads with wild mushrooms.

LE GRAIN DE SEL
2375 Rue Ste. Catherine East (near Fullum)
Telephone: (514) 522-5105
Open: Lunch, noon-2:30 P.M., Monday to Friday; dinner, 6 P.M.-10:30 P.M., Tuesday to Saturday
Reservations: Recommended
Price range: Starters, $5.25-$6.95; main courses, $16.95-$24.95; desserts, $3.95-$4.95

LE JARDIN DE PANOS

When it comes to brochetteries, there isn't another in Montreal that can hold a spanakopita to Avenue Duluth's Le Jardin de Panos. Take a look at the small open kitchen up front, and you'll see two burly fellows grilling up a storm. Brochetterie fare may be simple, but most every item here is delicious and satisfying (portions are generous). The decor completes the illusion of Greek authenticity. And if all that's missing is a bit of sunshine, there's a large, tree-filled terrace out back for summertime dining. Bring your own wine.

Favourite dishes: Fried calamari, moussaka, grilled lamb chops (epithelia), all brochettes, and Greek-style yogourt topped with Greek honey or cherries in syrup.

LE JARDIN DE PANOS
521 Rue Duluth East (near St. Hubert)
Telephone: (514) 521-4206
Open: 3 P.M.-midnight, daily
Reservations: Not accepted (expect a lineup on weekends)
Price range: Starters, $3.50-$6.50; main courses, $12.85-$19.85; desserts, $2.50-$3.50; table d'hôte menus, $16.85, $19.85, and $22.85

LE MAISTRE

Le Maistre is located in an old townhouse on the western end of Monkland Village. This unpretentious restaurant's popularity may be due to its trendy NDG location, but fair prices, friendly service, and solid bistro food obviously have something to do with it as well. Le Maistre's wine list is another of its strong points. With many diverse selections offered at no more than twice their retail price, the only difficulty is choosing, as so many bottles are perfectly suited to this style of cuisine.

Favourite dishes: Smoked salmon, cassoulet (when available), cheese course, and desserts.

LE MAISTRE
5700 Avenue Monkland (corner Harvard)
Telephone: (514) 481-2109
Open: Lunch, 11:30 A.M.-2 P.M., Thursday and Friday; dinner, 6 P.M.-9:30 P.M., Tuesday to Saturday
Reservations: Recommended
Price range: Starters, $9; main courses, $20-$23; desserts, $4.50; table d'hôte menu, $27-$30

LE MARGAUX

Set on a quiet corner in the Plateau Mont Royal, this charming 28-seat bistro offers lovingly prepared and presented French food in a bright little space framed by curtained windows, large mirrors, and a long, chintz-covered banquette. The short wine list (12 bottles) is priced to sell, with some fine selections — like Domaine de l'Hortus for a mere $28. The cheese course — three generous portions for seven dollars — is one of the best bargains in town.

Favourite dishes: Potage garbure, fondant de foie de canard (duck liver parfait), rabbit ballotine, gingerbread-crusted lamb chops, panfried marlin with sesame, and cheese course.

LE MARGAUX
371 Rue Villeneuve East (corner de Grands Près)
Telephone: (514) 289-9921
Open: Lunch, noon-2 P.M., Thursday and Friday; dinner,
5:30 P.M.-10 P.M., Tuesday to Saturday
Reservations: Recommended
Price range: Starters, $5-$8; main courses, $14-$18; desserts, $6

LE PARIS

A wildly popular downtown restaurant, Le Paris has been open since 1956. This flowery dining room has been the choice of affluent Montrealers looking for French "cuisine bourgeoise" in a casual and friendly setting. The old prints and posters, fresh flowers, wooden chairs, and a long burgundy banquette further enhance the air of a well-worn Paris bistro, and the closely spaced tables are ideal for eavesdropping. The no-frills French food (the peas are canned) is either described glowingly as "real" or dismissed by gourmets as "old-fashioned." But, for many, Le Paris isn't about food. The place is frequented mostly by regulars, so consider making numerous visits if you want to fit in and get a good table. The extensive French wine list is fairly priced and service is smooth.

Favourite dishes: Poached salmon with beurre blanc, brandade de morue, calf liver meunière, blood pudding, pepper steak, entre-côte bordelaise, tournedos chasseur.

LE PARIS
1812 Rue Ste. Catherine West (near St. Mathieu)
Telephone: (514) 937-4898
Open: Lunch, 11:30 A.M.-2:30 P.M., Monday to Saturday; dinner, 5:30 P.M.-10:30 P.M., Sunday to Thursday, and 5:30 P.M.-11:30 P.M., Friday and Saturday
Reservations: Recommended
Price range: Starters, $3-$7; main courses, $15-$23; desserts, $2.50-$5

LE P'TIT PLATEAU

With its patterned tin ceiling, dim lights, crowded wooden tables, and bustling open kitchen, this wildly popular, petite neighbourhood resto appears to have been transported from one of Paris's outer arrondissements. The southwestern French bistro food is superb, and the service, though brusque, is thoroughly professional. The room can be noisy, but with atmosphere like this, you'll hardly notice. Be sure to reserve well in advance, especially on weekends, when there are two seatings: 6:30 P.M. and 8:30 P.M.

Favourite dishes: Foie gras (hot and cold), fish soup, cassoulet, confit de canard, onglet, crème brulée, and chocolate mousse.

LE P'TIT PLATEAU
330 Rue Marie Anne East (corner Drolet)
Telephone: (514) 282-6342
Open: From 5:30 P.M., Tuesday and Wednesday, and 6:30 P.M. and 8:30 P.M. sittings Thursday to Saturday
Reservations: Essential
Price range: Starters, $7.50-$12; main courses, $22-$26; desserts, $6-$6.50

MONKLAND TAVERN

The Monkland Tavern is noisy and crowded. Reservations aren't taken, so arrive early or expect to stand in line for a table, especially in summer, when the cramped outdoor terrace is *the* place to be for local NDG residents. How did this place get to be so popular? Regulars love the groovy tunes, the enthusiastic wait staff, and the laid-back atmosphere. There's a definite bar scene here; regulars quaff whiskies, martinis, elaborate cocktails, or one of six beers on tap till the wee hours of the morning. But let's not forget that this is a restaurant, and the diverse, American-style menu created by chef Steven Leslie features California-style food made with Québécois ingredients. The pastas, salads, sandwiches, French fries, and grilled meats are all very good. There's also an interesting wine list filled with a good choice of international bottles at fair prices.

Favourite dishes: Squash soup, Caesar salad, Mediterranean grilled vegetable sandwich, BLT, salmon tartare, smoked chicken and Brie pasta, roasted butternut squash and Ricotta pasta medallions, shrimp-fennel-bacon-Sambucca pasta, pan-seared salmon with caramelized Savoy cabbage and crispy potatoes, and cheesecake.

MONKLAND TAVERN
5555 Avenue Monkland (corner Old Orchard)
Telephone: (514) 486-5768
Open: Lunch, 11:30 A.M.-3 P.M., Monday to Friday; dinner, 6 P.M.-11 P.M., daily; bar open until 1 A.M.
Reservations: Not accepted (no minors)
Price range: Starters, $6-$11; main courses, $14-$23; desserts, $5-$7; lunch table d'hôte menu, $10-$16, and dinner table d'hôte menu, $15-$24

PIZZERIA NAPOLITANA

One of Little Italy's most popular restaurants, Pizzeria Napolitana has been going strong for over 50 years now. Many consider this pizza to be the best in town. That's open to debate, but I'm sold. Try for yourself, but expect to line up for a table, bring your own wine, and share a table with strangers. High noise levels—the price of popularity—can also be a problem. If that's not your scene, pizza and pasta are available to take out.

Favourite dishes: Pizzas and pastas—especially penne (arrabbiata and Romana), gnocchi Fiorentina, and farfalle with smoked salmon.

PIZZERIA NAPOLITANA
189 Rue Dante (corner de Gaspé)
Telephone: (514) 276-8226
Open: 11 A.M.-11 P.M., Monday to Friday, 11 A.M.-1 A.M.,
Friday and Saturday, and noon-11 P.M., Sunday
Reservations: Accepted for groups of eight or more only
Price range: Starters, $4.50-$9.75; main courses, $8.75-$14.50;
desserts, $4.75-$6.75 (tax included)

PRONTO GASTRONOMIA

This basement restaurant has quickly become one of West-mount's best. Chef and owner Peppino Joe Perri has made the most of the small, cozy space by opting for a modern, elegant decor as opposed the standard checkered-tablecloth look. The food is authentic, no-frills Italian prepared with top-quality in-gredients and a lot of love. Chef Perri also offers a "cook your din-ner" class on Tuesdays ($39), along with catering services, take out, and a small selection of Italian condiments and coffees. The restaurant is licenced.

Favourite dishes: Pastas and baked pastas (especially lasagna), and veal dishes.

PRONTO GASTRONOMIA
4894 Rue Sherbrooke West (corner Prince Albert)
Telephone: (514) 487-9666
Open: 10 A.M.-10 P.M., Monday to Saturday,
and 4 P.M.-9 P.M., Sunday
Reservations: Recommended
Price range: Starters, $6-$15; main courses, $10-$36; desserts, $6-$8; table d'hôte menu, $22-$30

ROBERTO

Though this gelateria/wine bar may be off the beaten track for the downtown crowd, Rosemont residents know that Roberto is the place for homemade pastas, panini, and some of the best ice cream in the city. The bistro's table d'hôte offers fancy fare, but you might want to go easy on the pasta and veal dishes and splurge on one of the delicious ice cream desserts. The wine list is extensive, but there are too few selections offered by the glass for this to be a serious contender as a wine bar. On your way out, be sure to stop at Roberto's gourmet store next door for some fresh pasta, imported condiments, or cured meats. And don't forget to visit the takeout gelato counter for one of the 20 fabulous ice creams, such as Baci, nougat, or pistachio.

Favourite dishes: Sandwiches, arugula salads, grilled vegetables and mushrooms, pastas, gnocchi, veal scaloppini, and gelato.

ROBERTO
2221 Rue Bélanger (near St. Michel)
Telephone: (514) 374-9844
Open: Lunch, noon-3:30 P.M., Tuesday to Friday; dinner,
5 P.M.-10 P.M., Tuesday, Wednesday, and Sunday, and 5 P.M.-
11 P.M., Thursday to Saturday
Reservations: Recommended
Price range: Starters, $4.50-$8.50; main courses, $7.50-$18;
desserts, $3.50-$6.50; lunch table d'hôte menu, $10.95-$22.95,
and dinner table d'hôte menu, $16.95-$25.95

SCHWARTZ'S

A deli-lover's Mecca, Schwartz's has been around since your grandfather's day. The decor is—well, let's just say you don't come here for the decor. You come here for some of the best smoked meat—what Americans, and especially New Yorkers, might call "pastrami"—you've ever tasted. Aficionados rank it right up there with the best in the world. The secret is the spicing and smoking, which are done on the premises in a time-honoured fashion handed down by the Jewish immigrants who came to Montreal from Eastern Europe and Russia at the turn of the twentieth century. Menu, schmenu—ordering goes something like this: "Hi, folks. What can I get for you? A smoked meat sandwich? A steak? How do you like it? Lean? French fries? Pickle? And to drink? Cherry Coke?" One nice feature is the grab-it-where-you-can-find-it seating, which inevitably puts you shoulder to shoulder with strangers who, after a smoked meat sandwich and a pickle or two, are strangers no longer.

Favourite dishes: Smoked meat sandwich and rib steak.

SCHWARTZ'S
3895 Boulevard St. Laurent (near Napoléon)
Telephone: (514) 842-4813
Open: 9 A.M.-12:30 A.M., Sunday to Thursday, 9 A.M.-1:30 A.M., Friday, and 9 A.M.-2:30 A.M., Saturday
Reservations: Not accepted
Price range: Sandwich, French fries, and a drink, $8; rib steak with all the fixings (except the drink), $13

SCOLA PASTA

Neighbourhood bistros abound in the island city, and one of the best in Old Montreal is Scola Pasta, the cozy establishment on the corner of St. Jean and Notre Dame, a stone's throw from Notre Dame Cathedral. At this no-frills, two-floor Italian eatery the accent is on freshness and value and some of the friendliest service you'll ever encounter. A self-serve counter and an open kitchen are the main features of the simply decorated room, whose wraparound windows and uncluttered layout create a cheerful and airy space. Daily specials are listed on the small blackboard that takes the place of a printed menu. Choose one of the specials or customize your own pasta, antipasto plate, or sandwich (portions are invariably generous). Note: credit cards are not accepted.

Favourite dishes: Lunchtime sandwiches and homemade soups (available to take out as well), you-chose-the-ingredients pastas, heaping plates of antipasto (complete with cheese, salami, olives, and a mouthwatering array of macaroni, mushroom, tomato, cucumber, artichoke, and chickpea salads), and daily fish, chicken, or meat dishes.

SCOLA PASTA
260 Rue Notre Dame West (near St. Jean)
Telephone: (514) 842-2232
Open: Lunch, 11:30 A.M.-8:30 P.M., Monday to Friday
Reservations: Not accepted
Price range: Starters, $2.95-$6.95; main courses, $6.95-$9.95

SOFIA

Looking for a branché restaurant for an affordable dinner with friends or a meeting place for a light meal or glass of wine before a night on the town? Consider Sofia, a trendy Boulevard St. Laurent eatery with crackling ambience, industrial bistro decor, techno background music, superb simple food, and the kind of unpretentious service rarely associated with the Boulevard St. Laurent scene. Though Sofia tends to attract the twenty-to-thirtysomething crowd, diners of all ages should feel comfortable here, as the enticing menu and diverse wine list cater to sophisticated and novice palates alike. A word of warning: noise levels rise considerably after midnight, and when a guest DJ takes over the sound system, revellers have been known to dance on the tables.

Favourite dishes: Daily specials (such as grilled salmon and filet mignon), Italian sausage and roasted pepper pizza, grilled vegetable and goat's cheese sandwich, tuna Niçoise salad, polenta-crusted calamari, and homemade sorbets and ice creams.

SOPHIA

3600 Boulevard St. Laurent (near Prince Arthur)
Telephone: (514) 284-0092
Open: Lunch, noon-3 P.M., Monday to Friday;
dinner, 6 P.M.-11 P.M., Sunday to Wednesday, and 6 P.M.-1 A.M.,
Thursday to Saturday
Reservations: Recommended
Price range: Starters, $6-$12; main courses, $10-$25;
desserts, $4-$6

SOTTO SOPRA

A newcomer to the Little Italy restaurant scene, Sotto Sopra offers simply prepared Italian cuisine in a trendy, modern dining room. Its floor-to-ceiling windows overlook the fairy-light-illuminated park next door. In the open kitchen at the back of the room, you'll spot chef Mario Morabito, recruited from Rome, creating authentic Italian dishes with ingredients from the Jean Talon Market down the street. Add to this a fairly priced wine list (half the bottles cost less than $55), friendly service, and an upbeat atmosphere emanating from a central bar crowded with sharply dressed, cell-phone-toting twentysomething regulars, and you have one of the most dynamic new restaurants around.

Favourite dishes: Antipasto, fried calamari, grilled octopus salad, spinach and Ricotta ravioli and seafood ravioli, and roasted baby lamb.

SOTTO SOPRA
6700 Boulevard St. Laurent (corner St. Zotique)
Telephone: (514) 270-7792
Open: Lunch, noon-3 P.M., Monday to Friday; dinner, 6 P.M.-10:30 P.M., Monday to Friday, and 6 P.M.-11 P.M., Saturday
Reservations: Essential
Price range: Starters, $10-$28; main courses, $14-$33; desserts, $7

322 FLAVOURVILLE • LESLEY CHESTERMAN

STASH CAFÉ

An Old Montreal institution, Stash is *the* place for Polish home-cooked-style meals in a warm and welcoming atmosphere. It's popular with business types during the week, but the weekend crowd is made up primarily of tourists, who come to Stash to soak up borscht and nibble perogies in an Eastern European/ Old Montreal setting. The combination of old wooden church benches, stone walls covered with Polish art, candles, and fresh flowers lend an air of romance to any meal here. The retro-café ambience, laid-back wait staff, and large portions also make this a popular dinner destination for students. Stash is licenced.

Favourite dishes: Borscht, pierogis (dumplings filled with meat or cheese, served with sour cream), wild boar, kaczka (roast duck), apple strudel, and peach crisp.

STASH CAFÉ
200 Rue St. Paul West (near St. François Xavier)
Telephone: (514) 845-6611
Open: 11:30 A.M.-10 P.M., daily
Reservations: Recommended
Price range: Starters, $4-$8.75; main courses, $9.25-$15.75; desserts, $3-$4; four-course table d'hôte menu, $20.75-$28.50

VENTS DU SUD

Vents du Sud feels like a French village restaurant, with mismatched chairs, a cast of regulars, casually dressed friendly ladies uncorking your wine (bring your own), and a portly, moustached chef and owner (Gérard Couret) chatting up diners between courses. The cuisine is rustic Basque and Catalonian, and it features terrines, confits, grilled meats, and sauces laced with peppers, garlic, and tomatoes. In fall and spring, look for dishes with wild mushrooms, as chef Couret is an experienced mushroom gatherer. This popular bistro can get a bit out of hand when crowded (slow service, uneven food), so a meal early in the week is probably your best bet.

Favourite dishes: Grilled peppers, cassoulet, sweetbreads with girolle mushrooms, rabbit with prunes, and mixed garbure plate (which includes sausage, chicken, duck, and vegetables).

VENTS DU SUD
323 Avenue Roy East (corner Drolet)
Telephone: (514) 281-9913
Open: 5:30 P.M.-10 P.M., Tuesday to Sunday
Reservations: Essential
Price range: Starters, $5.75-$8.75; main courses, $16-$22.25; desserts, $6.25; table d'hôte menu, $19.95-$29.95

GEOGRAPHICAL INDEX